learning in the classroom
theory and application

richard d. olson
richard k. smith
gayle a. olson

Department of Psychology
Louisiana State University
New Orleans, Louisiana

McCutchan Publishing Corporation
2526 Grove Street
Berkeley, California 94704

Preface

 This book is designed for use as either a basic or supplementary text in educational psychology courses. It is designed to stress an application of the principles of learning in the classroom so that the prospective teacher may benefit from what we consider to be some of the more dynamic and efficient methods available for use. We feel that too often students teach as they have been taught, and not as they have learned to teach. Hopefully, the articles in this book will generate enough interest and knowledge so that every teacher will, at least to some degree, be able to benefit from the application of principles of learning as a means of achieving a more successful education for future students.

 Towards this end the book has been divided into four major sections. Section I presents a basic foundation for understanding the theories and procedures underlying the application of learning principles in the classroom. Section II discusses various techniques and considerations for actually initiating such a program. Section III is concerned with procedures for decreasing undesirable, especially disruptive, behavior. Section IV illustrates procedures for increasing desirable behavior, then brings them together in an article that describes an experimental school based on learning principles and procedures.

 So many people have contributed in various fashions to this book that it is impossible to recognize all of them at this time. However, we do want to acknowledge Mrs. E. J. Freymark and Miss Carolyn Wagner for their valuable assistance in preparing this book for publication.

Richard D. Olson
Richard K. Smith
Gayle A. Olson

New Orleans, Louisiana
May 1971

Contents

IV. Procedures for Increasing Desirable Behavior — 191

I

Basic Foundations

Just as important as knowing how to use a skill or technique is knowing when to use it and why it works. Accordingly, the article by Smith tries to prepare the reader for understanding the rationale and procedures used to evaluate the application of learning principles in the classroom, as well as to present a view of the philosophy in this area. The Olson and Olson article summarizes classical conditioning and presents some new ideas on operant and instrumental conditioning that are readily applicable to the classroom. Finally, Bijou writes on the topic, "What Psychology has To Offer Education—Now," which serves as the final preparation for understanding psychology's role in contemporary classroom instruction.

1

Educational technology: rationale and methodology

Richard K. Smith

There are many possible reasons that an educator might expect to find a course in educational psychology valuable. Unfortunately, it seems that expectations and actual encounters with psychology as a discipline exhibit numerous discrepancies. I would like to believe this is as much because teachers do not appreciate what is of value to be learned from psychology, as because they tend to expect too much from this discipline. Psychology is an area of knowledge and theory that has only recently developed to the point where practical applications may exceed theoretical implications. Unfortunately, what the education-oriented student needs to learn from psychology for professional competence or personal satisfaction may either not be available from psychologists, or not effectively communicable within the structures of the typical college course. Therefore, I will begin by presenting a brief and restricted view of what I feel psychology does have to offer education. For a broader overview, see Bijou's article (Reading no. 3).

It might prove interesting to ask ourselves what generally would most enhance a teacher's contribution to the student, the teaching profession, society—even himself. We assume the primary goal of the teacher (as for all of us as highly developed living systems) is to increase the capability of each individual to do most effectively what previously could be done only poorly or not at all. Whatever knowledge about how people behave that would increase this capability, *if appropriately applied* by the teacher, must be worth acquiring.

Accepting the premise that a teacher's function involves directed change in the characteristic behavior of the student implies, among other things, that the teacher knows: (1) what new or presently not occurring behavior is desired, (2) what behavior is occurring in place of the desired behavior, and (3) what relationships exist between present behavior capability and desired future capability. Emphasis here is on *knowledge based on observations* made by the instructor. Yet, observation as such simply does not provide appreciable knowledge; rather, it is the *interpretation* of what is observed within some logically consistent framework of interrelationships that yields suggestions for action that may prove fruitful. The conceptual schematization of human behavior that psychology offers comprises the greatest overall contribution to the educator.

2

Numerous and diverse ways of conceiving human actions and their inter-relations have been proposed in the past. These theories have spanned the spectrum from idealized speculations of what man should be to limited and uninspiring catalogs of physical characteristics of isolated responses. Our view is somewhere between these extremes and focuses the teacher's attention on the dynamic, functional properties of behavior; that is, behavior is defined by speci-fying the most direct *result* of whatever the person does. In general, if any living system or organism changes itself or acts to alter the environment in a specifiable way, we say the *function* of the behavior was to produce that particular result. Thus, a child's "play" behavior is classified in terms of the environmental changes (including in the child himself) that directly correlate with that set of actions. Technically, for the behavior of the child to be noticed at all implies that the observer has been changed in a particular way. The very fact of labeling one activity play, and another behavior nonplay, suggests a relationship between how the child acts and how the observer characterizes or interprets these behavioral changes. The *same* response occurring under different circumstances can result in different labels, which are used to describe fundamental aspects that carry great significance for a theory of behavior; likewise, *different* responses may be characterized as having the same aspect or function. For example, we may speak of "attention-getting" behavior, which could include very diverse actions with only one essential characteristic in common—they all get the attention of someone. Therefore, in what descriptive category we pigeonhole a particular action depends on much more than the physical spatio-temporal and isolated intermovement relationships observed. This latter aspect of behavior was often the focus of much of psychology's attempt to apply scientific objectivism to the study of man. We do not wish to deprecate systematic and unbiased observation; indeed, we consider it indispensable for dealing with mankind's problems. However, the preoccupation with behavior *per se,* isolated from the matrix of events in which the action is imbedded, is doomed to sterile stultifi-cation.

If this approach does have merit, both descriptively and on an explanatory level, the initial question then becomes, "What are the minimal functional classes of behavioral events necessary for an effective theory of behavior?" We have attempted to provide an acceptable answer to this question in a consistent, integrated, quasi-theoretical framework. Ideally, our goal is to make the teacher an effective problem-solver so that, when confronted by a situation in the class-room (or elsewhere), a reasonably systematic analysis of what is actually going on can be made and some tentative solutions can be tried out.

Behavior, especially human behavior, is often said to be very complicated. What is meant, usually, is that the reasons people do what they do are extremely numerous and varied. This diversity and multidimensionality exist mainly when one attempts to catalog the verbal rationalizations given by the doers, or if one focuses attention on the physical differences among the situations involved. With respect to the first so-called complication it is best to simply regard any state-ment of why one is behaving as one is as behavior that is itself subject to the fundamental laws governing all responses. That is, there need not be any great correspondence between the reasons given verbally and the actual reasons determined from application of behavior analysis techniques. In fact, it is even possible to apply the method of behavior analysis to the verbal behavior to determine why a person rationalizes what he does. For example, because of parental values and peer approval a girl might begin a career in nursing, stating her concern for human welfare as the reason for her choice; however, after marrying a busy doctor, her career strivings may disappear even though she has been given both the time and finances to pursue the problems of human welfare. It might be more realistic to ascribe the initiation and maintenance of her career activities to several classes of social interactions with other people which bear directly on *her* welfare or self-esteem.

It is my contention that behavior is really not as complicated as we often tend to make it. Certainly, when we fail to see that many different ways of behaving really serve the same functional end, it does seem that humans act for a myriad of reasons. For the purpose of simplification, then, it is necessary to define *classes* of behavior. The class is defined in terms of some relatively objective change in the environment, and *all* responses, no matter how varied, are included in this class if the defining criterion is met. On the other hand, many environmental events have remarkably similar effects on behavior, even though they differ in a multitude of ways. Again, these events must be seen as functionally equivalent and assigned to the same *stimulus* class. The fact that the same class of environmental events may have different effects or different responses for the same or another organism also adds to the apparent complexity; but if these different effects are specifiable as a function of other variables known to be operating, then the complexity can be easily handled as long as the number of moderating factors is not beyond the capacity of the information processor.

However, one class of events (such as a response class) cannot be defined solely in terms of another set of events (such as a stimulus class) *unless* the determination of each is *independent* of the other. Another way of looking at this is to emphasize that no new information is gained by interrelating two sets of events unless the properties of the two sets are separately evaluated, and the relation between them is a physical reality rather than just artificial language. We do not normally appreciate the extent to which the organization of our perceptions of the world is a product of using a language whose structure makes everything appear more consistent and orderly than it really is. It is easy, for example, to say that a person's religiousness is related to his belief in God. This could be interpreted in many ways and defended as an immutable truth or attacked as patently ridiculous. Whether or not the statement has a meaning that communicates some important relationship about the world and people's behavior depends on what the critical terms *religiousness* and *belief in God* are referring to. If these meaning referents cannot be specified, there is no way the relative truth of the original statement can be ascertained. For the nonscientist the meanings of such terms are often assumed to be self-evident; the science-trained individual knows that some procedure must be used to decide whether a person is religious (by the defining set of criteria chosen), and if he should be also classified as a believer in God. The procedures we go through to categorize people as belonging in one broad class rather than another are often formalized as a set of instructions called *operational definitions.*

For highly developed areas of inquiry, these operational definitions constitute measurement techniques for determining the amount of degree of the conceptual property exhibited by the person or event under consideration. Thus, we might be sophisticated enough to say that there are differences in religiousness among people of different sects, and even within the same denominational group belief in God might show considerable variation from person to person or for one person over a span of time. If the operational criterion for how religious a person was stemmed from analysis of an observable characteristic of his behavior such as church attendance, it should be obvious that the operational criterion of one's belief in God must constitute something other than the same data on church attendance. Otherwise, what at first appears to be a factual relationship between two separate aspects of an individual's life is, in actuality, merely the use of two different symbolic expressions to refer to the same phenomenon.

Unfortunately, those who are often most outspoken and verbose in their characterizations of man's true nature are also the least critical of the independent specification requirement of scientific constructs. A flagrant but common illustration involves the stated relationship between intelligence and achievement in school. Too often the extent of this correspondence is exaggerated because the operational criteria are similar; in fact, questions on achievement tests are sometimes "borrowed" intact from a test of intelligence.

In many of the subsequent articles there are statements relating classes of behavior change to classes of environmental change that follow the behavior. These relationships constitute the fundamental functional definitions of the reinforcement and punishment operations underlying a large proportion of our adaptation to our environment. What changes in the world actually reinforce, and what behavior is really altered, must be ascertained separately if we are not to delude ourselves by what we expect should be the case.

Everyone has their own ideas about what is important to other people and themselves. But again, we are easily misled if care is not taken. One of the most common failures among teachers who have the courage to try anything new in their procedures, is not establishing an appropriate reference point for later comparisons. In order to ascertain the effects of a new method of teaching, it is imperative that we know as exactly as possible what the effects of the previous activities were. None of us, especially those most familiar with a situation, are naturally accurate and reliable observers. We must employ many awkward devices and procedures to aid us in our objectivity. Perhaps first and foremost, we must decide what behavior we are interested in and how it tends to change naturally due to the many fluctuations in important external and internal conditions.

The establishment of such a reference condition is often referred to as "control" or "baseline" data collecting. If we have a good picture of how people behave under these conditions when no intentional changes are being made, we then get a good idea of how effective a single change in circumstances that immediately follow the control period actually is. Of course, we need not limit ourselves to alterations in only one aspect of the instructional environment *if* appropriate experimental and statistical principles are utilized. For the introduction of sequential changes of various kinds limited to one student or group of students, it is important that the original baseline of behavior is reestablished before each new procedural change. This allows each change to be compared with the same standard, and a fair comparison of the different effects with one another.

Of what does this baseline consist? Of students' behavior, of course. But how, exactly, is this behavior to be represented in a meaningful and useful fashion? What does *all* behavior have in common that is of really fundamental importance? The answer of one highly vocal and increasingly influential group of psychologists is that the relative frequency or rate of any response class is the most important aspect of behavior in general. Perhaps even more basic is whether or not the behavior occurred at all. This problem, discussed earlier, is resolved by having some technique that accurately determines if a change has actually occurred. Assuming the decision is valid, we can now attempt to see the extent to which these behavior modifications are correlated with other circumstances.

Consider a human action such as talking. At any given moment in time a person is either talking or not talking. Normally, this class of responses occurs in bunches or bursts of words (phonemic sequences) separated by pauses of various durations. If we simply examined the environment and the individual at isolated instants and attempted to see if anything in the environment was controlling the person's speech, we might be overwhelmed by the complexity of the information obtained. For one thing, extremely long and varied sequences or chains of responses are initiated and run through to completion on the basis of a single environmental stimulus event. But if we examine the *rate* of speech we may find that changes in the relative output are governed by some stimulus events in the organism's surroundings. Or, possibly, that some class of speech behavior such as descriptive adjectives or emotional references varies as a function of specifiable experiences.

An examination of rate changes, particularly when expressed as a cumulative record over time, can be highly informative. The rate existing before specific training manipulations is termed the *operant level*. The operant level is one kind of baseline often used in educational and psychological research. Perhaps this is because we are concerned not so much with whether some behavior occurs, as with how often it occurs under various conditions. For example, a large portion of the change in children's behavior attributable to our educational system involves socially approved and disapproved responses. Anger, lying, aggression, teasing, and many kinds of sexual behavior are not considered appropriate in the classroom; politeness, cooperation, sharing, pride, persistence, etc., are encouraged. Almost every child will exhibit some nonzero operant level of all of these behaviors and, more often forgotten, these are all appropriate in some sense at some time in the child's life. It is not so much that we wish to eliminate the possibility of certain classes of responses from the organism's repertoire or capability, as it is to teach the person to discriminate the circumstances under which the behavior should or should not occur. The cumulative recording of response frequency under such different conditions permits the observer to rate the differences that imply discrimination on the part of the student.

It is one of my primary theses that education has progressed so little during its long history because teachers have been unable accurately to assess their effect on students or to fit the effects they have observed into a meaningful framework. My hope is that the following materials will facilitate this dual requirement of an effective educational technology. I believe it is the teacher's— and, to a lesser extent, parents'—prerogative to decide what classes of observable behavior will comprise the ultimate goals of educational experiences. But these goals, often termed *behavioral objectives* or *terminal behavior,* must be clearly specified so that the teacher will know when the student's performance is approximating the goal to a greater degree. Thus, it may be concluded that the single most essential relation in teaching is the *loop* transmitting information about the effect of the teacher on the student *back* to the instructor.

Obviously, the only way that this feedback can exist is for the student's activity to be externalized and made public. This is why, even though ideally and eventually we have students who read silently to themselves, we must first bring reading aloud into the child's realm of accomplishment. Not only do younger people learn better when physically active, but the continuous information about performance change telling the teacher how well the student is doing is itself invaluable. Most of the contributions to education during the first half of this century stemmed from various procedures that made the student active in some directly observable form. Our educational system now produces adequately large amounts of active responding at the lower grades, and various programmed texts and related devices are bringing the desired behavior back out into the open in the long-suppressed higher grades.

The single greatest handicap for education of the masses is that we must, due to financial considerations, attempt teaching students en masse. But we do not wish to foster mass behavior; we are concerned with the relatively independent behavior of the individual. The success of any system of applied behavior modification, be it parental upbringing, psychotherapy, brainwashing, rehabilitation, or technical training, depends mainly on the extent to which the program can differentially stimulate the individuals involved according to their different capabilities. This is the reason the theory and illustrations in this book are almost exclusively devoted to dealing with people on an individual rather than group basis. Still, some of the planning recommendations are applicable, at least in the beginning, to undifferentiated groups.

Unfortunately, a theory of behavior, such as the one presented in the following section, does not provide a general strategy for the teacher. Even though changes in the teacher's behavior follow the same principles that are descriptive for students, what is perhaps most appreciated by teachers themselves is some idealized model of sequential action they can use for a pattern. Glaser (1962) has established what he calls a *Basic Teaching Model.* This design for instruction (discussed by DeCecco, 1968) is composed of four successive analytic activities engaged in by the teacher. Although discussion of these stages of analysis should indicate how essential it is to know what changes one is actually trying to achieve, no short article is adequate to provide the teaching behaviors appropriate to the innumerable choices that might be generated by such a breakdown. The components of Glaser's model are: (1) analysis of subject into performance objectives, (2) evaluation of the student's present level of competence *with regard to these objectives,* (3) selection and application of an instructional procedure that has a high probability of changing the student from a present relatively incompetent state to a more competent state, and (4) reevaluation of the student's level of competence.

Traditional educators have tended to characterize the first stage (instructional objectives) in nonbehavioral terms, thus making it extremely difficult to determine how well we are achieving those objectives. They have also fixed their attention mainly on the third stage (instructional procedures) without appreciating the extent to which decisions required in that stage depend on the outcomes of the previous component (entering behavior), plus the changes in competence suggested by the interrelations between the subsequent component (performance assessment) and the second and third stages.

These retroacting aspects are referred to as feedback into the system of the results of the system. The function of these feedback loops is to modify the action of the system to make it more congruent with the purpose or desired output, result specified, etc. If feedback sources are incorporated within one's teaching model in order to provide a high degree of flexibility for modifying instructional procedure, it is essential that objectives, entering behavior, and assessment all have a great deal in common. That is, goals and assessment must refer to the same classes of behavior rather than the common practice of using I.Q. test behavior as the entering evaluation basis, then stating objectives of education in terms quite divorced from standardized test performance. Ideally, the terminal instructional objectives should be defined by generating a test designed to answer the question of whether or not the goals being considered have, in fact, been attained. This set of ultimately desired behaviors should then be used to generate a set of tasks which would indicate appropriate entering behavior. Finally, the tasks (questions, skill requirements, etc.) comprising both entering and terminal behavior criteria should be employed for assessment of performance following instruction. The point here is that the behavior being observed and evaluated must be relevant to the goals of the *teacher.* It is, of course, hoped that the teacher's objectives are in agreement with parental and societal aspirations; in the final analysis, however, it is the person arranging the conditions of instruction who must ensure that methods of evaluation (both entering and terminal) are appropriate.

After finishing this set of readings, and probably well before, the reader should have concluded that we are in favor of actively deciding which of many alternative kinds of behavior are best for a particular instructional situation. This implies that educational technology has advanced to a point where many operating rules for effective teaching can be derived from the more general principles of behavior theory. If these premises are accepted as not only valid but also desirable, we believe this conceptual framework can be used with amazing success by an observant and concerned teacher. On the other side of this proposed vantage point is the spector of countless little automatons doing the bidding of a Big Brother contingency arranger. I would like to conclude by offering some comments on behavioral control, and the concepts of determinism and free will.

The control of behavior as a relation between the behavior of two persons (e.g., student and teacher) is symmetrical; that is, the controlling effect extends both ways—from teacher to student, and from student to teacher. This is always the case when someone is manipulating the consequences of the behavior of another person. For example, suppose a parent decides to reward or punish his child for a particular class of actions such as writing. For the reaction of the parent to have any effect, the consequence of the child's writing behavior must be of importance or value to the child. Thus, if the youngster is given praise, money, or television privileges for writing, and the payoff is really related to the occurrence of the desired behavior, it is clear that the child has been given a means of getting the things he values. If he wants whatever has been given as a reward in the past for writing, all he has to do is write. So, we might say that it is the parent's reward-giving behavior that is being controlled. An analogous account can be given for the control of behavior via aversive consequences. As long as the behavior of the controller produces an event of value to the controllee, such as punishment avoidance, the extent of control is essentially reciprocal. Yet, one might feel there is something lacking in such a characterization. Perhaps it is that there is no assurance the child *knows* this symmetricity exists, and therefore may not be able to use the information to his best advantage. And what about control of one's own behavior by oneself? Is not the concept of freedom incompatible with a highly arranged environment?

The answer to these queries depends greatly on the key role of *knowledge,* defined as the symbolic representation of relations among events. I am using the word knowledge as synonomous with being able to state an "if, then" relation which corresponds to actual conditions of the real world (usually termed *fact*). Thus, the typical scientific positivist says a *statement* of fact can be relatively true or false, but facts simply *are* whatever exists. Knowledge, to the extent it validly represents reality (i.e., facts), allows us to make predictions about what will happen under specified circumstances. This conception of knowledge as equivalent to predictability allows us to examine the so-called doctrine of *determinism.*

Philosophically, the doctrine simply says every effect has a cause. But this is deceptively simple, because cause and effect are then defined in terms of each other instead of independently, as was demanded earlier in this commentary. All that confronts the scientist, or anyone else, is a series of events we call life. It appears to us that some outstanding events are separated by gaps in time; but our conception of time is only a series of highly regular events used as a basis for comparison. Whether some happening, like an earthquake, is related causally to some other event, such as a tidal wave, or to "offending the gods" is not an easy matter to decide. In practice, there are two basic criteria: (1) Did the events occur close together in space or time, in which case the events tend to become behaviorally associated; and (2) is there any consistent reoccurrence of the second event when preceded by the first? This can be called *consistent togetherness*. Unfortunately, not all classes of events show consistent togetherness with some other event class. Even though the scientist cannot find any consistent pattern among the events, one might try to pretend or believe cause-effect relations somehow underlay the events but were, for whatever reasons, hidden. Although this kind of faith is comforting to the philosopher, it does not help the scientist trying to state these relationships. Therefore, we must distinguish between the metaphysical doctrine and the empirical state of affairs.

If we stick with the pragmatic scientific view that some events are deterministic (i.e., can be determined or known to occur) under certain conditions, while other happenings are only determinable in a probabilistic sense and some perhaps not at all, we see that determinism is simply how knowledgeable or informed we are. Using this meaning it should also be apparent that the opposite of determinism is not free will, but ignorance or lack of predictability in nature. The most accepted opposite of free will is compulsion, inability to impose constraints on oneself, or lack of control of one's behavior. Within this framework it is possible to predict or state in advance what you are going to do without being able to do anything about it. However, this is the exception among normal people in that knowledge of what probably will happen typically allows the person to imagine several alternate courses of action. At this point, once again, we are prone to come to the erroneous conclusion that thoughts are equivalents of actions.

Freedom, and its application to will (power of control over one's actions), implies lack of restraint or constraint of alternatives. But what is an alternative? What one can conceive of or imagine? In reality, there are many restraints and constraints on both our thoughts and actions. The imaginings of the most creative are beyond the conception of the least creative. Furthermore, even those of us who can imagine doing, saying, or feeling extraordinary kinds of experiences may find it impossible to actually engage in the behavior overtly in some noncognitive fashion. Thus, we see it means little to speak of hypothetical or ideal alternatives; only those ways of behaving that are actually producible have any existence for a scientist. Obviously, then, freedom is a concept rarely put to empirical test since most people would rather believe they are capable or incapable of something rather than face the harsh judgment of reality. This is a roundabout way of saying that freedom to produce alternate forms of behavior must be demonstrated.

The terms *demonstrate* and *producible* imply a strong relation between the situation under which the behavior is demanded and the action that results. This self-control or will power clearly requires that the individual *knows* how to make his own body behave; i.e., *if* the person interprets the situation as one for which aggressive and threatening responses are appropriate, *then* he can create or subdue such behavior. The fact that he can call the behavioral shots in advance is proof of some degree of control, while the generality of circumstances under which such prediction is possible indicates the breadth of control. It is not difficult to see that freedom to be the kind of person one wishes to be depends on knowing what is necessary to cause the desired behaviors. For example, if you have observed that you get mean-looking and angry if you recall some terrible injustice inflicted on you, there exists the potential for alternating between your normally jovial self and an aggressively threatening Mr. Hyde. Control is possible only where known deterministic relations exist; the control may be probabilistic in that it may be less than 100 percent effective, but it is still deterministic if *any* regularity can be achieved and specified.

Following this convoluted path of interrelated meanings we come to the somewhat startling conclusion that free will requires determinism! Actually, it is the *proof* or demonstration of free will that absolutely requires the individual to have knowledge of how he reacts to both external stimuli and his own internally provided cues generated by thoughts, movements, emotions, etc. It is the *knowledge* of the consistency in ourselves and of what behavior follows what stimulus situations that gives us the power over ourselves and makes us relatively free. This is, I believe, the justification for elevating education and the teaching of behavioral principles to the pinnacle of our value system, which emphasizes personal freedom so much. That behavior will be controlled, I have no doubts whatsoever. The only question is who will have the knowledge to achieve the control.

REFERENCES

DeCecco, J. P. *The Psychology of Learning and Instruction: Educational Psychology.* Englewood Cliffs, N. J.: Prentice-Hall, 1968. Pp. 11-13.

Glaser, R. Psychology and instructional technology. In R. Glaser (Ed.), *Training Research and Education.* Pittsburgh: University of Pittsburgh Press, 1962, Pp. 1-30.

2

Learning theory

Gayle A. Olson and Richard D. Olson

CLASSICAL CONDITIONING

Classical conditioning, or *respondent conditioning,* is a procedure in which an organism is subjected to a pair of stimuli. One of them, called the unconditioned stimulus (UCS), is a stimulus which, at the onset of an experiment or experience, evokes a regular and measurable response, designated as the unconditioned response (UCR). The other stimulus is the conditioned stimulus (CS) and is neutral in the respect that, at the beginning of the conditioning, it does not evoke an UCR. Often the CS has no particular significance for the subject and produces no response other than attention, although this property is not necessary for the definition of classical conditioning. After repeated pairings of UCS and CS, a response resembling the UCR will be evoked by the CS in the absence of the UCS. When this phenomenon occurs, it is called a conditioned response (CR).

Classical conditioning was originally demonstrated in a series of studies by the Russian physiologist Ivan P. Pavlov, begun in the late 1890's. Pavlov encountered the phenomenon of conditioning while conducting experiments into the nature of the digestive glands, and his explanations of it were limited to the physiological realm. His descriptions have been extended by countless others to include many types of learning procedures, including reinforcement, extinction, discrimination, and generalization, among others.

In the typical Pavlovian experiment, salivary secretion was the conditioned response. Pavlov devised an apparatus that could be attached to the subject's salivary glands with a minor operation, which diverted the saliva flow to outside the mouth where it could be collected and measured. The subject was a dog, who stood in a restraining harness facing a panel with a plate of food behind it, which acted as the UCS in the experiment. Pavlov sounded a bell (the CS) and immediately presented the plate with food powder to the dog. Since no salivation was evoked by the bell sound alone, the sound had no conditioned response associated with it; but there was copious salivation during eating when food alone was the UCS for the UCR of salivating. After pairing the sound of the bell with serving the food a few times, the strength of the response conditioned to the bell sound (CS) was tested by presenting the CS alone. Then more training trials were given. After 10 pairings of the CS (bell) and the UCS (food), slight amounts of salivation were measured in response to the CS alone. Additional pairings increased the strength of the CR. Figure 1 presents a schematic diagram of this experiment. The solid lines indicate a response that occurs without learning, or prior to the beginning of conditioning, while the dashed line represents learning acquired in this situation.

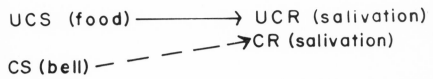

Fig. 1. A schematic representation of a simple classical conditioning procedure.

Another example of classical conditioning, which employs a motor response rather than a secretory response, is found in the work of another Russian physiologist, Vladimir M. Bekhterev. Besides the type of response studied, another difference between Pavlov's and Bekhterev's experiments involve the type of UCS. Bekhterev used as his UCS a noxious or unpleasant stimulus, a shock to the leg of the dog, whereas Pavlov employed food, which was attractive to the hungry subject. In Bekhterev's study, the UCR to the shock was a flexion of the leg that received the shock. When the CS evoked the flexion before the shock appeared, a CR was demonstrated. Thus, another differing feature in the two experiments was the use of test trials. Pavlov presented the CS alone, but this procedure was unnecessary in the shock study because the CR came before the shock (UCS), enabling the experimenter to assess the progress of conditioning on each trial.

Examples of classical conditioning often used with humans can be provided from eyelid conditioning experiments. Such studies usually employ an air puff to the cornea of the eye as the UCS to elicit an eyeblink (UCR). When the air puff has been paired with a CS, such as a bell, the bell alone can be seen to produce a blink. Another common situation involving human classical conditioning is one similar to the Bekhterev experiments. The UCS is a shock delivered to the hand or foot of the subject, producing a change in the electrical conductivity of the skin, as measured by the GSR (Galvanic Skin Response), which is influenced by sweating of the palm in emotional experiences. After pairing the UCS with any appropriate CS, like tone, the CS will produce the GSR changes by itself.

The ordering and spacing of stimuli in classical conditioning situations have been points of concern and study. The CS and UCS may occur simultaneously, but more typically, the UCS follows the CS by a definite interval of time. The time between presentation of the CS and onset of the UCS is known as the *interstimulus interval.* The optimal interstimulus interval varies with the situation and the kind of response used, but Pavlov found that about ½ sec between the CS and UCS was best for many responses.

Several arrangements of the interstimulus interval are possible. One of these is *delayed conditioning,* in which the CS appears prior to the UCS and lasts at least until the UCS appears. In *trace conditioning,* the CS comes on briefly and then goes off again before the UCS onset, so that the two never occur at exactly the same time. Another possible relationship between the CS and UCS is known as *backward conditioning,* in which the CS comes after the UCS. Conditioning is difficult, if not impossible, to accomplish with this method, however.

Figure 2 is a schematic representation of the relationships delineated above. Time is represented on the top line. The other lines represent stimulus onset and cessation, respectively, by upward or downward deviations of the lines. Note that there are several possible variations of delayed conditioning. These relationships can become important in applying classical conditioning procedures to classroom use.

The uses of responses from classical conditioning have been a matter of debate. Since Pavlov used reflex responses, many authors feel that classical conditioning considerations should be limited to built in, automatic responses, over which the subject has little or no control. Infant learning experiences as well as emotional learning provide examples of automatic responses, since most of these experiences are not under our control. A broader interpretation of classical conditioning involves any situation when two stimuli are paired with the result that a response formerly given to one (UCS), but not to the other (CS), eventually is evoked by the latter. Thus, the response does not have to be a reflex, although it may be. The second view of classical conditioning is the one applied most to everyday learning.

Besides the acquisition of learned responses, it is important to look at the weakening or disappearance of conditioned responses. In classical conditioning literature, *forgetting* refers to the loss of a response in the absence of practice. It is the reduction in response strength with lapsed time since the last exposure to the paired stimuli. Although few classical conditioning experiments directly investigate forgetting, it is necessary to note its occurrence and to take it into account.

More commonly studied is *extinction,* referring to decreases in response strength due to repeated presentations of the CS in the absence of the UCS. The decrease in response during extinction is not a mere passive disappearance of the response, but is instead an active inhibition. Extinction does not actually destroy the conditioned response; following a period of rest by the subject, the conditioned response returns even though no reinforcements have occurred in the interim. This phenomenon is called *spontaneous recovery.* A response which has so recovered is usually weaker than the original response, thus making it possible to totally remove a response by repeated reextinctions. Each time the response is extinguished, spontaneous recovery lessens, until it finally fails to reappear.

Another phenomenon investigated in classical conditioning situations is *generalization.* When a response has been conditioned to a particular stimulus, other physically similar stimuli will also evoke the response. Thus, if a dog

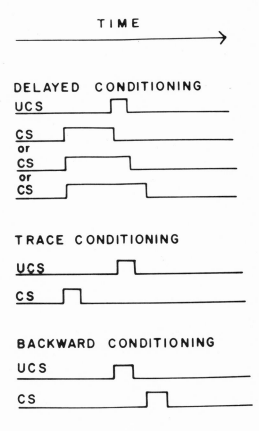

Fig. 2. Different procedures for classically conditioning a response: delayed conditioning, trace conditioning, and backward conditioning.

learned to salivate to a given tone, he will also salivate to higher and lower tones. The more nearly alike the new stimuli are to the original one, the more likely they are to evoke the conditioned response. This principle of generalization is the basis for one's ability to react to novel situations in much the same way as we have reacted to previously experienced or familiar ones. The amount of generalization falls off systematically as new stimuli become increasingly different from the original CS—known as a *gradient* of generalization (see Figure 3).

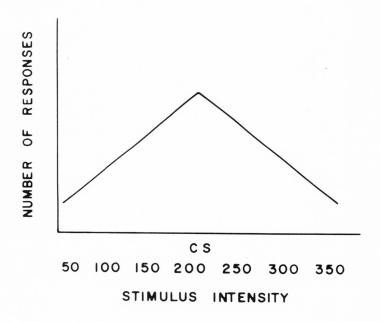

Fig. 3. Response strength along a stimulus dimension due to the phenomenon of stimulus generalization.

Inhibition associated with nonreinforcement or extinction also generalizes. If a stimulus has become inhibitory as a result of extinction, then other similar stimuli will also be inhibitory. There is a gradient of generalization for inhibition similar to the one noted above, with remoteness from the original stimulus producing decreasing amounts of inhibition.

A process complementary to generalization is *discrimination*. Whereas generalization is a reaction to similarities, discrimination is a response to differences. Discrimination is brought about by selective reinforcement and nonrein-forcement. Any response to the CS is reinforced, while a response to any other stimulus is extinguished, so that eventually the subject makes the response only in the presence of the CS.

Another procedure used in classical conditioning is *higher-order conditioning.* It involves more complicated behavior than the previous processes—the response conditioned to one stimulus is transferred to a conditioned stimulus. There are two or more stages to such an experiment. The first stage is a typical classical conditioning situation. In the second stage, the CS in the first stage becomes the UCS for the second stage. Such an experiment may be illustrated by a situation in which the first stage involves a typical salivation conditioning of a dog to a bell. In the second stage the bell is the UCS which elicits the UCR, the salivation. The CS is a light. After pairing the light and the bell, the light produces salivation when presented alone. A diagram of higher-order conditioning is shown in Figure 4.

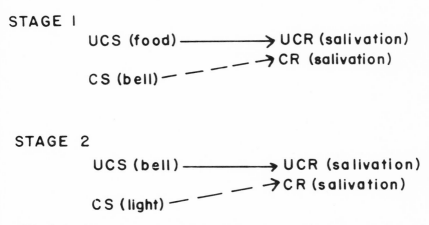

Fig. 4. A schematic representation of higher-order classical conditioning.

Higher-order conditioning is difficult to accomplish in the laboratory because during the second stage, the first stage learning is likely to be weakened. The first stage CS (the bell in our example) is paired with the light in the second stage, and never with food. Since extinction involves presentation of the CS in the absence of the UCS, and in the second stage the bell is presented in the absence of the food, the salivation to the bell is extinguished so that the bell can no longer serve as the UCS for salivation. This problem can be partially over-come by interspersing a few stage-one trials during the second-stage learning to prevent extinction entirely. With great difficulty, higher-order conditioning can be carried one more stage, using a third-order stimulus.

It seems probable that many of our emotional feelings are classically conditioned responses. A face, scene, or voice can act as the CS for an emotional response. Although the origin of a conditioned emotional response is obscure because the original UCS is forgotten or repressed, it is sometimes possible to discover the root of such a response. It might be possible, for example, to pin down the cause for a feeling of uneasiness or anxiety whenever a person passes a certain place, if it is discovered that the person had had an automobile accident there. The scene (CS) became paired with the accident (UCS), which produced numerous feelings of uneasiness, so that later the scene alone produced them. Or claustrophobia might be traced to an early experience of being trapped in a stuck elevator. The confinement (UCS) produced fear, and since the elevator was a stimulus associated with the confinement, the elevator alone began to evoke feelings of fear. This fear, then, could have generalized to all small enclosures.

Numerous experiments have been conducted to demonstrate that emotions can be classically conditioned. Probably the most famous and most often quoted study was that of Watson and Rayner (1920), in which they conditioned fear to furry objects in an infant named Albert. The nine-month old was allowed to play with a white rat, which elicited no fear from little Albert. Later in the experiment, while Albert was playing with the rat, a loud noise was sounded near him, startling him and causing him to cry. After that, Albert withdrew and whimpered at the sight of the rat. This fear of white rats generalized to all small furry animals, a fur coat, and even a Santa Claus mask. These responses persisted for more than a month, when the experiment was terminated, suggesting to the investigators that the conditioned fears might possibly be permanent.

The little Albert study caused an uproar among psychoanalysts, who claimed that Watson and Rayner had induced a lifelong fear that presented a highly disruptive influence on the subject's life. As a response to this problem, Jones (1924) conducted an experiment to demonstrate the removal of children's fears through the classical conditioning technique. An extinction procedure was not effective because the fear was so strong, thus requiring *deconditioning*. In deconditioning, the feared object (here, a rabbit) was presented into the playroom while the fearful child was playing. After numerous trials of pairing the rabbit (CS) with the playroom (UCS), the rabbit evoked the same response (i.e., approaching and playing) as did the playroom. The process was gradual, with the child first fearing, then ignoring, and finally approaching the rabbit. After the deconditioning, the child fondled the rabbit affectionately.

A similar procedure is *counterconditioning*. The desired CR is incompatible to the response originally elicited by the CS (i.e., fear). Such a conditioned response might be approach of the feared stimulus. This approach could be accomplished by presenting a pleasant UCS (e.g., candy) along with the CS (the feared stimulus), putting them side by side. In order to get the candy the subject must approach the feared object. If the UCS is desirable enough, the subject will go to it and discover that the CS is not really so bad after all. And after a number of such pairings, the subject should approach the CS when given alone. When this behavior occurs, the conditioning is complete and the fear is removed.

Kennedy (1971) extended the classical conditioning approach to emotional responding to what he called "classroom phobia." He defined this term as a reluctance to return to school after being out for a few days, especially in returning on Monday after being absent on the previous Friday. School phobia occurs as a result of separation anxiety, with separation (UCS) producing anxiety (UCR) being paired with school (CS), which itself comes to evoke anxiety or fear. The treatment of such school phobia involves forced school attendance, with praise after staying in school for the whole day. Since school attendance is used to produce reward, the original fear is counter-conditioned because the original CS (school) is now paired with attendance and evokes praise instead of fear.

Other emotional responses to school, such as those associated with the teacher, classmates, or learning, can be similarly affected by the classical conditioning paradigm. Therefore, it seems only logical that these school experiences should be paired with pleasant stimuli, or at least not paired with unpleasant ones.

The acquisition of new words for one's vocabulary can be considered a classical conditioning procedure. With young children the spoken word (CS) is often paired with the object it represents (UCS). The object itself produces in the child an image of the object. After such pairing, the spoken word alone will evoke the image of the object. The same process applies to learning written words. The written word (CS) is often pointed to and spoken (UCS) by the teacher or parent. If the spoken word has acquired the ability to produce an image of the object or event, then the written word will do likewise after pairing the two. This procedure is an example of higher-order conditioning, since the UCS in the second phase was a CS in the first stage.

Young children's dictionaries often use pictures to directly condition the meaning of the words. The written word (CS) is paired with a picture of the object (UCS), and since the picture gives the child an image of the object, the written word will do the same. For older children, dictionaries perform the same function, but use words already learned as the UCS, rather than pictures. After pairing the unknown word (CS) with the known one (UCS), the pupil learns the meaning of the formerly unknown one. Higher-order conditioning is again involved here.

Learning a foreign language follows the same lines. The foreign word (CS) is given alongside the English word (UCS), and after a number of such pairings, the meaning of the foreign word is associated with the meaning of the English word. Many educators feel, however, that it is better to go back to the original learning process of pairing a foreign word with the object it represents, bypassing English entirely. Either method, however, involves classical conditioning.

Another practical application of the classical conditioning paradigm is its use in the testing of hearing, as demonstrated by Aldrich (1928). He observed that hearing tests of infants are often inaccurate because they require some visible object that the baby has heard, such as a small dinner bell. These reactions are greatly affected by the visual-motor coordination of the child as well as his mood or attention. For this reason, Aldrich set up a classically conditioned response to the bell. The bell (CS) was rung just before he scratched the infant on the foot with a pin (UCS). After a dozen or so pairings, the bell alone produced withdrawal of the leg and crying. Thus, the infant demonstrated that he could, indeed, hear the bell. If he were deaf, no such conditioning could have occurred. Hardy and Bordley (1947) developed a similar test, but used a tone as the CS, a shock as the UCS, and the GSR as the UCR and CR.

Final applications of the classical conditioning technique were employed by Mowrer and Mowrer (1938) and Morgan and Witmer (1939) to extinguish bedwetting. The Mowrers used a special electrified sheet placed under the child. When the child began to urinate, the circuit in the sheet was completed, and a loud bell rang. The bell's ringing woke up the child, who then was instructed to go to the bathroom and finish urinating. The Mowrers assumed that the bedwetting was caused by faulty training in the child's ability to recognize bladder tension during the night. After pairing the noisy bell (UCS), which produced awakening (UCR), with the bladder tension (CS) for a while, the child can learn to awaken when his bladder is full, and can thus avoid bedwetting. This procedure would be of little help to a child with urological or psychological problems that contribute to the bedwetting, but it was found to be quite effective for those who had simply never learned adequate bladder control.

Since classical conditioning has been demonstrated to be involved in a number of animal and human learning experiences, its place in present-day considerations of psychological influences on behavior is assured. Of particular relevance to learning in the classroom are the acquisition of language and emotional learning by the classical conditioning technique.

OPERANT AND INSTRUMENTAL CONDITIONING

Although classical conditioning is important in the educational process, the great majority of classroom learning takes place through *operant* and *instrumental* conditioning. Typing, multiplication, spelling, and grammar are just a few examples to indicate the diverse nature of the types of behavior acquired through these processes. Accordingly, a foundation in these theoretical positions is also a necessary prerequisite for being an effective teacher.

Both operant and instrumental conditioning are concerned with a stimulus condition—an organism's reaction to the stimulus condition and the consequences of that response. The major methodological difference is that in operant conditioning the learner is free to respond at any time, while in instrumental conditioning the use of discrete trials requires responses to be made at specified intervals. The main interest variable in operant conditioning is the rate of responding, which may be defined as the number of responses made in a given unit of time. For instance, in learning to type, one would be concerned with the

---

*The basic ideas concerning the origin of the 16 behavioral paradigms and the definition of extinction as applied to a preference continuum were originally presented by Dr. D. Gene Davenport, Professor of Psychology, in a colloquium to the Department of Psychology, St. Louis University, in May, 1969. The authors of the present paper are responsible for the application to the classroom situation.

number of words per minute. Such variables as response latency and number of problems correct would be examples of measures used in instrumental conditioning. However, even though these differences exist, the basic paradigm of stimulus-response-results is the same in both cases. Accordingly, the following analysis of learning will be applicable to either as long as allowances are made for variations in methodology.

The first consideration is the stimulus. Does the individual respond to the environment as a whole or to some discriminable aspect of it? In *discriminated stimulus learning* (DSL) a discriminable stimulus (e.g., light) is introduced to signal the appropriateness of the response; this stimulus is termed an S^D. Verbal statements, bells, lights, etc., are examples of S^D's, which represent stimulus conditions that may be intermittently present and absent in the environment, but when present signal to the learner that now is the time to make the response. When the S^D is absent from the environment the stimulus condition is termed S^Δ.

Responding to the general environment rather than a specific cue is termed *nondiscriminated stimulus learning* (NDSL). Typically the NDSL condition is characterized by the fact that any time a response is made the expected results will occur; this stimulus condition can be represented simply by an S.

Thus, the two alternatives are (1) that the stimulus that signals reward is specific and present only occasionally (DSL), or (2) that the stimulus is general and present rather consistently (NDSL).

The second consideration is the response. A response may cause certain results to occur (RC), i.e., an individual may make a response in an attempt to produce a desired outcome. For example, a student may raise his hand in an attempt to be called on by the teacher. Responses may also occur in an attempt to prevent something from happening (RP). For example, a child will study to keep from failing a course.

The final consideration is the result that occurs after the response has been made. It is generally acknowledged that the results of any behavior may be represented by a stimulus event that is reinforcing (S^+) or that is punishing (S^-). Further, the stimulus event may be initiated because of the response ($_+S$) or it may be terminated because of the response ($_-S$). Accordingly, four outcomes are possible: (1) the initiation of a good stimulus event ($_+S^+$), (2) the initiation of a bad stimulus event ($_+S^-$), (3) the termination of a good stimulus event ($_-S^+$), or (4) the termination of a bad stimulus event ($_-S^-$).

By considering all possible combinations of the above contingencies, 16 different paradigms of operant/instrumental conditioning may exist. This is clearly indicated in Figure 5.

Each of the paradigms will now be considered in terms of their existence in the classroom and their effect on behavior.

1. $S^D \longrightarrow RC \longrightarrow _+S^+$ = *Discriminated Reward.* In this paradigm the individual is taught that in the presence of a discriminative stimulus the performance of the response will result in the initiation of a positive stimulus event. The response is reinforced and becomes more frequent since it causes a positive

situation. For example, a child is told by his teacher that if he spells his vocabulary words correctly he will get five extra minutes of gym time. After correct spelling has happened once it will be even more likely to happen in the future because it has been reinforced. The teacher's verbal statement is the S^D, the child's spelling is the RC, and the extra gym time he will get is the $_+S^+$.

2. $S^D \longrightarrow RC \longrightarrow_+S^-$ = _Discriminated Punishment._ In this paradigm the individual is taught that in the presence of a discriminative stimulus the performance of the response will result in the initiation of a negative stimulus event. The response is punished and becomes less frequent since it causes a negative situation. For example, a child is told by his teacher that if he hits anyone he will have to stay after school and do extra work. After this has happened once it will be less likely to happen in the future because the behavior has been punished. The teacher's verbal statement is the S^D, the child hitting a classmate is the RC, and having to stay after school to do extra work is the $_+S^-$.

3. $S^D \longrightarrow RC \longrightarrow S^+$ = _Discriminated Reward Termination._ In this paradigm the individual is taught that in the presence of a discriminative stimulus the performance of the response will result in the termination of a positive stimulus event. The response is punished and becomes less frequent since it terminates a positive situation, which is a type of punishment. For example, a child is playing in the gym and is told by his teacher that if he hits any of his classmates he will forfeit his gym period. After the child does hit someone he will be less likely to do it again because forfeiting his gym period is a type of punishment. The teacher's verbal statement is the S^D, the child hitting a classmate is the RC, and having to forfeit gym is the S^+.

4. $S^D \longrightarrow RC \longrightarrow S^-$ = _Discriminated Escape._ In this paradigm the individual is taught that in the presence of a discriminative stimulus the performance of the response will result in the termination of a negative stimulus event. The response is reinforced and becomes more frequent since it terminates a negative situation. For example, a child is punished by not getting recess for a week; however, his teacher tells him that if he does not make any errors on his spelling test he will no longer be punished. After he makes the perfect score and gets to play during recess he is likely to try harder at spelling because this behavior has now been reinforced. The teacher's verbal statement is the S^D, the child making a perfect score is the RC, and the termination of his punishment is the S^-.

5. $\overline{\lfloor S^D \underline{\hspace{2cm}} \atop RP\rfloor} \longrightarrow_+S^+$ = _Discriminated Omission Training._ In this paradigm the individual is taught that in the presence of a discriminative stimulus signaling the future initiation of a positive stimulus event the performance of the response will prevent the initiation of that event. The response is punished and becomes less frequent since it prevents the initiation of a positive situation. For example, a child is told he will get to play in the gym on Friday afternoons unless he gets into a fight. He does fight and does not go to the gym; however, this behavior is now less likely to occur again since it has been punished. The teacher's verbal statement is the S^D, the child's hitting someone is the RP, and the Friday gym period is the $_+S^+$.

6. $\boxed{-S^D \xrightarrow[\text{RP}]{} {}_+S^-}$ = _Discriminated Avoidance._ In this paradigm the individual is taught that in the presence of a discriminative stimulus signaling the future initiation of a negative stimulus event the performance of the response will prevent the initiation of that event. The response is reinforced and becomes more frequent since it prevents the initiation of a negative situation. For example, a child is told that he is going to fail spelling unless he gets an A on the last test. He does earn an A and does not fail spelling. This behavior is now more likely to occur again since it has been reinforced. The

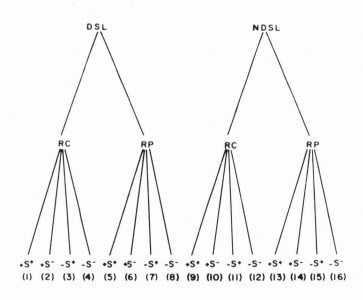

Fig. 5. The schematic origin of the 16 different paradigms of instrumental and operant conditioning.

teacher's verbal statement is the S^D, the child's earning an A is the RP, and the failing of spelling is the $_+S^-$.

7. $\boxed{-S^D \xrightarrow[\text{RP}]{} S^+}$ = _Discriminated Avoidance of Reward Termination._ In this paradigm the individual is taught that in the presence of a discriminative stimulus signalling the future termination of a positive stimulus event the performance of the response will prevent the termination of that event. The response is reinforced and becomes more frequent since

it prevents the termination of a positive situation. For example, a child reads a notice that he will lose his position on the baseball team unless he arrives at practice on time. He does get to practice on time and does not lose his position. This behavior is now more likely to occur again since it has been reinforced. The written notice is the S^D, the child's getting to practice on time is the RP, and the losing of his position is the S^+.

8. $\llcorner_S{}^D \underset{RP \lrcorner}{\overline{\quad\quad\quad\quad\quad}} \rightarrow \underline{S}^{-}\lrcorner$ = _Discriminated_ _Aversive_ _Stimulus_

Extension. In this paradigm the individual is taught that in the presence of a discriminative stimulus signaling the future termination of a negative stimulus event the performance of the responses will prevent the termination of that event. The response is punished and becomes less frequent since it prevents the termination of a negative situation. For example, a child is punished for talking and is told by his teacher that he must read for 30 minutes without talking, then the punishment will end. However, he talks to his friend and continues to be punished, even after the original 30 minutes has passed. This behavior is now less likely to occur again since it has been punished. The teacher's verbal statement is the S^D, the child's talking is the RP, and the termination of punishment is the S^-.

9. $S \longrightarrow RC \longrightarrow {}_+S^+$ = _Reward_. In this paradigm the individual is taught that in the presence of a nondiscriminative stimulus the performance of the response will result in the initiation of a positive stimulus event. The response is reinforced and becomes more frequent since it causes a positive situation. For example, a child learns that by studying hard every night he will receive good grades. There is no specific, discriminable stimulus that controls his behavior. Rather, it appears that his behavior is a function of the total stimulus complex present in his environment and is thus representative of what is termed the nondiscriminated stimulus learning situation. The child's studying is the RC, and the earning of good grades is the ${}_+S^+$.

10. $S \longrightarrow RC \longrightarrow {}_+S^-$ = _Punishment_. In this paradigm the individual is taught that in the presence of a nondiscriminative stimulus the performance of the response will result in the initiation of a negative stimulus event. The response is punished and becomes less frequent since it causes a negative situation. For example, a child falls down on the floor in the gym and gets a wood burn. The stimulus is all of the stimuli present when the child falls, the child's falling is the RC, and the wood burn is the ${}_+S^-$.

11. $S \longrightarrow RC \longrightarrow {}_-S^+$ = _Reward_ _Termination_. In this paradigm the individual is taught that in the presence of a nondiscriminative stimulus the performance of the response will result in the termination of a positive stimulus event. The response is punished and becomes less frequent since it causes the termination of a positive situation. For example, a child learns that any day he fails to turn in his homework he will lose his recess for that day. The stimulus is all of the stimuli present when he fails to turn in his homework, the child's failure to do his homework is the RC, and the loss of his recess for the day is the S^+.

12. $S \longrightarrow RC \longrightarrow S^- = $ *Escape.* In this paradigm the individual is taught that in the presence of a nondiscriminative stimulus the performance of the response will result in the termination of a negative stimulus event. The response is reinforced and becomes more frequent since it causes the termination of a negative situation. For example, a child learns that when he is punished by being kept after school, if he helps the teacher clean up the classroom she will let him go home. The stimulus is all of the stimuli present when he stays after class, the child's helping with the cleaning of the classroom is the RC, and the permission to go home is the S^-.

13. $\boxed{{}_-S \underset{RP \rfloor}{\quad\quad\quad} \longrightarrow {}_+S^+} = $ *Omission Training.* In this paradigm the individual is taught that in the presence of a nondiscriminative stimulus signaling the future initiation of a positive stimulus event the performance of the response will prevent the initiation of that event. The response is punished and becomes less frequent since it prevents the initiation of a positive situation. For example, a teacher plans to let her class go to the library in the afternoon as a surprise, to let them read for pleasure. However, one child starts a fight and does not get to go to the library. The nondiscriminated stimulus is all of the stimuli present when the response occurred, the child's starting the fight was the RP, and the going to the library was the $_+S^+$.

14. $\boxed{{}_-S \underset{RP \rfloor}{\quad\quad\quad} \longrightarrow {}_+S^-} = $ *Avoidance.* In this paradigm the individual is taught that in the presence of a nondiscriminative stimulus signaling the future initiation of a negative stimulus event the performance of the response will prevent the initiation of that event. The response is reinforced and becomes more frequent since it prevents the initiation of a negative situation. For example, a child learns that the bullies in his class hang around the baseball shed at recess time and, therefore, he does not go to the baseball shed. This behavior is likely to occur again and again since it has now been reinforced. The stimulus is all of the stimuli present by the baseball shed at recess time, the child's going somewhere besides the baseball shed is the RP, and the bad time that the bullies would give him is the $_+S^-$.

15. $\boxed{{}_-S \underset{RP \rfloor}{\quad\quad\quad} \longrightarrow {}_-S^+} = $ *Avoidance of Reward Termination.* In this paradigm the individual is taught that in the presence of a nondiscriminative stimulus signaling the future termination of a positive stimulus event the performance of the response will prevent the termination of that event. The response is reinforced and becomes more frequent since it prevents the termination of a positive situation. For example, a teacher has decided to take away a child's gym periods for one week because he has been doing poorly in the classroom. However, he gets a very high grade on his next test and does not lose his gym periods. This behavior is now more likely to occur again since it has just been reinforced. The stimulus is all of the stimuli present at the time of the response, the earning of the high grade is the RP, and the loss of the gym periods is the $_-S^+$.

16. $\boxed{}$ S————— RP ——→ S⁻ = _Aversive Stimulus Extension_. In this paradigm the individual is taught that in the presence of a nondiscriminative stimulus signaling the future termination of a negative stimulus event the performance of the response will prevent the termination of that event. The response is punished and becomes less frequent since it prevents the termination of a negative situation. For example, a student is punished for talking by having to do extra multiplication problems after school. The teacher is just about to let him go home when he yells to his friend who is walking down the hall. Because of this response the teacher continues to make him do multiplication problems. This behavior is now less likely to occur again since it has just been punished. The stimulus is all of the stimuli present when the student yelled to his friend, his yelling is the RP, and the termination of his punishment is the S⁻.

To extinguish a response one simply sets up the paradigm so that the response is ineffective; i.e., regardless of whether or not the response is made no reward or punishment is presented.

With the various paradigms under consideration it becomes extremely important to determine what is a positive or negative stimulus event for an individual, because individuals do not interpret stimulus events in the same fashion. While missing a music lesson may punish one child, it may reward another. Accordingly, some means of determining individual preferences is necessary.

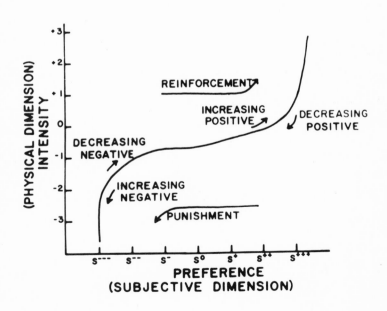

Fig. 6. A theoretical representation of a preference continuum based on the physical and subjective aspects of the stimulus.

As indicated in Figure 6, the interpretation of events is typically negative or positive. Any response producing a movement to the left (more negative) is punished and less likely to occur again. Any response producing a movement to the right is reinforced and more probable to occur again. Physical differences have their greatest effects on subjective judgments around the neutral point and their smallest effects at either extreme. Changes do not have to cross the neutral point to become positive or negative; any movement to the left is punishing and any movement to the right is reinforcing, regardless of the distance. Extinction of a response occurs when the response fails to produce any movement on the continuum.

REFERENCES

Aldrich, C. A. A new test for hearing in the new-born: the conditioned reflex. *American Journal of Diseases of Children,* 1928, 35, 36-37.

Hardy, W. G., and Bordley, J. E. Special techniques in testing the hearing of children. *Journal of Speech and Hearing Disorders,* 1951, 16, 122-131.

Jones, M. C. The elimination of children's fears. *Journal of Experimental Psychology,* 1924, 7, 382-390.

Kennedy, W. A. *Child Psychology.* Englewood Cliffs, N. J.: Prentice-Hall, Inc., 1971.

Morgan, J. J. B., and Witmer, F. J. Treatment of enuresis by the conditioned reaction technique. *Journal of Genetic Psychology,* 1939, 55, 59-65.

Mowrer, O. H., and Mowrer, W. M. Enuresis: a method for its study and treatment. *American Journal of Orthopsychiatry,* 1938, 8, 436-459.

Watson, J. B., and Rayner, R. Conditioned emotional reactions. *Journal of Experimental Psychology,* 1920, 3, 1-12.

3

What psychology has to offer education—now

Sidney W. Bijou

Some day, the question, "What does psychology have to offer education—now?" will be answered by psychologists with some measure of agreement. But at present the answer to this question depends almost entirely on the particular orientation of the individual to whom the question is put, for psychologists differ enormously in their conception of the subject matter and objectives of their discipline. Some say its subject matter is the domain of the mind, others, that it is the observable interaction of an individual's behavior with environmental events. When the question of the objectives of psychology arises, some claim them to be the understanding and explanation of psychological phenomena, others, the prediction and control of behavior. Psychologists also differ markedly in their choice of research methodology, with one segment stressing statistical designs that compare achievement of groups, and others emphasizing changes in the behavior of an individual organism. In addition, psychologists vary greatly in their approach to theory construction, with some favoring the hypothetic-deductive method, and others, the empirico-inductive procedure.

In spite of these great individual variations, there would probably be three basic approaches to the question of what psychology has to offer education: that which would be taken by the *great majority,* that of the *large minority,* and that of the *small minority.* The great majority would probably say that psychology presently offers education something like this: "We can offer an impressive collection of facts about the abilities of the child and his growth and

From *Journal of Applied Behavior Analysis,* 1970, 3, 65-71. Copyright 1970 by the Society for the Experimental Analysis of Behavior, Inc. Reprinted by permission.

Invited address, Division of School Psychologists, American Psychological Association, 76th Annual Convention, September 1, 1968, San Francisco, California. Dedicated to Professor B. F. Skinner in his sixty-fifth year. The analysis presented was generated in large measure from research supported by the U. S. Office of Education, Division of Research, Bureau of Education for the Handicapped, OEG-0-9-2322030-0762(032). Reprints may be obtained from S. W. Bijou, Child Behavior Laboratory, 403 East Healey, Champaign, Illinois 61820.

development; we can offer an extensive literature on the analysis of stimuli, on the psychology of simple and complex learning, and on perception; we can offer a considerable body of knowledge on measurement, test construction, and statistical procedures for the experimental study of groups; and we can offer some promising theories of intelligence, socialization, personality, development, and psychopathology."

The concept and principles of this large majority have accrued not only from psychology, but from sociology, anthropology, and physiology as well. They have evolved from many theories, mostly from psychoanalytic, cognitive, and learning theory. They have been established on findings from many research methods, experimental, correlational, clinical, and field observational or ecological. Consequently, many of the concepts and principles are not rooted in objectively defined raw data, nor are they systematically related to each other. Those with this orientation are eclectic with respect to a research methodology. In general, group experimental designs serve to test theories and hypotheses while correlational methods serve to assess traits and abilities. Since these psychologists, for the most part, view teaching as an intuitive art, their predominant view is that psychology can offer educators the kind of information and ideas that will help them evaluate their philosophy of education, and can acquaint teachers with recent research findings and their possible implications for instruction.

If, on the other hand, another group of psychologists, whom we shall call the large minority, were asked what psychology can offer education, the reply might be: "We can offer some tentative ideas about the nature of the child; we can present firm convictions about the stages of cognitive and intellectual development; and we can offer theoretical formulations about perception, learning, the will to learn, and the general mechanisms of coping and defending. We can also offer a philosophy of science which postulates that behavior is determined both by observable and by hypothetical internal variables."

Subgroups in this large minority attempt to relate their concepts and principles in a systematic manner. However, the concepts and principles developed by one group do not synchronize with those developed by the others, mainly because these systematists do not anchor all of their terms to objectively verifiable data. Research, as with the first group, is designed mainly to test a theory or an hypothesis and consists for the most part of comparing the achievements of groups. Practical application often involves terms and processes that are not related to the principles applied. That is to say, attempts to apply research findings to classroom practices are all too often bolstered by hypothetical variables or precepts. Because hypothetical variables and processes are central to the theories in this group, educators who subscribe to this approach are prone to attribute school failures to such presumed internal conditions as lack of drive, perceptual disability, or clinically inferred brain damage.

Still another group of psychologists, which at present is only a small minority, responding to the question of what psychology can contribute to education now would say: "We can offer a set of concepts and principles derived exclusively from experimental research; we can offer a methodology for applying these concepts and principles directly to teaching practices; we can offer a research design which deals with changes in the individual child (rather than inferring them from group averages); and we can offer a philosophy of science which insists on observable accounts of the relationships between individual behavior and its determining conditions."

Faced with this complex state of affairs—a house of psychology divided on what it has to offer education—I should like to elaborate on the offer of the last-mentioned group of psychologists, the behavioral analysis group. I shall discuss what I believe to be the promise of this approach, its influence on the role of the school psychologist, and what educators can do if they choose to pursue the leads offered by this group.

THE OFFER OF THE SMALL MINORITY

The offer of the behavioral analysis will be presented in terms of its philosophy of science, concepts and principles, core research method, and procedure for the application of concepts and principles to teaching.

The Philosophy of Science

The philosophy of science (assumptions) of any approach merits close scrutiny because it influences the kinds of problems selected for study, the basic method of gathering data, the forms in which the data are presented, and the interpretation of the findings. For the purpose of this paper, I shall limit my discussion to only five of the basic assumptions of a behavioral analysis. More comprehensive accounts may be found in Kantor (1959) and Skinner (1947, 1953, and 1963).

1. The subject matter of psychology is the interaction between the behavior of an integral organism and environmental events. These interactions are analyzed in *observable, measurable,* and *reproducible* terms and therefore are amenable to scientific investigation.

2. The interactions between the behavior of an individual and environmental events are lawful. Given an individual with his unique biological endowment, changes in his psychological behavior are a function of his interactional history and the current situation in which he is behaving.

3. As in all of the sciences, the subject matter of psychology exists in *continuities.* Continuities are assumed to exist in the stages of development, in the rates of development (normal, retarded, and accelerated), in the relationships between normal and pathological development, in the problems and procedures of basic and applied research, and in the analysis of psychological phenomena from raw data to theoretical formulation.

4. Complex interactions evolve from simple interactions and begin with the infant's initial relationships with people and objects. This does not mean that complex behaviors are assumed to be sums of simple behaviors. How a specific form of complex behavior, such as mathematical problem solving, is established

is a problem for experimental study. The final analysis of any class of complex behavior would probably involve many concepts and principles such as minute stimulus control, subtle variations in setting conditions, and intricate schedules of reinforcement.

5. A psychological theory and its technology are open and flexible systems. That is, a new concept, a new principle, or a new technique may at any time be added to the existing list, provided that it can display the proper credentials: it must be tied unequivocally to observable events; it must be functional; and it must not overlap with the concepts, principles, or techniques already cataloged.

The Concepts and Principles

The concepts of behavioral analysis refer only to observable behavioral events and environmental conditions, and to the relationships between them. Furthermore, these concepts, derived entirely from experimental investigations, are functional in character; that is to say, behavioral events are defined by their effects on the environment, such as producing or removing a stimulus, and environmental events are defined by their effects on the behavior, such as providing an occasion for a class of operant behavior.

The behavioral concepts of this approach are, for the most part, divided on the basis of whether they are sensitive to antecedent or consequent stimulus events; the former are referred to as respondent behavior, and the latter as operant behavior. There is, among adherents to this approach, an acknowledged penchant for measuring respondent behavior in terms of its latency or magnitude and operant behavior in terms of its rate of frequency of occurrence (Skinner, 1966a).

The environmental concepts also fall into two categories: stimuli with functional properties, and setting factors. A conditioned stimulus in a respondent interaction and a discriminative stimulus in an operant interaction are examples of stimulus functions. Satiation and deprivation of reinforcing stimuli, disruption of sleep cycles, and drug intervention are examples of setting factors.

The principles of the behavioral approach are statements describing demonstrated relationships among behavioral and environmental variables. These statements, which have been accumulating steadily over the past sixty years, are the *facts* of the science of psychology as generated by an experimental analysis of behavior. They have been organized variously, but with slight differences among them (e.g., Ferster and Perrot, 1968; Millenson, 1967; Reynolds, 1968; and Skinner, 1953). Reynolds (1968), for example, groups the principles as follows: acquisition and extinction of operant behavior, stimulus control of operant behavior, conditioned reinforcers, schedules of reinforcement, respondent behavior and respondent conditioning, aversive control, and emotion and motivation.

Research

Experimental analysis of the interactions between changes in individual behavior and environmental events is the core strategy in research (Sidman, 1960). Here, research is not planned to test a theory or an hypothesis but to demonstrate functional relationships (Skinner, 1966b), or to evaluate a practical application of the concepts and principles (Baer, Wolf, and Risley, 1968).

The strategy of teaching-oriented applied research does not consist of designing a study to determine whether Method A is better than Method B for the teaching of subject-matter X. It is, instead, a search for ways to engineer an educational environment so that each child can learn specified tasks, and then, after that goal is attained, to compare achievement in that engineered situation with achievement in some other school situation.

Application to Education

The concepts and principles of behavioral analysis are applied directly to the classroom teaching situation: to the observable behavior of the pupil in relation to the teacher's techniques of instruction, the instructional materials, the contingencies of reinforcement, and the setting conditions. The analysis of teaching and the methodology of application are clearly set forth by Skinner in *The Technology of Teaching* (1968).

Teaching, according to Skinner, is a situation in which the teacher arranges the contingencies of reinforcement to expedite learning by the child. The teacher is the arranger, and since she generally works in the classroom by herself, we may think of her as the "Lone Arranger". The teacher arranges the contingencies to develop appropriate study behavior, for example, attending to the materials to be learned, and hopefully she arranges the contengencies so that this behavior becomes part of a child's way of dealing with future study tasks. She also arranges contingencies by scheduling the formal academic subjects (the visible programs), and manners and moral behavior (the invisible programs) in such a way that each child makes progress at approximately his own pace and with minimum frustration or aversive consequences. She finds it necessary, at some times, also to arrange contingencies to reduce or eliminate behaviors that compete with acquiring the desired academic and social behaviors.

Two comments about arranging the educational environment are appropriate at this point; one pertains to scheduling the contingencies of reinforcement; the other, to scheduling the stimulus material. The fact that academic and social behaviors are operants, and hence sensitive to consequent stimulation, has led many teachers and researchers to use, indiscriminately, contrived contingencies such as tokens, candies, points, stars, etc. Such artificial reinforcers are not always necessary, and in many instances in which they have been used, they have not been functional. In other words, a child's rate of learning has not increased through the use of candies, or by whatever else he receives in exchange for a collection of tokens or a sum of points. Contrived reinforcers are appropriate only when the usual reinforcers applied in the classroom (confirmation, indications of progress, privileges, preferred work, approval, and the like) are not meaningful to a child. If, at times, contrived reinforcers are considered necessary in order to initiate learning, they can be scheduled so that they are gradually replaced by the reinforcers indigenous to the situation and the activity being learned. These are called by Ferster (1970) "natural," "intrinsic," or "automatic" reinforcers. As Skinner (1968) pointed out, the critical task in most teaching is not the incorporation of more and more new reinforcers but the effective utilization of those currently available to the teacher.

Let us turn to the scheduling of stimulus materials. The fact that a school task can be learned with a minimum of frustration and on the basis of positive reinforcement via a program of differential reinforcement of successive approximations to the ultimate form of a response (skill), or the desired response in the proper situation (knowledge), has led to an over-emphasis on the role of teaching machines, and to a misconception about the school subjects that can be properly programmed. Teaching machines, from the most primitive to the most elaborate, are of value in teaching only insofar as they assist the teacher in arranging the contingencies that expedite learning, i.e., aid the teacher in presenting the material properly, in providing for explicit responses, and in arranging for optimum timing of effective contingencies of reinforcement. The programming of any academic subject for a child is straightforward: (1) state in objective terms the desired terminal or goal behavior, (2) assess the child's behavioral repertory relevant to the task, (3) arrange in sequence the stimulus material or behavioral criteria for reinforcement, (4) start the child on that unit in the sequence to which he can respond correctly about 90% of the time, (5) manage the contingencies of reinforcement with the aid of teaching machines and other devices to strengthen successive approximations to the terminal behavior and to build conditioned reinforcers that are intrinsic to the task, and (6) keep records of the child's responses as a basis for modifying the materials and teaching procedures.

The research to date suggests that behavioral principles can be applied to the teaching situation with gratifying results. Further advances in basic and technological knowledge should, of course, lead to even more effective application.

IMPLICATIONS FOR THE SCHOOL PSYCHOLOGIST

Now let us look briefly at the offer from the mini-minority of psychologists as it relates to the school psychologist. Let us suppose that we have a school in which the teachers are happily applying behavioral principles to all aspects of education. In such a situation, the school psychologist would perform at least four functions.

First, he would work in close cooperation with kindergarten and first-grade teachers to help newly admitted children make a smooth transition from their homes to the classroom, with the objective of preventing school retardation and behavior problems. Specifically, the school psychologist would help these teachers to assess the repertories of their children and would help them to arrange suitable individual pupil programs. He would also help these teachers and their assistants to modify the programs when the child encounters difficulties and to assess their reinforcement contingency practices.

Second, he would work with counselors, teachers, school social workers, and parents on mitigating or eliminating problem behavior, setting up remedial programs that would be based on the same set of concepts and principles that are applied to teaching. In other words, the school psychologist would be engaging in behavior modification or *action counseling* as described and practiced by Krumboltz and his colleagues (1966).

Third, the school psychologist would assist teachers in dealing with problems of classroom management and subject-matter programming. His efforts with respect to classroom management would be comparable to the work of Thomas, Becker, and Armstrong (1968). On request from the teacher, he would observe the behavior of a problem child or group of children in the classroom, and on the basis of data collected he would analyze the contingencies that are operating in the situation, work out a course of action with the teacher, and evaluate it in terms of data from observational procedures. Data indicating that the new procedure was ineffective would lead to reassessment and alteration of the plan until a satisfactory solution is found. In helping the teacher to program instructional material, the school psychologist's task would consist of analyzing each child's daily academic records and modifying teaching procedures, contingency arrangements, and sequences of materials. With respect to assisting the teacher to develop and maintain other essential school behavior, such as paying attention, his procedures would be similar to those described by Hall, Lund, and Jackson (1968).

Fourth, and finally, the school psychologist would conduct in-service training for the teacher's assistants. In many instances these people would be clerks, like the instructional material clerks in the University of Pittsburgh type of programming; or they might be aides who would conduct individual and small group tutorials. The school psychologist would also be responsible for keeping the teachers and others informed of advances in technology of teaching and the specific ways of incorporating them into the school system.

It is obvious that the school psychologist described here would not be simulating the role of a child psychiatrist, would not be performing as a part-time clinical psychologist, would not be a full-time psychometrician; rather, he would be a person informed and skilled in the application of behavioral principles to all aspects of teaching both normal and handicapped children.

REQUIREMENTS FOR THOSE IN
EDUCATION WHO WISH TO
ACCEPT THE OFFER

Now I should like to suggest what educators might do if they wish to accept the offer of psychologists with a behavioral analysis orientation.

First, they should learn with precision the more specific aspects of this approach. A thorough grounding is necessary because behavioral analysis does not offer a touchstone. It is necessary because the approach has an apparent simplicity that can be deceptive, and many alluring features that can be misleading. Lastly, it is necessary because effective application requires a minute analysis of the teaching situation, and ingenuity in rearranging contingencies in order to eliminate difficulties and to expedite the establishment and maintenance of the desired behavior. It is therefore essential that the practitioner learn from *first sources:* (1) the nature of the concepts and principles and referential supporting data, (2) the methodology of practical application and the basic literature on the behavioral technology of teaching, (3) the individual research methodology, and (4) the assumptions of behavioral analysis and their implications for educational practices.

Second, the practitioners should obtain experience in applying these principles. Those who would use this approach should arrange to observe demonstrations in actual educational settings and should seek out opportunities to practice the techniques under supervision. Such first-hand experience provides occasions in which one must face and deal with the problems of contingency management and subject-matter programming; it also provides opportunities to be reinforced by the visible changes that result from one's efforts. If there are no preschool or elementary school demonstration classes within easy reach, educators who teach in colleges and universities might apply these principles to their classes (Ferster, 1968; and Keller, 1968). They might do this even if there are opportunities to observe the application of behavioral principles to the education of young children. Not only will it give them a new source of satisfaction but their students would probably appreciate a learner-centered approach to instruction.

SUMMARY AND CONCLUSIONS

A small but rapidly growing group of psychologists can now offer educators (1) a set of concepts and principles derived entirely from the experimental analysis of behavior, (2) a methodology for the practical application of these concepts and principles, (3) a research method that deals with changes in individual behavior, and (4) a philosophy of science that says: "Look carefully to the relationships between observable environmental and behavioral events and their changes."

Application of behavioral principles to education would revise the role of the teacher; she would become a facile manager of the contingencies of reinforcement and an effective instructional programmer. Application would also change the style of educational research from comparing the achievement of groups of children to analyzing the specific conditions and processes in the teaching of a particular subject as they relate to the behavior of an individual pupil, and application of these principles would change the role of the school psychologist. He would be an expert in the behavioral technology of teaching. As such, he would collaborate with kindergarten and first-grade teachers to prevent school problems by arranging remedial procedures for individual children. He would also serve as a consultant to all teachers on problems of classroom management and programming, and through in-service classes would train teacher's aides to assist the teacher in reaching her goals.

To act on this offer from the small minority of psychologists, educators are advised to learn the details of this approach from primary sources. In addition, they should seek firsthand experiences in applying the techniques so they can understand the problems involved and the approaches to their solutions.

What sorts of changes would be expected to result from an acceptance to this offer? It is difficult to foresee all the details of the changes but certain broad indications are clear. First, the teacher would probably derive new satisfaction from teaching because she would be in a situation that allows her to see concretely the progress of each child in her class, and she would know what to do when a child is not making reasonable progress. She could not help but gain new confidence in herself as a teacher because she would know *what* she is doing and *why* she is doing it. She would in addition be more secure in the knowledge that her teaching practices are based on demonstrated principles, and that with the help of the school psychologist she can refine and extend her methods in accordance with new research findings. Finally, she would have opportunities to try new ways of teaching standard subjects, and to explore ways of teaching subjects not now programmed.

Second, putting this offer into operation would probably provide a common basis for the discussion of problems among those working with the teacher—the principal, the psychologist, the counselor, and the school social worker. It would make no difference whether the problem were the persistent deviant behavior of a child, curriculum difficulties, an unruly classroom, an uncooperative parent, or the behavior of groups of children in the cafeteria or on the playground. A common approach to all aspects of education, especially one based on experimental concepts and principles, would certainly advance teaching as a profession.

Third, systematic application of behavior principles would be expected to reduce dramatically the number of children who reach the fourth grade without learning to read at a socially functional level. Present estimates of this group range from 20% to 40% of the school population. In terms of numbers, this is a staggering figure. With its emphasis on the prevention of academic and behavioral retardation, it is not unrealistic to think that the behavioral analysis approach could reduce that percentage to almost zero. And for the same reason, it would be expected to reverse the trend of spiralling increases in budgets for remedial services.

Fourth, the ultimate result, of course, would be a better educated community—the first requisite in equipping an industrial society to manage the advances of science and technology to achieve *humanitarian goals* (MacLeish, 1968).

REFERENCES

Baer, D. M., Wolf, M. M., and Risley, T. R. Some current dimensions of applied behavior analysis. *Journal of Applied Behavior Analysis,* 1968, 1, 91-97.

Ferster, C. B. Arbitrary and natural reinforcement. *Psychological Records,* 1967, 17, 341-347.

Ferster, C. B. Individualized instruction in a large introductory psychology college course. *The Psychological Record,* 1968, 18, 521-532.

Ferster, C. B., and Perrott, Mary C. *Behavior principles.* New York: Appleton-Century-Crofts, 1968.

Hall, R. V., Lund, Diane, and Jackson, Deloris. Effects of teacher attention on study behavior. *Journal of Applied Behavior Analysis,* 1968, 1, 1-12.

Kantor, J. R. *Interbehavioral psychology.* (2nd rev. ed.) Bloomington, Ind.: Principia Press, 1959.

Keller, F. S. "Good-bye, teacher . . ." *Journal of Applied Behavior Analysis,* 1968, 1, 79-90.

Krumboltz, J. (Ed.) *Revolution in counseling.* New York: Houghton Mifflin, 1966.

MacLeish, A. The great American frustration. *Saturday Review,* 1968, 51, No. 28, 13-16.

Millenson, J. R. *Principles of behavioral analysis.* New York: Macmillan, 1967.

Reynolds, G. S. *A primer of operant conditioning.* Glenview, Ill.: Scott, Foresman, 1968.

Sidman, M. *Tactics of scientific research.* New York: Basic Books, 1960.

Skinner, B. F. Behaviorism at fifty. *Science,* 1963, 140, 951-958.

Skinner, B. F. Current trends in experimental psychology. In W. Dennis (Ed.), *Current trends in psychology.* Pittsburgh: University of Pittsburgh Press, 1947. Pp. 16-49.

Skinner, B. F. Operant behavior. In W. K. Honig (Ed.), *Operant behavior: Areas of research and application.* New York: Appleton-Century-Crofts, 1966. Pp. 12-32. (a)

Skinner, B. F. *Science and human behavior.* New York: Macmillan, 1953.

Skinner, B. F. *The technology of teaching.* New York: Appleton-Century-Crofts, 1968.

Skinner, B. F. What is an experimental analysis of behavior? *Journal of Experimental Analysis of Behavior,* 1966, 9, 213-218 (b).

Thomas, D. R., Becker, W. C., and Armstrong, M. Production and elimination of disruptive classroom behavior by systematically varying teacher's behavior. *Journal of Applied Behavior Analysis,* 1968, 1, 35-45.

II

Implementation: Considerations and Techniques

How does a new teacher apply the principles of learning? Madsen, Becker, and Thomas suggest the efficacy of these general rules: Make explicit classroom rules, praise behavior that should be repeated, and ignore undesirable behavior whenever possible. More specifically, Hall, Panyan, Rabon, and Broden discuss the procedures for instructing beginning teachers in operant techniques and present favorable case studies. The final articles in this section offer slightly different ideas. Surratt, Ulrich, and Hawkins make it clear that one does not have to be a Ph.D. to apply operant techniques. Their data clearly shows that a well-trained, fifth-grade student can also have success. Cantrell, Cantrell, Huddleston, and Woolridge discuss another contemporary technique that lends itself to behavioral engineering: contingency contracting.

4

Rules, praise, and ignoring: elements of elementary classroom control

Charles H. Madsen, Jr., Wesley C. Becker, and Don R. Thomas

An attempt was made to vary systematically the behavior of two elementary school teachers to determine the effects on classroom behavior of Rules, Ignoring Inappropriate Behaviors, and showing Approval for Appropriate Behavior. Behaviors of two children in one class and one child in the other class were recorded by observers, as were samples of the teachers' behavior. Following baseline recordings, Rules, Ignoring, and Approval conditions were introduced one at a time. In one class a reversal of conditions was carried out. The main conclusions were that: (a) Rules alone exerted little effect on classroom behavior, (b) Ignoring Inappropriate Behavior and showing Approval for Appropriate Behavior (in combination) were very effective in achieving better classroom behavior, and (c) showing Approval for Appropriate Behaviors is probably the key to effective classroom management.

Modern learning theory is slowly but surely increasing its potential for impact upon social problems. As problems in social development and interaction are more closely examined through the methods of experimental analysis, the importance of learning principles in everyday life becomes clearer. The potential contribution of these developments to childrearing and education appears to be especially significant. This report is a part of a series of studies aimed at demonstrating what the teacher can do to achieve a "happier," more effective classroom through the systematic use of learning principles. The study grows out of a

From *Journal of Applied Behavior Analysis*, 1968, 1, 139-150. Copyright 1968 by the Society for the Experimental Analysis of Behavior, Inc. Reprinted by permission.

We wish to express our appreciation to the teachers involved, Mrs. Barbara L. Weed and Mrs. Margaret Larson, for their cooperation in a study which involved using and applying procedures which at times made their teaching duties very difficult. Gratitude is expressed to the Director of Elementary Education, Unit District no. 116, Urbana, Illinois, Dr. Lowell M. Johnson, and to the principals of Thomas Paine and Prairie Schools, Richard Sturgeon and Donald Holste. This study was supported by Grant HD-00881-05 from the National Institutes of Health. Reprints may be obtained from Wesley C. Becker, Bureau of Educational Research, 284 B Education Bldg., University of Illinois, Urbana, Illinois 61801 body of laboratory and field research demonstrating the importance of social reinforcers (smiles, praise, contact, nearness, attention) in establishing and maintaining effective behaviors in children. Extensive field studies in experimental nursery schools by Wolf, Bijou, Baer, and their students (e.g., Hart, Reynolds, Baer, Brawley, and Harris, 1968; Allen, Hart, Buell, Harris, and Wolf, 1965; Bijou and Baer, 1963) provided a background for the extension of their work by the present authors to special and typical elementary classrooms. In general, we have found to date that teachers with various "personalities" and backgrounds can be trained systematically to control their own behavior in ways which will improve the behavior of the children they are teaching. (Becker, Madsen, Arnold, and Thomas, 1967). We have also found that teachers can "create" problem behaviors in the classroom by controlling the ways in which they respond to their pupils (Thomas, Becker, and Armstrong, 1968); Madsen, Becker, Thomas, Koser, and Plager, 1968). It is hoped that field studies of this sort will contribute to more effective teacher training.

The present study is a refinement of an earlier study of Becker et al. (1967), in which the behavior of two children in each of five classrooms was recorded and related to experimentally controlled changes in teacher behaviors. The teachers were instructed and guided to follow a program which involved making classroom rules explicit, ignoring disruptive behaviors unless someone was getting hurt, and praising appropriate classroom behaviors. Under this program, most of the severe problem children under study showed remarkable improvements in classroom behavior. However, that study lacked certain controls which the present study sought to correct. First, the teachers in the earlier study were in a seminar on behavior theory and practice during baseline conditions. Some target children improved during baseline, apparently because some teachers were beginning to apply what they were learning even though they had been requested not to do so. Second, public relations and time considerations did not make it possible to introduce the components of the experimental program one at a time (rules, ignoring, and praise) to better study their individual contributions. Third, a reversal of teacher behavior was not attempted. Such a reversal would more conclusively show the importance of teacher's behavior in producing the obtained changes. Fourth, extensive recordings of teacher behavior under all experimental conditions were not undertaken in the earlier study. The present study attempted to deal with each of these problems.

METHOD

Procedures

Teachers in a public elementary school volunteered to participate in the study. After consultation with teachers and observation of the children in the classroom, two children with a high frequency of problem behavior were selected for study in each class. Previously developed behavioral categories (Becker et al., 1967) were modified for use with these particular children and baseline recordings were made to determine the frequency of problem behaviors.

At the end of the baseline period the teachers entered a workshop on applications of behavioral principles in the classroom which provided them with the rationale and principles behind the procedures being introduced in their classes. Various experimental procedures were then introduced, one at a time, and the effects on the target children's behaviors observed. The experiments were begun in late November and continued to the end of the school year.

Subjects

Classroom A. There were 29 children in Mrs. A's middle-primary (second grade) room who ranged in school progress from mid-first-grade level to early-third-grade level. Cliff and Frank were chosen as the target children.

Cliff was chosen because he displayed no interest in school. In Mrs. A's words, "he would sit throughout entire work periods fiddling with objects in his desk, talking, doing nothing, or misbehaving by bothering others and walking around the room. Lately he has started hitting others for no apparent reason. When Cliff was required to stay in at recess to do his work, he would complete the work in a short time and it was usually completely accurate. I was unable to motivate him into working on any task during the regular work periods." Cliff is the son of a university professor who was born in Europe and immigrated when Cliff was 5-yr old. Cliff scored 91 on an early (CA 5-3) intelligence test. This score was discounted by the examiner because of language problems. His group IQ scores rose steadily (CA 5-9, IQ 103; CA 6-2, IQ 119; CA 7-1, IQ 123). His achievement scores indicated a low second-grade level at the beginning of the present study. Cliff was seen by the school social worker throughout the entire first grade and throughout this entire study.

Cliff was observed early in the year and it was noted that he did not respond once to teacher's questions. He played with his fingers, scratched himself repeatedly, played in his desk, paid no attention to the assignment and had to stay in at recess to finish his work. Almost continually he made blowing sounds and talked to himself. On occasions he was out of his seat making noises and talking. He would leave the room without permission. Before the study began the observers made the following notes: "What a silly kid, writing on the bottom of his shoes, writing on his arms, blowing kisses at the girls. He was vying for the attention of the girl behind him, but she ignored him. . . . Poor Cliff! he acts so silly for his age. He tried to talk to the other kids, but none of them would pay attention to him. . . . Cliff seems concerned with the little girl beside him (girl behind him last week). He has a sign on his desk which reads, 'Do you love me?' . . . ."

Frank was described by his teacher as a likable child. He had a record of misbehavior in the classroom and intense fighting on the playground. He was often out of his seat talking to other children and did not respond to "discipline." If someone was reprimanded for doing something, Frank would often do the same thing. Test scores indicated an IQ of 106 (Stanford-Binet) and achievement level just under beginning second grade at the start of school (average California Achievement Test scores 1.6 grades). The school psychologist noted that Frank's mother was a person "who willingly permitted others to make decisions for her and did not seem able to discipline Frank." Father was absent from the home during the entire year in the Air Force.

Classroom B. Twenty children were assigned to Mrs. B's kindergarten room. Two children were observed initially; one moved from the community shortly after baseline was taken, leaving only Stan for the study.

Stan was described as coming from a truly pathetic home environment. The mother was not married and the family of four children subsisted on state aid. One older brother was enrolled in a special class for the educable retarded. At the beginning of the year, Stan's behavior was characterized by the teacher as "wild." She reported that, "Stan would push and hit and grab at objects and at children. He had no respect for authority and apparently didn't even hear directions. He knew how to swear profusely, and I would have to check his pockets so I would know he wasn't taking home school equipment. He would wander around the room and it was difficult to get him to engage in constructive work. He would frequently destroy any work he did rather than take it home."

The difficult home situation was made manifest during the month of March. Stan has been absent for two weeks and it was reported that his mother was taking her children out of public school and placing them in a local parochial school. Investigation by school personnel indicated that Stan's mother had moved the children into a relative's home and had gone to the hospital to have another illegitimate baby. A truancy notice was filed for all four children including Stan. Following legal notice the children were returned to school.

Rating of Child Behavior

The same rating schedule was used in both classrooms except that Isolate Play was added to the list of Inappropriate Behaviors for the kindergarten. Since the children were expected to be involved in structured group activities during observation periods, going off by oneself to play with the many toys or materials in the room was considered inappropriate by the kindergarten teacher. Inappropriate Behavior was defined as the occurrence of one or more of the behaviors listed under Inappropriate Behavior in Table 1 during any observation interval.

Observers were trained in the reliable use of the rating schedule before baseline recordings began. Training consisted of practice in use of the rating schedule in the classroom. Two observers would each rate the same child for 20 min and then return to the research office to compare their ratings and discuss their differences with their supervisor. Training was continued until reliability was above 80% on each behavior code. Training lasted approximately two weeks. Reliability was determined periodically throughout the study by dividing the number of agreements by the number of agreements plus disagreements. An agreement was defined as a rating of the same behavior class in the same observation interval. Average reliability over children, behavior classes, and days for the 69 occasions (out of 238) on which it was checked was 81%. Single day reliabilities ranged from 68% to 96%. Reliabilities were checked in each phase of the study.

Table 1. Behavioral coding categories for children.

I. Inappropriate Behaviors

A. *Gross Motor.* Getting out of seat, standing up, running, hopping, skipping, jumping, walking around, moving chair, etc.

B. *Object Noise.* Tapping pencil or other objects, clapping, tapping feet, rattling or tearing paper, throwing book on desk, slamming desk. Be conservative, only rate if you can hear the noise when eyes are closed. Do *not* include accidental dropping of objects.

C. *Disturbance of Other's Property.* Grabbing objects or work, knocking neighbor's books off desk, destroying another's property, pushing with desk (only rate if someone is there). Throwing objects at another person without hitting them.

D. *Contact (high and low intensity).* Hitting, kicking, shoving, pinching, slapping, striking with object, throwing object which hits another person, poking with object, biting, pulling hair, touching, patting, etc. Any physical contact is rated.

E. *Verbalization.* Carrying on conversation with other children when it is not permitted. Answers teacher without raising hand or without being called on; making comments or calling out remarks when no questions have been asked; calling teacher's name to get her attention; crying, screaming, singing, whistling, laughing, coughing, or blowing loudly. These responses may be directed to teacher or children.

F. *Turning Around.* Turning head or head and body to look at another person, showing objects to another child, attending to another child. Must be of 4-sec duration, or more than 90 degrees using desk as a reference. Not rated unless seated. If this response overlaps two time intervals and cannot be rated in the first because it is less than 4-sec duration, then rate in the interval in which the end of the response occurs.

G. *Other Inappropriate Behavior.* Ignores teacher's question or command. Does something different from that directed to do, including minor motor behavior such as playing with pencil or eraser when supposed to be writing, coloring while the record is on, doing spelling during the arithmetic lesson, playing with objects. *The child involves himself in a task that is not appropriate.* Not rated when other Inappropriate Behaviors are rated. Must be time off task.

H. *Mouthing Objects.* Bringing thumb, fingers, pencils, or any object in contact with the mouth.

I. *Isolate Play. Limited to kindergarten* free-play period. Child must be farther than 3 ft from any person, neither initiates or responds to verbalizations with other people, engages in no interaction of a nonverbal nature with other children for the entire 10-sec period.

II. Appropriate Behavior

Time on task; e.g., answers question, listens, raises hand, works on assignment. Must include whole 10-sec interval except for Turning Around responses of less than 4-sec duration.

Instructions to observers followed those used by Becker et al. (1967). In essence, the observers were not to respond to the children, but to fade into the background as much as possible. Teachers, as well as children, quickly learned not to respond to the observers, although early in the study one observer was attacked by a kindergarten child. The observer did not respond to the behavior and it quickly disappeared. Experimental changes were initiated without informing observers in an attempt to control any observer bias. However, the changes were often dramatic enough that observer comments clearly reflected programmed changes in teacher's behavior.

The target children were observed for 20 min per day, three days a week. In the middle-primary class, observations were taken when the children were engaged in seat work or group instruction. In the kindergarten class, observations were made when structured activities, rather than free play, were expected. Each observer had a clipboard, stopwatch, and rating sheet. The observer would watch for 10 sec and use symbols to record the occurrence of behaviors. In each minute, ratings would be made in five consecutive 10-sec intervals and the final 10-sec would be used for recording comments. Each behavior category could be rated only once in a 10-sec interval. The primary dependent variable was percentage of intervals in which an Inappropriate Behavior occurred. Since the varieties of Inappropriate Behavior permitted a more detailed analysis with the schedule used, the presentation of results is focussed on them, even though functionally their converse (Appropriate Behavior) was the main behavior being manipulated.

Ratings of Teacher Behavior

Ratings of teacher behavior were obtained to clarify relationships between changes in teacher behavior and changes in child behavior. Recordings of teacher behavior were also used by the experimenters to help the teachers learn the contingent use of Approval and Disapproval Behaviors. The teacher rating schedule is presented in Table 2. Teacher behaviors were recorded by subclasses in relation to child behaviors. That is, the record would show whether a teacher response followed Appropriate child classroom behavior or whether it followed one of the categories of Inappropriate Behavior. Responses to all children were rated. Teacher behavior was scored as the frequency of occurrence of a specified class of behavior during a 20-min interval. Teacher ratings were either recorded during one of the periods when a target child was being rated by another observer, or immediately thereafter when only one observer made both ratings. Teacher behavior was rated on the average of once a week, except during experimental transitions, when more frequent ratings were made. The number of days teacher behavior was rated under each condition is given in Table 3. Most recorded teacher behavior (about 85%) fell in the *Verbal* Approval or Disapproval categories. For this reason we have used the term *Praise* interchangeably with Approval Behaviors and *Criticism* interchangeably with Disapproval Behaviors.

Reliability of measures of teacher behavior were checked approximately every other rating day (21 of 42 occasions for the two teachers) by dividing the

Table 2. Coding definitions for teacher behaviors.

Appropriate child behavior is defined by the child rating categories. The teacher's rules for classroom behavior must be considered when judging whether the child's behavior is Appropriate or Inappropriate.

I. Teacher Approval following Appropriate Child Behavior

    A. *Contact.* Positive physical contact such as embracing, kissing, patting, holding arm or hand, sitting on lap.

    B. *Praise.* Verbal comments indicating approval, commendation or achievement. Examples: that's good, you are doing right, you are studying well, I like you, thank you, you make me happy.

    C. *Facial attention.* Smiling at child.

II. Teacher Approval following Inappropriate Child Behavior

Same codes as under I

III. Teacher Disapproval following Appropriate Child Behavior

    A. *Holding the child.* Forcibly holding the child, putting child out in the hall, grabbing, hitting, spanking, slapping, shaking the child.

    B. *Criticism.* Critical comments of high or low intensity, yelling, scolding, raising voice. Examples: that's wrong, don't do that, stop talking, did I call on you, you are wasting your time, don't laugh, you know what you are supposed to do.

    C. *Threats.* Consequences mentioned by the teacher to be used at a later time. If _____ then _____ comments.

    D. *Facial attention.* Frowning or grimacing at a child.

IV. Teacher Disapproval following Inappropriate Child Behavior

Same codes as under III.

V. "Timeout" Procedures

    A. The teacher turns out the lights and says nothing.

    B. The teacher turns her back and waits for silence.

    C. The teacher stops talking and waits for quiet.

    D. Keeping in for recess.

    E. Sending child to office.

    F. Depriving child in the classroom of some privilege.

VI. Academic Recognition

Calling on a child for an answer. Giving "feedback" for academic correctness.

These are procedural definitions of teacher behaviors possibly involving the withdrawal of reinforcers as a consequence of disruptive behaviors which teacher could not ignore.

agreements as to time interval and behavior codes by the agreements plus disagreements. Average reliability over behavior classes, teachers, and days was 84% with a range from 70% to 96% for individual day measures.

Experimental Conditions

In the middle-primary class (Class A) the experimental conditions may be summarized as consisting of *Baseline;* introduction of *Rules; Rules* plus *Ignoring* deviant behavior; *Rules* plus *Ignoring* plus *Praise* for appropriate behavior; return to Baseline; and finally reinstatement of *Rules, Ignoring,* and *Praise.* In the kindergarten class (Class B) the experimental conditions consisted of *Baseline;* introduction of *Rules; Ignoring* Inappropriate Behavior (without continuing to emphasize rules); and the combination of *Rules, Ignoring,* and *Praise.*

The various experimental procedures were to be used by the teachers for the classroom as a whole throughout the day, not just for the children whose behavior was being recorded, and not just when observers were present.

Baseline. During the Baseline period the teachers conducted their classes in their typical way. No attempt was made to influence their behavior.

Rules. Many people would argue that just telling children what is expected should have considerable effect on their behavior. We wished to explore this question empirically. Teachers were instructed individually and given written instructions as follows:

The first phase of your participation in the use of behavioral principles to modify classroom behaviors is to specify explicit rules of classroom conduct. When this is done, there is no doubt as to what is expected of the children in your classroom. However, do not expect a dramatic shift in classroom control, as we all know that knowing the prohibitions does not always keep people from "sin." This is the first phase in the program and inappropriate behavior should be reduced, but perhaps not eliminated. The rules should be formulated with the class and posted in a conspicuous location (a chart in front of the room or a special place on the chalkboard where they will not be erased). Go over the rules three or four times asking the class to repeat them back to you when they are initially formulated and use the following guidelines:

(a) Make the rules short and to the point so they can be easily memorized.

(b) Five or six rules are adequate. Special instructions for specific occasions are best given when the occasion arises. Children will not remember long lists of rules.

(c) Where possible phrase the rules in a positive not a negative manner (for example, "Sit quietly while working," rather than, "Don't talk to your neighbors"). We want to emphasize positive actions.

(d) Keep a sheet on your desk and record the number of times you review the rules with the class (strive for at least four to six repetitions per day). Remember that young children do not have the retention span of an adult and frequent reminders are necessary. Let the children recite the rules as you ask them, rather than always enumerating them yourself.

(e) Remind the class of the rules at times other than when someone has misbehaved.

(f) Try to change no other aspects of your classroom conduct except for the presentation of the rules at appropriate times.

Teacher tally sheets indicated that these instructions were followed quite explicitly. The average number of presentations of rules was 5.2 per day.

Ignoring Inappropriate Behavior. The second experimental phase involved Ignoring Inappropriate Behavior. In Class A, repetition of rules was also continued. Individual conferences to explain written instructions were given both teachers. Both teachers were given the following instructions:

The first aspect of the study was to make expectations explicit. This you have been doing over the past few weeks. During the next phase of the study you should learn to *ignore* (do not attend to) behaviors which interfere with learning or teaching, unless of course, a child is being hurt by another, in which case use a punishment which seems appropriate, preferably withdrawal of some positive reinforcement. Learning to ignore is rather difficult. Most of us pay attention to the violations. For example, instead of ignoring we often say such things as the following: "Johnny, you know you are supposed to be working"; "Sue, will you stop bothering your neighbors"; "Henrieta, you have been at that window for a long time"; "Jack, can you keep your hands off Bill"; "Susie, will you please sit down"; "Alex, stop running around and do your work"; "Jane, will you please stop rocking on your chair."

Behaviors which are to be ignored include motor behaviors such as getting out of seat, standing up, running, walking around the room, moving chairs, or sitting in a contorted manner. Any verbal comment or noise not connected with the assignments should also be ignored, such as: carrying on conversations with other children when it is not permitted, answering questions without raising hands or being called on, making remarks when no questions have been asked, calling your name to get attention, and extraneous noises such as crying, whistling, laughing loudly, blowing noise, or coughing. An additional important group of behaviors to be ignored are those which the student engages in when he is supposed to be doing other things, e.g., when the child ignores your instructions you are to ignore him. Any noises made with objects, playing with pencils or other materials should be ignored, as well as, taking things from or disturbing another student by turning around and touching or grabbing him.

The reason for this phase of the experiment is to test the possiblity that attention to Inappropriate Behavior may serve to strengthen the very behavior that the attention is intended to diminish. Inappropriate Behavior may be strengthened by paying attention to it even though you may think that you are punishing the behavior.

Praise for Appropriate Behavior. The third phase of the experiment included individual contacts with teachers to encourage and train Praising of Appropriate Behavior. The Praise instructions to the teachers were as follows:

The first phase included specifying explicit rules, writing them on the board and reviewing them 4-6 times per day. The second phase was designed to reduce the amount of attention paid to behaviors which were unwanted by ignoring them. This third phase is primarily directed toward *increasing* Appropriate

Behaviors through praise and other forms of approval. Teachers are inclined to take good behavior for granted and pay attention only when a child acts up or misbehaves. We are now asking you to try something different. This procedure is characterized as "catching the child being good" and making a comment designed to reward the child for good behavior. Give praise, attention, or smile when the child is doing what is expected during the particular class period in question. Inappropriate Behavior would not be a problem if all children were engaging in a great deal of study and school behavior, therefore, it is necessary to apply what you have learned in the workshop. Shape by successive approximations the behavior desired by using praise and attention. Start "small" by giving praise and attention at the first signs of Appropriate Behavior and work toward greater goals. Pay close attention to those children who normally engage in a great deal of misbehavior. Watch carefully and when the child begins to behave appropriately, make a comment such as, "You're doing a fine job, (name)." It is very important during the first few days to catch as many good behaviors as possible. Even though a child has just thrown an eraser at the teacher (one minute ago) and is now studying, you should praise the study behavior. (It might also decrease the rate of eraser throwing.) We are assuming that your commendation and praise are important to the child. This is generally the case, but sometimes it takes a while for praise to become effective. Persistence in catching children being good and delivering praise and attention should eventually pay off in a better behaved classroom.

Some examples of praise comments are as follows:
I like the way you're doing your work quietly (name).
That's the way I like to see you work _____.
That's a very good job _____.
You're doing fine _____.
You got two right _____ , that's very good (if he generally gets no answers right).

In general, give praise for achievement, prosocial behavior, and following the group rules. Specifically, you can praise for concentrating on individual work, raising hand when appropriate, responding to questions, paying attention to directions and following through, sitting in desk and studying, sitting quietly if noise has been a problem. Try to use variety and expression in your comments. Stay away from sarcasm. Attempt to become spontaneous in your praise and smile when delivering praise. At first you will probably get the feeling that you are praising a great deal and it sounds a little phony to your ears. This is a typical reaction and it becomes more natural with the passage of time. Spread your praise and attention around. If comments sometimes might interfere with the ongoing class activities then use facial attention and smiles. Walk around the room during study time and pat or place your hand on the back of a child who is doing a good job. Praise quietly spoken to the children has been found effective in combination with some physical sign of approval.

General Rule: Give *praise* and *attention* to behaviors which facilitate learning. Tell the child what he is being praised for. Try to reinforce behaviors incompatible with those you wish to decrease.

The teachers were also instructed to continue to ignore deviant behavior and to repeat the rules several times a day.

Additional training given teachers consisted of: (a) discussion of problems with suggested solutions during weekly seminars on behavior analysis, and (b) specific suggestions from the experimenter on possible alternative responses in specific situations based on the experimenter's observations of the teachers during experimental transitions, or based on observer data and notes at other times when the data showed that the teachers were not on program.

Additional cues were provided to implement the program. Cards were placed on the teachers' desks containing the instructions for the experimental phase in which they were engaged.

Reversal. In Class A the final experimental conditions involved an attempt to return to Baseline, followed by a reinstatement of the *Rules, Praise,* and *Ignore* condition. On the basis of the earlier observations of Teacher A, we were able to specify to her how frequently she made disapproving and approving comments. The success of this procedure can be judged from the data.

RESULTS

Percentage of observation intervals in which Inappropriate Behaviors occurred as a function of conditions is graphed in Fig. 1 and 2. Major changes in Inappropriate Behaviors occurred only when Praise or Approval for Appropriate Behaviors was emphasized in the experimental procedures. A t test, comparing average Inappropriate Behavior in conditions where Praise was emphasized with those where Praise was not emphasized, was significant at the 0.05 level ($df = 2$).

Before examining the results more closely, it is necessary to inspect the data on teacher behavior. Table 3 gives the frequency of classes of teacher behaviors averaged within experimental conditions. Since day-to-day variability of teacher behavior was low for the measures used, these averages fairly reflect what went on.

Introduction of Rules into the classroom had no appreciable effect on Inappropriate Behavior.

Ignoring Inappropriate Behaviors produced inconsistent results. In Class A the children clearly became worse under this condition; in Class B little change was apparent. Both teachers had a difficult time adhering to this condition, and Teacher A found this phase of the experiment very unpleasant. Table 3 shows that Teacher A was only able to reduce critical comments from an average of one per 1 min to an average of three in 4 min. Teacher B cut her critical comments in half. In view of these difficulties, the present results cannot be taken as a clear test of the effects of responding with Disapproval to Inappropriate Behaviors.

The failure to eliminate Disapproval Reactions to Inappropriate Behaviors in Phase Three of the experiment, adds some ambiguities to the interpretation of the Phase Four data for Teacher A. The Rules, Ignore, and Praise condition for Teacher A involved both a reduction in critical comments (Ignoring) as well as a marked increase in Praise. As demonstrated previously (Becker et al., 1967), this combination of procedures is very effective in reducing inappropriate classroom behaviors, but we still lack a clear isolation of effects. The data for Teacher B are

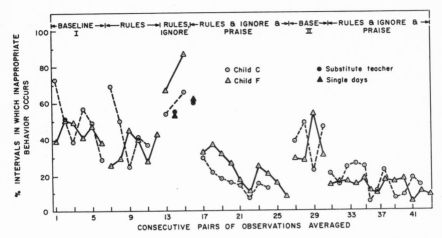

Fig. 1. Inappropriate behavior of two problem children in Classroom A as a function of experimental conditions.

not confounded with a simultaneous shift in frequency of Disapproval and Approval Reactions, but they are made less interpretable by a marked shift in Academic Recognition (defined in Table 2) which occurred when the shift in Praise was made. Since Academic Recognition does not show any systematic relations to level of Appropriate Behaviors elsewhere in the study, we are not inclined to interpret this change as showing a causal effect. A best guess is that the effective use of Praise gave the teacher more time to focus on academic skills.

The reversal operation for Teacher A quite clearly shows that the combination of Praising and Ignoring exerts a strong control over Appropriate Behaviors.

As with Academic Recognition, no attempt was made to control how frequently the teacher used procedures labelled "Timeout" (defined in Table 2). The frequency data reported in Table 4 indicates that during Baseline, Teacher A, especially, used "Timeout" procedures to try to establish control (usually turning off the lights until the children were quiet). The changes in the frequency of use of "Timeout" procedures are not systematically related to the behavior changes graphed in Fig. 1 and 2.

In summary, the main results indicate: (a) that Rules alone had little effect in improving classroom behavior, (b) the functional status of Ignoring Inappropriate Behavior needs further clarification, (c) the combination of Ignoring and Praising was very effective in achieving better classroom behavior, and (d) Praise for Appropriate Behaviors was probably the key teacher behavior in achieving effective classroom management.

The effects of the experimental procedures on individual classes of behavior for the two children in Class A are presented in Table 4. The data in Table 4 illustrates that with a few exceptions the effects on individual classes of behavior are similar to those for Inappropriate Behavior as a whole.

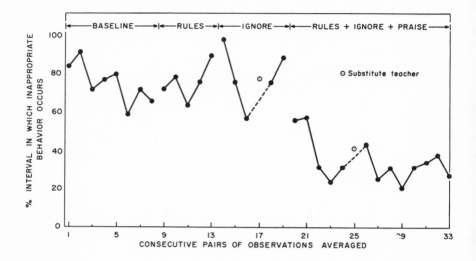

Fig. 2. Inappropriate behavior of one problem child in Classroom B as a function of experimental conditions.

DISCUSSION

Technical Considerations

The problems of gaining good data and maintaining adequate experimental control in an ongoing classroom in a public school have not all been recognized as yet, much less solved. The greatest difficulty encountered was that of maintaining stable control over some important variables while others were being changed. When these variables involve aspects of teacher behavior, the problem becomes one of helping the teacher maintain discriminative control over her own behavior. Daily feedback from the experimenter, based on the observer ratings, can help in this task (i.e. show the teacher the up-to-date graph of her behavior). Also, providing the teacher with a small counter to help monitor her own behavior can be helpful (Thomas et al., 1968). Most difficult to control in the present study was teacher's Disapproving Reactions to Inappropriate Behaviors during the Ignore Phase of the experiment. Teacher A became very "upset" as her classroom became worse. One solution to this problem might be a prestudy in which the teacher is trained in effective management techniques, and then taken through a series of short periods where both Approval and Disapproval are eliminated and one or the other reinstated. The teacher would then have confidence that she can effectively handle her class and be better able to tolerate short periods of chaos (if such periods did occur). She would also have had sufficient training in monitoring her own behavior to permit more effective control.

No attempt was made to program the frequency of various classes of Academic Recognition behaviors. Since such behavior may be important in interpreting results, and was found to vary with some experimental conditions, future work should strive to hold this behavior constant also.

Table 3. Teacher behavior—averages for experimental conditions (frequency per 20-min observations).

Teacher A Behavior Classes	Experimental Conditions					
	Baseline I	Rules	Rules + Ignore	Rules + Ignore + Praise I	Baseline II	Rules + Ignore + Praise II
Approval to Appropriate	1.2	2.0	0.0	18.2	2.5	12.5
Approval to Inappropriate	8.7	0.8	2.0	1.2	4.0	5.1
Disapproval to Inappropriate	18.5	20.5	15.7	4.1	9.8	3.5
Disapproval to Appropriate	0.9	0.7	1.0	0.3	0.9	0.0
Timeout	3.3	1.4	1.7	0.4	0.0	0.1
Academic Recognition	26.5	23.6	46.3	52.4	45.4	45.6
Days observed	15	8	3	11	4	9

Teacher B Behavior Classes	Baseline	Rules	Ignore	Rules + Ignore + Praise
Approval to Appropriate	19.2	14.1	19.3	35.2
Approval to Inappropriate	1.9	0.9	0.3	0.0
Disapproval to Inappropriate	16.9	22.1	10.6	10.8
Disapproval to Appropriate	0.0	0.0	0.0	0.0
Timeout	1.5	1.5	0.3	0.4
Academic Recognition	14.5	5.1	6.5	35.6
Days observed	8	6	6	10

The present study emphasized the importance of contingencies between student and teacher behaviors, but did not measure them directly. While producing similar effects on two chilcren in the same classroom and one child in another classroom, and showing correlated changes in teacher behaviors (including a reversal operation), more powerful data are potentially obtainable with a different technology. Video-tape recordings could enable the use of present coding techniques to obtain contingency data on all classroom members over longer observation periods. Just as the children adapted to the presence of observers, a class could be adapted to the presence of a TV camera man. Costs could be trimmed by saving only some sample tapes and reusing others after reliability ratings are obtained. The current observation procedures (short of having an observer for each child) cannot readily be extended to include simultaneous coding of teacher and child behavior without overtaxing the observers.

The present findings, and related studies in this series, are sufficiently promising to warrant an investment in more powerful recording equipment.

Teacher Reactions

Teacher A. Initially, Mrs. A generally maintained control through scolding and loud critical comments. There were frequent periods of chaos, which she handled by various threats.

When praise was finally added to the program, Mrs. A had these reactions: "I was amazed at the difference the procedure made in the atmosphere of the classroom and even my own personal feelings. I realized that in praising the well-behaved children and ignoring the bad, I was finding myself looking for the good in the children. It was indeed rewarding to see the good rather than always criticizing. . . . I became convinced that a positive approach to discipline was the answer."

Teacher B. During Baseline Mrs. B was dispensing a great deal of praise and approval to her classroom, but it was not always contingent on Appropriate Behavior. Her timing was wrong and inconsistencies were apparent. For example, on one occasion two children were fighting with scissors. The instigator was placed under a table away from the rest of the class and left there for 3 min. After 3 min Mrs. B took the child in her arms and brought her back to the group even though she was still emitting occasional loud screams. Mrs. B would also ignore behavior for a period of time and then would revert to responding to Inappropriate Behavior with a negative comment; she occasionally gave Approval for Inappropriate Behavior. The training given in seminar and discussions with the experimenter led to an effective use of contingencies. Teacher B was also able to use this training to provide instructions and training for her aide to eliminate problems which arose in the final phase of study when the aide was continuing to respond to Disruptive Behaviors.

Changes in the Children

Cliff showed little change until Mrs. A started praising Appropriate Behavior, except to get worse during the Ignore phase. He was often doing no academic work, talking to peers, and just fiddling away his time. It took considerable effort by Mrs. A to catch Cliff showing praiseworthy behavior. As the use of praise continued, Cliff worked harder on his assigned tasks, learned to ignore other children who were misbehaving, and would raise his hand to get teacher's attention. He participated more in class discussions. He was moved up to the fastest arithmetic group.

Frank showed little change in his "hyperactive" and "inattentive" behaviors until praise was introduced. Frank responded rapidly to praise. After just two days in the "praise" phase, Frank was observed to clean his desk quietly and quickly after completing a handwriting assignment. He was able to finish a task and study on his own until the teacher initiated a new activity. He began to ask for extra assignments and volunteered to do things to help his teacher. He had

Table 4. Percentage of intervals in which behaviors occur:
averages for two children in classroom A by experimental conditions.

Behavior Classes[1]	Experimental Conditions					
	Baseline I	Rules	Rules + Ignore	Rules + Ignore + Praise I	Baseline II	Rules + Ignore + Praise II
Inappropriate Behavior[2]	46.8	39.8	68.5	20.5	37.6	15.1
Gross Motor	13.9	11.3	32.7	5.9	15.5	4.1
Object Noise	3.5	1.4	1.3	0.5	1.9	0.8
Disturbing Other's Property	3.3	1.8	1.9	0.7	0.7	0.3
Turning Around	21.6	9.9	11.4	9.1	12.8	7.6
Verbalizations	12.0	16.8	21.8	6.5	8.0	3.5
Other Inappropriate Behavior	10.9	7.8	16.5	3.9	7.8	2.6
Mouthing Objects	5.5	2.9	3.5	0.7	0.2	0.1

[1]*Contact* occurred less than 1% of the time and is not tabulated here.

[2]The sum of the separate problem behaviors will exceed that for Inappropriate Behavior, since the latter measure does not reflect the possibility that more than one class of problem behaviors may occur in an interval.

learned to sit quietly (when appropriate), to listen, and to raise his hand to participate in class discussion, the latter occurring quite frequently.

Stan slowly improved after contingent praise was instituted, but some of the gains made by Mrs. B were in part undone by the teacher aide. The aide was described as playing policeman and it took special efforts by the teacher to get her to follow the program. Mrs. B summarized the changes in Stan as follows: "Stan has changed from a sullen, morose, muttering, angry individual into a boy whose smile seems to cover his whole face." He became very responsive to teacher praise and learned to follow classroom rules, to pay attention to teacher-directed activities for long periods of time, and to interact with his peers in a more friendly way.

Implications

This replication and refinement of an earlier study by Becker et al. (1967) adds further confidence to the assertion that teachers can be taught systematic procedures and can use them to gain more effective behaviors from their students. Unless teachers are effective in getting children "ready to learn," their technical teaching skills are likely to be wasted. Knowledge of differential social reinforcement procedures, as well as other behavioral principles, can greatly enhance teachers' enjoyment of the profession and their contribution to effective development of the students.

The reader should note that while we formally recorded the behavior of a few target children, teacher and observer comments indicated dramatic changes in the whole "atmosphere" of the classroom and in the teachers' enjoyment of their classes.

REFERENCES

Allen, K. E., Hart, B. M., Buell, J. S., Harris, F. R., and Wolf, M. M. Effects of social reinforcement on isolate behavior of a nursery school child. In L. P. Ullmann and L. Krasner (Eds.), *Case studies in behavior modification.* New York: Holt, Rinehart, & Winston, 1965. Pp. 307-312.

Becker, W. C., Madsen, C. H., Jr., Arnold, Carole R., and Thomas, D. R. The contingent use of teacher attention and praise in reducing classroom behavior problems. *Journal of Special Education,* 1967, 1, 287-307.

Bijou, S. W. and Baer, D. M. Some methodological contributions from a functional analysis of child development. In L. P. Lipsitt and C. S. Spiker (Eds.), *Advances in child development and behavior.* New York: Academic Press, 1963. Pp. 197-231.

Hart, Betty M., Reynolds, Nancy J., Baer, Donald M., Brawley, Eleanor R., and Harris, Florence R. Effect of contingent and non-contingent social reinforcement on the cooperative play of a preschool child. *Journal of Applied Behavior Analysis,* 1968, 1, 73-76.

Thomas, D. R., Becker, W. C., and Armstrong, Marianne. Production and elimination of disruptive classroom behavior by systematically varying teacher's behavior. *Journal of Applied Behavior Analysis,* 1968, 1, 35-45.

Madsen, C. H., Jr., Becker. W. C., Thomas, D. R., Koser, Linda, and Plager, Elaine. An analysis of the reinforcing function of "Sit Down" Commands. In Parker, R. K. (Ed.), *Readings in educational psychology.* Boston: Allyn and Bacon (in press).

5

Instructing beginning teachers in reinforcement procedures which improve classroom control

R. Vance Hall, Marion Panyan, Deloris Rabon, and Marcia Broden

Systematic reinforcement procedures were used to increase study behavior in the classrooms of three beginning teachers experiencing problems of classroom control. Classroom study rates were recorded during a baseline period. During subsequent experimental periods, the teachers changed one or more reinforcement contingencies (teacher attention, length of between-period break, a classroom game) to bring about increased study rates and concomitant reductions in disruptive behaviors. A brief reversal period, in which these contingencies were discontinued, again produced low rates of study. Reinstatement of the contingencies resulted once again in marked increases in study behaviors.

Previous studies (Hall, Lund, and Jackson, 1968; Evans and Ozwalt, 1968; Thomas, Becker, and Armstrong, 1968) have shown that teacher-applied contingencies could be used to increase or decrease study rates and academic performance of dawdling or disruptive pupils in regular school classrooms. These studies, like almost all of those which have demonstrated that teacher-applied contingencies can be effective in special education classrooms (Wolf, Giles, and

From *Journal of Applied Behavior Analysis,* 1968, 1, 315-322. Copyright 1968 by the Society for the Experimental Analysis of Behavior, Inc. Reprinted by permission.

The authors wish to express appreciation to Dr. O. L. Plucker, Dr. Bertram Caruthers, Alonzo Plough, Curtis Reddic, and Barbara Gaines of the Kansas City, Kansas Public Schools and Kenneth Tewell, Robert Clark, and John Beougher of the Bonner Springs, Kansas Public Schools without whose cooperation and active participation these studies would not have been possible. We are also indebted to Dr. R. L. Schiefelbusch, Director, and R. H. Copeland, Associate Director of the Bureau of Child Research, who provided essential administrative support and counsel. Reprints may be obtained from R. Vance Hall, Juniper Gardens Children's Project, 2021 North Third Street, Kansas City, Kansas 66101.

The research was carried out as a part of the Juniper Gardens Children's Project, a program of research on the development of culturally deprived children and was partially supported by the National Institute of Child Health and Human Development: (HD 03144-01) and the Office of Economic Opportunity: (CG 8180) Bureau of Child Research, University of Kansas.

Hall, 1968; Clark, Lachowicz, and Wolf, 1968; O'Leary and Becker, 1967; Hall and Broden, 1967; McKenzie, Clark, Wolf, Kothera, and Benson, 1968), were carried out by experienced teachers. Often, the teachers had been selected because of their excellent classroom management skills and the high probability that they could carry out the experimental procedures successfully.

These demonstrations have been important, but they have not addressed themselves to one of the most significant aspects of classroom management in education: the training of beginning teachers in the principles and procedures which will bring about classroom control.

The present studies were carried out in the classrooms of three first-year teachers. Not only were they initially unfamiliar with learning theory principles and the systematic application of contingencies, but each was experiencing significant problems of general classroom control.

Teacher One

The first teacher had received his B.A. in education the previous year. His first teaching assignment was a class of 30 sixth-graders in a public school located in a low socioeconomic area of Kansas City, Kansas. His class was selected for study on the principal's recommendation because of continued high rates of disruptive and other student non-study behaviors. In the principal's words, the class was, "completely out of control."

Data were recorded every day during the first hour of the school day during the reading period. The recording system was essentially that used in previous studies with individual pupils in which an observer recorded pupil behavior every 10 sec during a 30-min observation session, except that instead of observing the same pupil throughout the session, each was observed for 10 sec on a consecutive rotating basis. If the pupil being observed was out of his seat, or if he talked without being recognized by the teacher any time during the 10-sec interval, an "N" for nonstudy was scored for the interval. Otherwise, the student's behavior at the end of the 10 sec determined the rating. If he was looking out the window, playing with cards, fighting or poking a classmate, tapping pencils on books, cleaning out his desk or engaging in any of a variety of other such behaviors, an "N" was recorded. If there was no "N" behavior an "S", indicating study, was scored for the interval. Study behaviors included writing the assignment, looking in the book and answering the teacher's questions.

When every class member had been observed in turn, recording began again with the first child, until all were observed again in the same order. From this time-sampling procedure the per cent of study for the entire class was computed by dividing the number of study intervals by the total number of observation intervals and multiplying by 100.

The teacher's verbal attention, defined as a verbalization directed to a pupil or pupils, was also analyzed. The teacher's comment was recorded as a "+" if it followed appropriate study behavior, and a "−" if it followed an instance of nonstudy behavior. These comments were recorded when they occurred. Almost without exception those that followed study behavior were approving and those that followed nonstudy behavior were in the form of a verbal reprimand. See Broden (1968) for a more detailed description of these interval recording procedures.

Periodically, and at least once during every experimental condition, a second observer made a simultaneous observational record. Correspondence of the two records interval-for-interval yielded the percentage of interobserver agreement. For this study, the percentage of agreement for class study behavior and for teacher attention ranged from 87 to 93%.

Figure 1 presents the class study rates for the various phases of the experiment and the frequency of teacher comments following study and nonstudy behaviors. The broken horizontal lines indicate the mean study rates for each experimental condition.

During Baseline, the mean class study rate was 44%. The mean number of intervals in which the teacher made comments following study behavior was 1.4 per session. The class study rate rose to 90% when the helping teacher presented a demonstration lesson. The points at which the teacher met with the principal to discuss organizational procedures are indicated. After the first meeting, the teacher began writing all assignments on the board. After the third, he changed the class seating arrangements. As can be seen, these counseling procedures seemed to have some beneficial effects, but the improvement was not enough to eliminate concern.

Before the first day of the second phase, reinforcement principles and procedures used in other studies which had been effective in increasing study behavior of individual pupils were discussed with the teacher. He was shown the class baseline study record and the record of the frequency of teacher comments following study behavior. He was instructed to increase the frequency of positive comments for appropriate study. Each day he was shown the records of the class study rates and the frequency of his comments following appropriate study. Under these conditions the mean frequency of teacher comments following study behavior increased to 14.6 per session. There was a dramatic and sustained concomitant increase in study behavior to a mean rate of 72%. According to the subjective observations of the teacher, principal, and the observers, the class was under better control and classroom noise had decreased significantly.

During a brief Reversal phase, the teacher provided almost no reinforcement for study behavior. This resulted in a sharp decrease in study, which by the sixth session was well within the Baseline range. According to the subjective judgments of the teacher, principal, and observers, disruptive behaviors and high noise levels also returned.

During the Reinforcement$_2$ phase, an immediate sustained increase in study to a mean rate of 76% accompanied an increase of "+" teacher comments to a mean frequency of 14 per session. In the final nine sessions (43 to 52) of the Reinforcement$_2$ phase, the teacher was instructed to continue reinforcing study behavior but to discontinue making comments following nonstudy behaviors. Up to that point, the level of these "−" comments had remained fairly constant, occurring in about 12 intervals per session. When the teacher decreased "−" comments so that they occurred in only 4.5 intervals per session there was no significant change in the class study rate. Therefore, study behavior seemed to be unaffected by comments (usually reprimands) following nonstudy.

Continuous observation was terminated at the end of the Reinforcement$_3$ phase when the primary observer, who was a student intern, returned to her university classes. Post checks taken at one-, three-, and five-month intervals, however, indicated that the relatively high rates of study and teacher attention for study were being maintained.

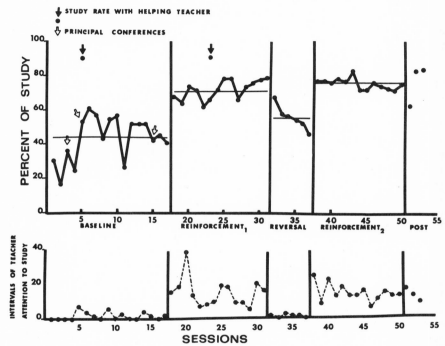

Fig. 1. A record of class study behavior and teacher attention for study behavior during reading period in a sixth-grade classroom: Baseline—before experimental procedures; Reinforcement$_1$—increased teacher attention for study; Reversal—removal of teacher attention for study; Reinforcement$_2$—return to increased teacher attention for study; Post—followup checks up to 20 weeks after termination of experimental procedures.

Teacher Two

The second teacher was also a recent college graduate and in her first year of teaching. She had been assigned to teach a first-grade class of 24 pupils in the same Kansas City, Kansas school. Again the principal and helping teacher had recommended and demonstrated procedures to the teacher for improving classroom management. The results were deemed unsatisfactory because both principal and teacher felt nonstudy behaviors were still too high.

Data were recorded every day the first 30 min of the morning reading period. This time was selected at the request of the teacher because of her concern about the low study rate of pupils at their desks doing "seatwork" while she was working with one or another of the three classroom reading groups in a circle at the front of the room.

The recording procedures were essentially those used with Teacher One. The percentage of agreement between observers for class study behavior and teacher attention ranged from 85 to 88%.

Figure 2 presents the class study rates for the various phases of the experiment. Mean rates for each condition are shown by a broken horizontal line. During the Baseline phase, the mean study rate of pupils at their desks not participating in reading circle was 51%. The mean frequency of intervals of teacher attention following study behavior was 1.6.

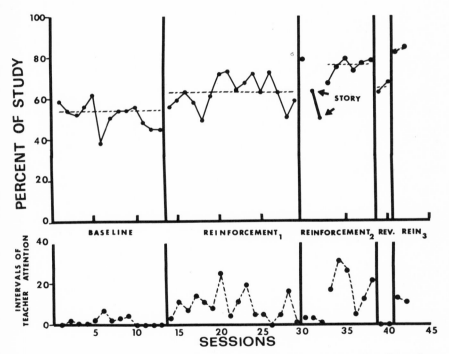

Fig. 2. A record of study rates and teacher attention for study of pupils at desks during a first-grade reading period; Baseline—before experimental procedures; Reinforcement₁—increased teacher attention for study; Reinforcement₂—study game following reading period; Reversal—removal of study game and attention for study; Reinforcement₃—reinstatement of study game and attention for study.

Before the first experimental phase (Reinforcement$_1$) reinforcement principles and procedures were explained to the teacher and she was shown the Baseline study record and the record of her verbal attention following study behavior. She was asked to increase the frequency of her attention for appropriate study of pupils working at their desks. As a result of these instructions, the frequency of teacher attention following appropriate study was increased to nine per session. The mean rate of appropriate study increased to 62%. The teacher, however, was still not satisfied with this study rate. So a second condition, the study game, was introduced as a contingency.

The study game was the simple classroom game, familiar to many teachers, commonly called "7 Up." In it the teacher selects seven pupils, in this case the seven best studiers, to go to the front of the room. Then the rest of the class members put their heads down on their desks and close their eyes. The seven tiptoe around the room, touch one of the seated pupils lightly on the head and return to the front of the room. The seated pupils then open their eyes. The seven who were touched stand and in turn attempt to guess which of those who are up in front touched them. If they succeed they get to go to the front of the room and be "it" on the next round. "7 Up" was renamed the "study" game. It was used because it is a favorite of elementary pupils up through the sixth grade, it is quiet, and it requires little or no teacher supervision.

The "study" game was introduced to the children before reading period on the first day of the Reinforcement$_2$ phase. This was a priming procedure similar to that described by Allyon and Azrin (1968). Teacher judgment was the sole criterion as to whether or not pupils studied enough to play the "study" game.

When the "study" game followed the reading period in the Reinforcement$_2$ phase, study rose to 79%. An unplanned reversal effect was observed in the next two sessions of Reinforcement$_2$ when the teacher read a story to her students after the reading period in lieu of the "study" game. By the second session, study had dropped to 50%. When the "study" game was reinstituted as a contingency for study, the class study rate rose to higher levels.

The next phase was a planned reversal in which the teacher was instructed not to reinforce study and told the pupils they could not play the "study" game. The mean study rate for Reversal was 63%.

The mean rate of study during the two days of the Reinforcement$_3$ phase, when the "study" game was again used as reinforcement for appropriate study, was 82%. Since these last two sessions were during the last week of the school year, the teacher was particularly pleased at the high study rate achieved and the almost complete lack of disruptive behavior in the class.

Teacher Three

In the third study, the teacher taught a class of 30 seventh graders enrolled in an afternoon unified studies (English and social studies) class in the small town of Bonner Springs, Kansas which is just outside Kansas City. The class met daily for 40 min with a 5-min break and then met for another session of 45 min.

The class was selected on the principal's recommendation because the teacher was in his first year and there was concern because of the high rate of disruptive behaviors. These included talking without permission, being out of their seats, fighting, and throwing paper. The noise level was so high and so constant that the teacher kept the classroom door closed and the shade over the door window pulled at all times.

Observations were made daily during the first 30 min of the period before the 5-min break.

The recording system was essentially that used in the first two experiments, except that the recording interval was 5 sec rather than 10. Thus, the recorded behavior for the first pupil was that which was occurring after the first 5 sec of observation, the behavior of the second pupil was recorded after the next 5 sec of observation, and so on, so that the behavior of a different pupil was recorded at each 5-sec interval until the entire class had been observed. Then the observation sequence was repeated. Teacher attention for both study and nonstudy was also recorded as it occurred. Reliability checks made during each phase of the study showed an interobserver agreement which ranged from 80 to 90%.

Figure 3 shows that the mean class study rate for the baseline period of 25 days was 47%. The mean frequency of teacher attention following study behavior was six times per session. The frequency of attention for nonstudy was over 20 per session; most often this attention was in the form of the command, "Let's have it quiet in here."

During the first Reinforcement phase, the teacher was asked to try to increase the amount of attention to study and decrease the amount of attention for nonstudy. As a result, teacher attention for study increased to nine times per session while attention for nonstudy decreased to about nine per session. The study rate under these conditions increased to 65%. According to the subjective judgment of the teacher, principal, and the experimenters, however, the classroom noise still remained at a disruptive level.

In the next phase (Reinforcement$_2$), the teacher added an additional condition. He placed a chalk mark on the chalk board if any student got out of his seat without permission or disturbed the class. For each mark placed on the board 10 sec were deducted from the five-min between-period break. If as many as 24 marks were accumulated there was to be no break. The teacher paused about 5 sec before placing a mark on the board. If the class became quiet and the disruptions stopped within the 5-sec period, no mark was put on the board.

Under these conditions study increased to 76%. A marked decrease in classroom noise was noticed by the observers and the teacher began to leave the door to the room open. He also, for the first time, left the room for brief periods without losing control.

After the first two days of Reversal, when punishment of noisy behavior was discontinued the rate of study behavior dropped sharply. At the same time, teacher attention for nonstudy behaviors increased, as did the high level of classroom noise, according to the judgment of the observers.

During the final reinforcement phase, the study behavior rose immediately to 81% and was maintained at that level to the end of the study.

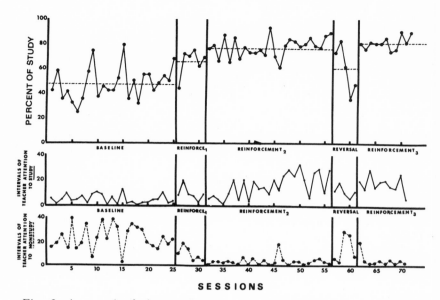

SESSIONS

Fig. 3. A record of class study rates and teacher attention for study and nonstudy during a seventh-grade unified studies period: Baseline—before experimental procedures; Reinforcement₁ —increased attention for study; Reinforcement₂ —increased attention for study and shortened between-period break for disruptive behavior; Reversal—removal of punishment for disruptive behavior; Reinforcement₃ —reinstatement of punishment for disruptive behavior.

DISCUSSION

The beginning teacher faces a formidable challenge. Except for a brief exposure to student teaching, where the classroom is organized and supervised by an experienced teacher, he or she has had no pedagogical experience. Often the practice teaching is at a different grade level than the one assigned the new teacher when he gets his own classroom. Thus, on the first day of school the teacher suddenly finds himself alone, facing a classroom of 30 or so pupils with responsibility for providing them an effective learning environment. All too often he finds that he is ill-prepared to cope with the management and control problems which face him, for his professors have not specified precisely enough what procedures should be followed to bring about classroom control.

Most teachers do learn over time the techniques which are effective in getting pupils to study, rather than to engage in nonstudy behaviors. Often another teacher, the principal, or in some districts a helping teacher, suggest or demonstrate ways for achieving classroom control. Even this help, however, is often ineffective. Sometimes it is well into the year before a semblance of good classroom control has been achieved. Some new teachers never make it and drop out during or after that first year. Those that do succeed, often look back and realize that both they and their pupils wasted a great deal of time and energy that first year until they "caught on" on how to manage a class.

The results of the present experiments showed that beginning teachers of three different grade levels experiencing problems of classroom control could be taught to use systematic reinforcement procedures to increase classroom study behavior even when previous attempts at assistance by principals and helping teachers had been relatively ineffective.

In the first experiment, before the changes brought about, the principal had termed the sixth-grade teacher's status as "precarious." He had contemplated replacing him during the year and certainly could not have offered him a contract for a second year if. considerable improvement in control had not occurred. The teacher's awareness of his situation was reflected in a remark made to the observer after the third day of the first reinforcement phase, when an improved classroom atmosphere was already evident. He said: "You know, I think I'm going to make it." He did make it, and was offered and accepted a contract to continue teaching.

In the cases of the first- and seventh-grade teachers there was less immediate concern about imminent failure. Even so, both the teachers and the principals reported that the improvements seen in class control were dramatic.

One notable aspect of all three studies is that the teachers were able to carry out the procedures after an initial explanatory session of between 15 and 30 min at the beginning of each experimental period and daily feedback of the results. The feedback sessions were also used to provide social reinforcement to the teacher for carrying out the procedures. It seems likely that for all three teachers, the fact that their classes became more manageable served to reinforce and thus maintain the changes in the teacher's reinforcement behavior. They reported it was actually less work to teach using the procedures than when they had not used them. In the case of the seventh-grade teacher, this was borne out by the fact that, whereas he provided attention (mostly verbal reprimands) almost once a minute during Baseline, he was able to maintain a much higher study rate during the reinforcement phases with about half as much total teacher attention.

We are well aware that good teachers (who had "caught on") had been using these same techniques effectively long before B. F. Skinner formulated the principles of operant conditioning. Even these teachers, however, had not looked at behavior closely enough and with enough understanding to be able to specify precisely what they had done and what the ineffective teacher needed to do to bring about desired pupil behavior. These studies indicate that a behavior analysis approach will allow educators, including principals and helping teachers, to help the beginning teacher who otherwise may have been doomed to failure or at least to a fumbling and frustrating trial and error period, quickly to learn to manage his classroom through systematic use of the reinforcing contingencies available to him.

Furthermore, college instructors should now be able to give prospective teachers functional information regarding the relationship of their behavior to that of their pupils. This information can be specific and precise enough so that the new teacher can apply it in the classroom.

Finally, it should be noted that the procedures were carried out with telling effect within the existing school structure. Teacher attention, a classroom game, and access to a between-period break were used rather than reinforcers extrinsic to the situation. The procedures described (or others that are similar) which use the reinforcers already available in the schools can be employed by teachers in any classroom without added expense and without major administrative revision.

REFERENCES

Allyon, T. and Azrin, N. H. Reinforcer sampling: a technique for increasing the behavior of mental patients, *Journal of Applied Behavior Analysis,* 1968, 1, 13-20.

Broden, Marcia. Notes on recording. *Observer's Manual for Juniper Gardens Children's Project.* Bureau of Child Research, 1968.

Bushell, D., Wrobel, P. A., and Michaelis, M. L. Applying "group" contingencies to the classroom study behavior of preschool children. *Journal of Applied Behavior Analysis, 1968,* 1, 55-61.

Clark, M., Lachowicz, J., and Wolf, M. M. A pilot basic education program for school dropouts incorporating a token reinforcement system. *Behavior Research and Therapy,* 1968, 6, 183-188.

Evans, G. and Ozwalt, G. Acceleration of academic progress through the manipulation of peer influence. *Behaviour Research and Therapy,* 1967, 5, 1-7.

Hall, R. Vance and Broden, Marcia. Behavior changes in brain-injured children through social reinforcement. *Journal of Experimental Child Psychology,* 1967, 5, 463-479.

Hall, R. Vance, Lund, Diane, and Jackson, Deloris. Effects of teacher attention on study behavior. *Journal of Applied Behavior Analysis,* 1968, 1, 1-12.

McKenzie, Hugh; Clark, Marilyn; Wolf, Montrose; Kothera, Richard, and Benson, Cedric. Behavior modification of children with learning disabilities using grades as token reinforcers. *Exceptional Children,* 1968, 34, 745-752.

O'Leary, K. D. and Becker, W. C. Behavior modification of an adjustment class: a token reinforcement system. *Exceptional Children,* 1967, 33, 637-642.

Thomas, Dan R., Becker, Wesley C., and Armstrong, Marianne. Production and elimination of disruptive classroom behavior by systematically varying teachers' behavior. *Journal of Applied Behavior Analysis,* 1968, 1, 35-45.

Wolf, Montrose M., Giles, David K., and Hall, R. Vance. Experiments with token reinforcement in a remedial classroom. *Behaviour Research and Therapy,* 1968, 6, 51-64.

6

An elementary student as a behavioral engineer

Paul R. Surratt, Roger E. Ulrich, and Robert P. Hawkins

Four first-grade public school students exhibited nonstudy behaviors during a period when all children were to study individually. A fifth-grade student modified the maladaptive behaviors of the four first-grade students. Lights on the four students' desks, which were associated with opportunity for reinforcement, rapidly brought study behavior under stimulus control. Differential reinforcement of other behaviors dramatically decreased studying. Reinforcement was reinstituted and studying returned to a high and stable rate. Surreptitious post--experimental observation using closed-circuit TV indicated that the behavioral changes effected during the experimental phases were partially maintained by the regular classroom environment. A replication of the baseline phase with the observer in the classroom produced an increase in the rate of study behavior, indicating that the observer's presence acted as a discriminative stimulus for studying. An additional contingency requiring improved academic behavior was imposed before the fifth grader was given the opportunity to engage in the behavior modification experiment.

From *Journal of Applied Behavior Analysis,* 1969, 2, 85-92. Copyright 1969 by the Society for the Experimental Analysis of Behavior, Inc. Reprinted by permission.

This research was supported by a grant from the Michigan Department of Mental Health entitled In-School Treatment Program. The authors wish to express their gratitude to Mr. Kenneth Otis, Superintendent, Vicksburg Community Schools, and to Mrs. Francis Smink, Principal; Mrs. Judy Berghuis, First-Grade Teacher; Mr. Brent Lehmkuhl, Student Engineer; and entire staff of Indian Lake Elementary School for their cooperation and support throughout this experiment. Appreciation is also extended to Dr. Donald Whaley and Mr. Marshall Wolfe for their comments and criticisms throughout the study and in preparation of the manuscript. Gratitude is also expressed to Miss Lois Huey, Miss Brigette Symannek, Mr. Richard Cole, Miss Cheri Yeager, Miss Madeline Lewis, Miss Marilyn Arnett, and Miss Sylvia Delaney for their aid in preparation of the manuscript and graphs. Reprints may be obtained from Paul R. Surratt, Rehabilitation Institute, Southern Illinois University, Carbondale, Illinois 62901.

The use of behavior modification techniques in regular public school classrooms has recently received considerable attention (Hall, Lund, and Jackson, 1968; Thomas, Becker, and Armstrong, 1968; Madsen, Becker, and Thomas, 1968). In each of these cases, the teacher was utilized as a behavioral engineer, which necessitated that he or she selectively observe the behavior of each of the children in question. Within a normal classroom, there are times when such observations are not practical. For example, when a teacher is working intensively with a small reading group, it is frequently not possible to attend closely to the behaviors of other class members located in another part of the room.

If time, personnel, and adequate funds were available, the optimal condition within a school would be for a trained behavioral therapist to work with children who are exhibiting mild problems. Because of the prohibitive cost involved in hiring special personnel and the lack of individuals with sufficient training, many problems are allowed to exist and to develop until it is only after a severe behavioral problem is well established that any student is given professional attention.

In a setting where the teacher is unable to work with the behaviors in question, he or she must utilize the resources at hand. In the typical school setting, an abundant resource available for the modification of student behavior, is other students.

It has been shown that nurses and hospital attendants (Ayllon and Michael, 1959), parents (Zeilberger, Sampen, and Sloane, 1968; Hawkins, Peterson, Schweid, and Bijou, 1966), as well as many other diverse populations can be trained effectively in a short period of time to modify the behavior of others (Ulrich, Stachnik, and Mabry, 1966; Homme, 1966). Ulrich and Kent (1966) have suggested the use of college students as instructors for less advanced students.

Many behavior modification studies (i.e., Hawkins et al., 1966) have attempted to assess the long-term effects of their experimental manipulations by returning the observer to the setting in which the manipulations took place. That observer then records the behavior that is occurring and these data are presented as the residual effect of the experimental manipulations. It would seem feasible that in varying degrees an observer-modifier could become a discriminative stimulus for the behavior in question. The validity of standard post-check methodologies would be in some doubt if such a discriminative function could experimentally be attributed to the presence of the observer-manipulator within the classroom.

The present study investigated the behaviors of four first-grade students in response to controls exerted by a fifth grader functioning as a student engineer. In addition, the effect of the presence of the student engineer during post-check was assessed.

METHOD

Subjects

Four students, enrolled in the first grade of a rural public school, had been described by the teacher as students who did not complete work assignments during study times, but engaged in incompatible behaviors such as talking, walking around the room, and "day dreaming." All four of these children were reported to be experiencing some trouble with their classwork. Two of the four had repeated at least one grade and were being considered by school personnel as candidates for a special remedial classroom. The behavioral engineer in the present study was a fifth grader from the same school.

Apparatus

The experiment was conducted in the first-grade room of a public school which was equipped with the usual classroom facilities and accommodated 29 students and a teacher.

The apparatus consisted of a console designed and constructed to record the behaviors in question and to give feedback to the subjects as to whether they were meeting criteria for those behaviors. Power to the entire console was controlled by a Gra-Lab Session Timer, Model 176, that determined session length. Four silent, single throw, mercury switches each controlled a Cramer Running Timer Meter, Model 636, as well as current to an outlet on the back of the console. When a subject engaged in the behavior being monitored, the console operator would place that student's switch in the "ON" position, which would activate the running-time meter and provide current to the outlet for that particular student. During Phases II through VI, electric lights were plugged into the outlets on the console which were illuminated when the student's switch was in the "ON" position.

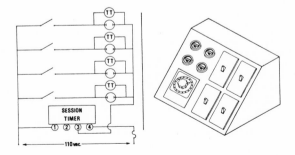

Fig. 1. A schematic and line drawing of console.

Throughout all phases, the student engineer wore dark sunglasses with narrow eye openings to prevent direct eye-to-eye contact between the engineer and the pupils being observed.

Procedure

Sessions were conducted each weekday morning between 9:40 and 10:00. During this time the teacher conducted a small reading group in one corner of the room and the remaining students were assigned arithmetic problems to be completed individually at their desks.

"Working" was the behavior recorded and was operationally defined as any of the following: (1) looking at the blackboard; (2) counting on fingers, pencils, crayons, etc.; or (3) writing on paper. When the student was engaged in any of these behaviors, his or her timer was turned "ON," and recorded "time working." When the student was engaged in behaviors other than "working," the switch was kept in the "OFF" position. These data were converted into "per cent time working" by dividing total number of minutes spent working by the total session length in minutes, times 100.

For several days before the first session, the student engineer operated the console within the classroom without lights in order to become proficient in its use and to allow the students to adapt to the observer's presence.

The study was conducted in eight phases, which will be discussed in order. During the first phase, baseline data were collected to determine the amount of time spent "working" during each session. In the second condition, lights were placed on the desks of Ricky and Dennis which were individually illuminated when either of the students met a criterion for "working." Tim and Lisa, without lights, continued in the baseline phase. This phase allowed an assessment of: (1) the effect of response-contingent lights (with Ricky and Dennis) and (2) the effect of seeing another student receive response-contingent light (with Tim and Lisa).

During Phase III, Ricky and Dennis were told: "If you study a great deal during class today, you will get a little blue ticket. On that ticket you may write anything that you want to do tomorrow morning such as _____." In this blank the students could have written any activity in which they desired to engage, such as going to the gym, going to the playground, performing janitorial tasks around the school building, or any other activity that could be arranged by the experimenter. The duration of each of these activities was 15 min. On the first day, the criterion for reinforcement for Dennis or Ricky was 12 min of work out of a total session length of 20 min. For the next three days, the criterion was raised 2 min per day and on the fourth day was raised 1 min; thus, the successive criteria were 12, 14, 16, 18, and 19 min. From that point on, the criterion remained at 19 min. That is, Ricky and Dennis had to emit working behaviors during 95% of the session in order to receive a blue ticket exchangeable for a chosen activity. At the onset of this phase, lights were placed on Tim's and Lisa's desks, but no reinforcement contingencies were stated; nor were reinforcements given for increased study time. This allowed for the assessment of the effects of response-contingent lights where reinforcement was not available and where the behaviors of the two other subjects were being reinforced for increased study time.

At the onset of the fourth condition, Tim and Lisa were told: "If you study a great deal during class today, you will get a little blue ticket. On that ticket you may write anything that you want to do tomorrow morning such as _____ ." The same increasing sequence of reinforcement criteria, beginning with 12 min of working behavior, was utilized with Tim and Lisa as had been used with Ricky and Dennis.

During the fifth phase, a differential reinforcement of other behavior (DRO) contingency (Bijou and Baer, 1966) was put into effect for all four children. Under this contingency, all behaviors except "working" were reinforced.

Following the DRO condition, the reinforcement contingencies for appropriate "working" behaviors that had been in effect, were reinstated. When this phase was completed, the students and the student engineer were told that the study was completed. They were thanked for their help and participation, and the experimenters, with their equipment, left the building. After this phase and before the onset of the post-check TV condition, a time lapse of 37 days occurred. During this period, the four children, along with remaining class members, continued to work individually on arithmetic problems while the teacher was working with a reading group.

Before the post-check TV condition, a closed-circuit television camera, which scanned the seats of the four subjects, was installed in the classroom. This installation was accomplished on a weekend when classes were not in session. The camera and tripod were so concealed that the only portion visible to the class was an opening for the lens. The morning after the camera was installed, the teacher told the class that it was a piece of scientific apparatus to be used in a night class held in the room, and it was generally disregarded thereafter. In a small enclosed booth outside the classroom, a television monitor was installed whereby the student engineer, utilizing the console, again monitored time spent "working" by the four children for six consecutive school days without their knowledge.

In the final condition, a replication of baseline was conducted by having the student enginner walk into the room with the console and measure time "working." No lights were on the subjects' desks.

At the end of each session during phases when reinforcement was available, the students would gather around the console and compare their timer against their criterion time, which was written on the data sheet. If they met or exceeded criterion for reinforcement, they were given the small blue ticket. The following morning, immediately after classes began, the children who had tickets from the day before were allowed 15 min in which to engage in the activity that they had chosen. To avoid social isolation, the children were given the option of taking a friend with them for the 15-min reinforcement periods. If, at the end of the daily sessions, the students had not met the criterion, they were told: "I'm sorry, you did not keep your light on long enough today. Please take your seat." Thus, the following morning, they would not have the necessary blue ticket to be excused from class. After the four students returned from their reinforcing activity, the class was instructed in the daily arithmetic session and the experimental session commenced.

The student engineer was a fifth-grader whose own classroom was operated on a token economy. The student engineer evidenced a great deal of interest in his role in this study, which led the experimenters to speculate that the Premack Principle (Premack, 1965) could be utilized to modify his academic behavior. Thus, before each of the experimental sessions, each of his teachers was consulted about his academic performance for the previous day. If his performance was above average in all classes, he was given a token by the experimenter for good academic achievement and at the end of the session was given an additional token for operating the console. If, on any occasion, his work was not above average in any of his classes, he was not given a token for academic performance but was given a token for operation of the console. The student engineer was told also that he would not be allowed to operate the console if his teachers reported that his academic performance in any classes was less than above average for any two consecutive days. The latter situation never occurred.

Reliability checks were conducted throughout the study by having a second observer record "time working" for one of the four subjects. These observations were made by the classroom teacher and the experimenters. The larger of the two "times" thus derived was then divided into the smaller and the quotient multiplied by 100, yielding per cent agreement. Reliability checks for the entire study averaged 95% agreement, with a range of 89% to 99%.

RESULTS AND DISCUSSION

Figure 2 shows the percentage of time spent "working" for each of the four subjects. The results of the study will be presented and discussed in the successive order of the eight phases.

During the baseline, "working" time ranged from 15% to 78%, with a mean of 52.8%. In all four subjects there is a downward trend in "working" time as the baseline progresses. A possible explanation for this decline is that the introduction of the student engineer and the console into this classroom a few days before the baseline produced a "Hawthorne effect" on working behavior; that is, the mere change in the stimuli of the classroom brought on a temporary increase in productive behaviors. The baseline data of Fig. 2 would then represent the decline of this effect, or the gradual return to "normal" productivity as the subjects adapted to the new stimuli. The fact that the student engineer was in the classroom for less than an hour per day would be likely to make this adaptation gradual, as the data show the change to be.

The introduction of the lights for Ricky and Dennis, in the second phase, and their response-contingent operation appears to have produced a slight (and perhaps transient) increase in Ricky's working behavior and little or no effect on Dennis'. However, the effect on Ricky's behavior cannot readily be interpreted as evidence that the light's operation had a reinforcing function for this subject, because there was also an apparent increase in Tim's and Lisa's working behavior, even though there were no lights on their desks.

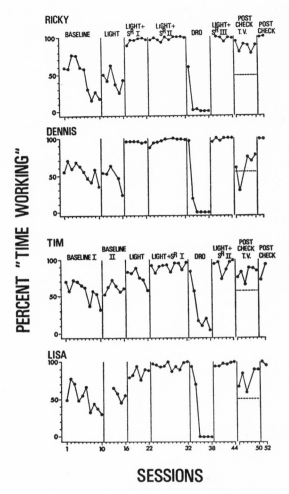

Fig. 2. Graph showing per cent "time working" for all students.

In the third phase, Tim and Lisa were given lights that were turned on when the subjects emitted "working" behaviors. This resulted in a clear increase in these behaviors from Lisa and a smaller (perhaps temporary) increase from Tim. It seems unlikely that all of this increase was due to the simple introduction of a novel stimulus. First, the lights could not be very novel because similar ones had been on Ricky's and Dennis' desks for six days. Second, it is improbable that the high performance produced in Tim and Lisa above their baseline performance in both cases would result from such a minor stimulus change. Therefore, it appears that at least part of the increase in Tim's and Lisa's performance in the third phase could be due to the response-contingent nature of the lights' operation. The turning on of the lights may have been a reinforcer in this phase for Tim and Lisa because they observed Ricky and Dennis being recognized and receiving reinforcements for increased "working" time, via the same light system. Thus, seeing Ricky and Dennis receive a reinforcing consequence may have served as a setting event (Bijou and Baer, 1966) that increased the reinforcing function of response-contingent lights alone for Tim and Lisa.

Before and during study, these four students were seated together in one portion of the room. Another plausible explanation, which might partially account for the increase in time "working" on the part of Tim and Lisa, is that Ricky and Dennis, who were now working, provided fewer distractions. Typically, during the baseline phase when any one student began emitting deviant behavior, it appeared as if the other students attended to that behavior. In addition, many of the nonworking behaviors, such as conversation, required two or more individuals. It could be that part or all of the increase in time "working" on the part of Tim and Lisa could be attributed to: (1) the fact that Ricky and Dennis no longer provided distractions, (2) that Ricky and Dennis did not attend to Tim or Lisa when they emitted some distracting behavior, or (3) a combination of these two.

For Ricky and Dennis, the response-contingent lights combined with the special privileges for studying "a great deal" clearly served to increase their working behavior during the third phase. They averaged 95.8% and 95.5% working time, respectively, in this phase.

In the fourth phase, the same conditions were continued for Ricky and Dennis and their high level of performance continued. The same conditions were also applied to Tim and Lisa, and their performance improved as well.

The DRO contingency, applied to all four subjects in the fifth phase, produced a rapid decline in "working" time for each child. In the last three sessions of this phase, the mean "working" time for the four subjects combined was 2.8%. This effect, combined with the effect of the conditions of the next phase, when lights and special activities were again contingent upon "working" behaviors, suggests that the reinforcement contingencies were highly effective and were indeed responsible for the high performance attained by the four subjects during reinforcement phases. In addition, the results of the DRO condition suggest that neither the presence of novel stimuli in the room nor the status of being singled out as subjects for special treatment were variables powerful enough (at this time in the study) to exert much control over the behaviors being measured. Any tendency of these variables to increase (or decrease) the behaviors was clearly overridden by the control exerted by the reinforcement contingency.

When the subjects were surreptitiously observed via closed-circuit TV approximately six weeks after the last application of the contingent lights and special activities, their performance was generally better than it had been during the baseline. Mean "time working" was 76.7%.

To facilitate comparison between baseline performance and performance during the post-experimental follow-up, each subject's mean working time from the baseline is presented as a dashed line in the segment of Fig. 2 depicting the results of the TV followup. According to the data collected by TV, three of the four children showed a better performance six weeks after the experiment than during the baseline, suggesting that the brief application of special reinforcement contingencies during the experiment produced a lasting improvement in working behaviors.

Evidently the conditions existing before the experiment were insufficient to produce a high level of performance in these four children; but once sufficient contingencies were applied to strengthen working behaviors, the pre-experimental contingencies were adequate to maintain those working behaviors in moderate strength. This conclusion assumes, of course, that the environment after the experiment was essentially the same as it had been before. It is possible that the experiment inadvertently changed some important behavior of the teacher's, or of the subjects' peers, and that these new behaviors served to maintain the subjects' performance after the experimental contingencies were removed; however, no such changes were observed by the experimenters. Others in this class, who were described by the teacher as "good" students, were observed to be studying a comparable amount of time.

Patterson, Jones, Whittier, and Wright (1965) suggest that schedules of reinforcement and punishment on the part of parents and peer group can be critically important in maintaining behaviors of students within classrooms. It could also be that very subtle interactions were occurring along these lines that were not apparent to the experimenters.

In the second post-check, "time working" was generally found to be as high as it had been during the phases when "working" behaviors were being systematically reinforced. As is evident in Fig. 2, "time working" was lower during the TV post-check than during the post-check when the observer was present in the classroom. There are at least two possible explanations for the difference between the results of the two followup phases, and both explanations would seem to hold implications for behavior modification research that utilizes observers to obtain data.

The first explanation is that the student engineer and his console were discriminative stimuli whose presence occasioned working behaviors. The student engineer served both as an observer and a dispenser of consequences for the subjects, and would thus be likely to acquire a discriminative function. As each child took readings from the console at the end of the session to determine whether or not he or she had met the criterion, it also seems feasible that the console itself could have acquired a discriminative function. If this explanation of the difference in the data of the last two phases is valid, it raises a question regarding the interpretation of certain previous studies. For example, Hawkins et al. (1966), in order to teach a mother to be therapeutic toward her own child, had the observer signal the mother when to reward or punish the child. In addition, they instructed the mother to limit the therapeutic procedures to the times when the experimenter-observer was present. These conditions could have resulted in the observer becoming a discriminative stimulus for appropriate behaviors, in which case the favorable data obtained by the same observer in a later followup may not have represented the child's "usual" behavior. These followup data may reflect, at least partially, the appropriate behavior occasioned by the observer's presence. This interpretation can be made of any followup data obtained by an observer whose presence has been (or may have been) correlated with experimental procedures (as in Hall et al., 1968). Certainly it is highly probable that the student engineer in the present study would become a discriminative stimulus for the behavior in question, as he was directly connected with both the observation of the behavior in question and its subsequent reinforcement. While these data do not suggest that a more passive observer (i.e., no direct contact with subjects) would become an equally strong discriminative stimulus in another setting, they do seem to raise some question as to whether and to what degree such events might occur. In order to separate the effects of observer presence, not only during post-check but throughout studies of this nature, the ideal observational medium would seem to be one where the subject is unaware of the observer's presence. The TV method of obtaining data in the present study may be one solution of this problem.

The second explanation of the difference between the findings of the two post-experimental checks is that "working" behaviors may have been more difficult to discriminate via TV than by direct observation. To determine the feasibility of this hypothesis, additional data were recorded in a similar classroom by both TV and direct observation, allowing comparison between data obtained through these two media. The subject was an adult imitating the kind of behavior exhibited by the four subjects in the experiment. A TV camera was located in the room at approximately the same distance from the subject as had been employed in the experiment. Four sessions of approximately 5 min each were held and were recorded on videotape for later viewing. The subject's behavior was also recorded by an observer located approximately 10 ft away. At the end of a session, the observer did not look at the stopwatch on which he recorded "working" time, but handed it to the experimenter who made a record of the time. The observer then watched the videotape recording of the same session and again recorded the subject's "working" time, making it possible to determine intraobserver reliability. In addition, a second observer later viewed this same recording, making it possible to assess interobserver reliability. This second measure of accuracy of data recording was considered important to control for any "practice effect" or retention of how a particular response had been recorded during the intraobserver reliability phase.

The four sessions, each with a new observer, all yielded intraobserver reliabilities above 99%. Interobserver reliabilities in the four sessions were obtained with four different pairs of observers and were all above 97%. These results suggest that the "working" behaviors defined in the present experiment could be recorded as accurately via TV as they could be by direct observation. Thus, it appears that the performance of the four children in the second followup was actually better than during the TV followup, rather than an artifact of the difference in media of observation.

The "working" behaviors modified in the present experiment are assumed to be correlated with the actual accomplishment of assigned work and ultimately with academic achievement. Some evidence was obtained that this assumption may be valid. The teacher reported that the four children completed a greater number of problems, and that a higher proportion of problems completed were correct during the phases of the study when "working" behaviors were reinforced than during other phases (except the followup phase); and that these gains were at least partially maintained after the study terminated. She also reported that the subjects exhibited more "working" behavior and less disruptive behavior throughout the day than during the experiment. Surprisingly, Tim was considered by the teacher to have shown the greatest improvement outside the arithmetic period, even though his "working" behavior in this experiment showed the least improvement and he appeared rather apathetic about the blue tickets and the special activities obtained in exchange for them.

In general it appears that the present technique has considerable promise for helping some children in school settings. It is capable of modifying the behavior of several children at one time and yet involves very little professional time. In fact, it should tend to release the teacher from some of the time she spends attempting to stop disruptive behavior for the acceleration of more adaptive behaviors. Techniques based on this one should be useful to teachers, principals, school psychologists, school social workers, and others faced with the problem of helping children more consistently to exhibit more adaptive classroom behavior.

REFERENCES

Ayllon, T. and Michael, J. The psychiatric nurse as a behavioral engineer. *Journal of the Experimental Analysis of Behavior,* 1959, 2, 323-334.

Bijou, S. W. and Baer, D. M. Operant methods in child behavior and development. In W. Honig (Ed.), *Operant behavior: areas of research and application.* New York: Appleton-Century-Crofts, 1966. Pp. 718-789.

Hall, R. V., Lund, D., and Jackson, D. Effects of teacher attention on study behavior. *Journal of Applied Behavior Analysis,* 1968, 1, 1-12.

Hawkins, R. P., Peterson, R. F., Schweid, E., and Bijou, S. W. Behavior therapy in the home: amelioration of problem parent-child relations with the parent in a therapeutic role. *Journal of Experimental Child Psychology,* 1966, 4, 99-107.

Homme, L. Contingency management. *Educational Technology Monographs,* 1969, 2, No. 2.

Madsen, C. H., Jr., Becker, W. C., and Thomas, D. R. Rules, praise, and ignoring: elements of elementary classroom control. *Journal of Applied Behavior Analysis,* 1968, 1, 139-150.

Patterson, G. R., Jones, R., Whittier, J., and Wright Mary A. A behavior modification technique for the hyperactive child. *Behaviour Research and Therapy,* 1965, 2, 217-226.

Premack, D. *Reinforcement theory.* Paper read at the Nebraska Motivation Symposium, Lincoln, 1965.

Thomas, D. R., Becker, W. C., and Armstrong, M. Production and elimination of disruptive classroom behavior by systematically varying teacher's behaviors. *Journal of Applied Behavior Analysis,* 1968, 1, 35-45.

Ulrich, R. and Kent, N. D. *New tactics for the education of psychologists.* Paper presented at the American Psychological Association, New York, 1966.

Ulrich, R., Stachnik, T., and Mabry, J. *Control of human behavior.* Glenview, Ill.: Scott, Foresman and Company, 1966.

Zeilberger, J., Sampen, S., and Sloane, H., Jr. Modification of a child's problem behaviors in the home with the mother as therapist. *Journal of Applied Behavior Analysis,* 1968, 1, 47-53.

7

Contingency contracting
with school problems

Robert P. Cantrell, Mary Lynn Cantrell,
Clifton M. Huddleston, and Ralph L. Wooldridge

Contingency contracting procedures used in managing problems with school-age children involved analyzing teacher and/or parental reports of behavior problem situations, isolating the most probable contingencies then in effect, the range of reinforcers presently available, and the ways in which they were obtained. The authors prepared written contracts delineating remediative changes in reinforcement contingencies. These contracts specified ways in which the child could obtain existing individualized reinforcers contingent upon approximations to desired appropriate behaviors chosen as incompatible with the referral problem behaviors. Contract procedures were administered by the natural contingency managers, parents and/or teachers, who kept daily records of contracted behaviors and reinforcers. These records were sent to the authors and provided feedback on the progress of the case. Initial results of this procedure have been sufficiently encouraging to warrant recommending an experimental analysis of contingency contracting as a clinical method.

This paper discusses our adaptation of operant methodology to deal with school children's problem behaviors in the setting of a diagnostic and remediation center. The methods described are based primarily on the structuring of available reinforcement contingencies to reinforce approximations to the desired appropriate school behaviors. The data presented are preliminary but suggest that systematic research in these methods might be very fruitful. The term "contingency contract" was borrowed from L. P. Homme (1966), who used written contracts with adolescent potential dropouts to spell out the reinforcers that were to follow completion of academic tasks. The present contract involved a somewhat different procedure. The contingency contract was a written explanation of the changes in contingencies to be used by the natural contingency

From *Journal of Applied Behavior Analysis,* 1969, 2, 215-220. Copyright 1969 by the Society for the Experimental Analysis of Behavior, Inc. Reprinted by permission.

Reprints may be obtained from Robert P. Cantrell, Center for Developmental and Learning Disorders, 1919 Seventh Avenue South, Birmingham, Alabama 35233.

managers, parents and/or teachers. It usually also contained: (1) a written schedule of desired behaviors (such as approximations to school attendance or behaviors involved in appropriate school achievement) with assigned point values, and (2) a written schedule of high probability behaviors (Premack, 1965) (individually defined rewards, privileges, preferred activities) with assigned exchange values.

The efficacy of structuring reinforcement contingencies to shape or maintain adaptive behavior in children is evident in a growing volume of behavior studies (Staats, Minke, Finley, Wolf, and Brooks, 1964; Ullmann and Krasner, 1965; Homme, 1966; Nolen, Kunzelmann, and Haring, 1967; O'Leary and Becker, 1967; Bushell, Wrobel, and Michaelis, 1968; Wolf, Giles, and Hall, 1968; McKenzie, Clark, Wolf, Kothera, and Benson, 1968; Hewett, Taylor, and Artuso, 1969). The present procedure was devised to see if viable changes in child behavior could be brought about by guiding parents and teachers in procedures of contingency control where frequency counting, direct observation, and direct manipulation by professionals were not immediately possible. Problems with which these procedures have been used have ranged from persistent school runaway behavior, school nonattendance, hyper-aggressivity, and stealing, to achievement motivation in underachieving students. Subjects were public school children, first through eleventh graders, from the seven parish areas served by the Louisiana Tech Special Education Center; all lived at a distance of 10 to 85 miles from the Center. The procedures described were initially the result of the need to deal with situational difficulties of sometimes near-crisis dimensions for the families and schools involved. Since most of these problems were of situational origin, the primary intervention procedures thought necessary were those of minimal prescriptive restructuring to alleviate the immediate problem.

Formulation of a contingency contract generally approximated the following pattern. Initially, referral information indicated if a problem might be largely one of motivation rather than academic programming. In considering the use of a contract, some sign was needed that the child could actually do or had done what was expected of him (such as inconsistent grades, intelligence test results, or adequate achievement test scores). If the child was badly in need of special academic programming, motivation by means of a contract might have been detrimental, unless that programming could have been provided in that setting. Also, if special programming would have been sufficient for motivation in and of itself, there would obviously have been no need for a contract.

After referral, the first step was to interview the child's adult agents. If the school appeared incapable of following the exigencies of a contract explicitly, only the parents and home were involved. If the home was unlikely to cooperate and the school would, only the school was involved. In most cases both agencies entered in, even though personal interviews might have been only with parents. Parents who had exhausted all available external sources of remediation and who were still concerned about their child's problems appeared to be the most willing to restructure their child-management contingencies.

Parents and teachers were told that it would be better not to attempt to write a contract unless they definitely wanted such help and were willing to involve their own personal effort in its success. This was done for at least two reasons: (1) If the system were to be attempted half-heartedly, it would not be enforced consistently and whatever extinction procedures were necessary would not occur. (2) If the agents were to give up on the system at the point where the child was testing it most severely, they would probably terminate with the maladaptive behavior at a higher peak and one even more resistant to change than before.

Initial interviews with the natural contingency managers were used to provide answers to the following questions:

1. What specifically were the key problem behaviors and how often did they occur? These primary behaviors were isolated and some provisions for counting their preintervention frequency were made to provide "baseline" data.

2. What was the typical or occasional consequence of these problem behaviors? Careful interviewing at this point provided a fairly complete list of usual consequences and some estimate of the schedules of their usage which appeared to be maintaining the maladaptive behavior.

3. What were the events, privileges, pastimes, foods, and material possessions which already served as reinforcements for this child? These were usually obtained by asking the parents or teachers what the child liked to do if he had the opportunity, what he spent the most time doing, what he would work for, and if any other consequence might possibly serve as a reinforcing event. Parents and teachers were usually able to provide a fairly complete list of reinforcers for their children in a roughly hierarchical arrangement of value to the child. For each reinforcer the parent was queried as to how the child at that time gained access to these reinforcers. In almost all cases, access to desired reinforcers was not being made contingent upon approximations to the desired behavior.

4. What might be used as a definite punishment or extinction consequence of an undesirable behavior if needed? This question was usually posed to the parents in the form of asking what the child would work to avoid, what seemed to be the most effective punishment if punishment were needed, and how easily might the parents or teachers be able to legislate specific punishing contingencies if they were found to be necessary. Here again, parents or teachers were usually able to identify a rough hierarchy of events which the child would work to avoid.

Once these basic questions were answered, the problem became one of how to change the contingencies in order to utilize reinforcers already available. The written contract had to be clear, complete, useful as ongoing data to judge its effectiveness, and simple enough to carry out that its demands did not make it aversive to the agents enforcing it. The child was presented with the record sheets and the new regimen by his parents or teacher. In most cases he took his weekly sheet of earned points to school where his teacher gave him points as earned and then brought it home where his parents gave him points earned at home. Points earned at school and home were spent on a daily and weekly basis. His weekly record sheet of points spent was kept at home for easy reference by the child.

Behavioral change was monitored by building into the contract methods of measuring the problem behavior before the contract went into effect, of graphing progress continually, and of measuring the problem behavior after intervention with the contract had been completed. Independent records from the schools (such as grades, attendance records, incidences of maladaptive behavior) were obtained in addition to parental report forms.

The contracts generally fell into two ways of arranging contingencies once the problem behaviors and available reinforcers had been delineated. In the first, receipt of the reinforcers was simply made contingent on adaptive behaviors that were incompatible with the problem behaviors. For example, R's parents and teachers complained that he did not complete homework or class assignments unless he did so very carelessly and that he did not work or listen to directions without constant reminders and "pushing". R's contract was formulated as follows.

Contingency Contract

This contract defines the ways in which R can earn points by doing specific things at school and at home that would be necessary for his academic growth (i.e., completing class assignments and homework). He exchanges these points for preferred activities or money (i.e., going places, watching television, Coke money, etc.). He can earn an approximate maximum of 50 points per day or 250 points per week under this schedule.

R's teacher marks his points earned each day on his weekly record sheet of points earned (Fig. 1) and sends home an average of one graded paper per day for which he gets additional points. His mother gives him points for homework done at home and keeps a record of points spent on the appropriate weekly sheet (Fig. 2). When R wants to spend his points, he is allowed to and given verbal praise for having worked well enough at school to have enough points. When he does not have suffcient points for something he wants, a simple statement that he does not yet have enough points is made. It is crucial that R receive these privileges only when he has the required number of points already on his chart.

It appears that R's nonworking at school results in getting more attention from adults than his working ordinarily does. Switching the tables on him should result in increased effort on his part. Efforts should be made to give R attention and approval when he is working and behaving as we would hope. Inappropriate behavior or nonworking should result in little attention (punishment, reminders, scolding included) given to him. Insofar as possible, R should learn that he will be ignored when he is not working or behaving appropriately, but when he does put forth effort and behave appropriately, people are proud of him and give him attention.

Week of: _____

R earned points for:	Mon.	Tues.	Wed.	Thurs.	Fri.	TOTALS

Homework:
    completed (3 points)
    well done* (5 additional)						

Class assignments:
    completed   (1 point each)
    well done* (2 additional)
    with no more than 2 misspelled words or
        careless arithmetic errors
                    (1 additional)						

Listening and complying to directions without reminder (1 point each time)						

Daily grades:
    A (10 points)
    B (6 points)
    C (3 points)
    D (1 point)						

Homework:
    started with no warnings (5 points)
                one warning (3 points)
                two warnings (2 points)
                three warnings (1 point)
    completed by supper time (2 additional)						

TOTALS						

*Bonus: Baseball glove as soon as R earns 75 points total in these two "well done" categories

Fig. 1. Weekly record sheet of points earned.

Week of: _____

R exchanged his points for:	Mon.	Tues.	Wed.	Thurs.	Fri.	Sat.	Sun.	TOTALS
Outdoor time (5 points per ½ hour)								
Television viewing time (5 points per ½ hour)								
Kitchen time (cooking privileges) (5 points per ½ hour)								
Driving (as parents direct) (10 points per ½ hour)								
Going out privilege (10 points per event)								

Staying with friend all night
    or having one over for night
    (25 points per event)								

Money (up to limit set by parents) (5 cents per point)								
TOTALS								

Fig. 2. Weekly record sheet of points spent.

In comparing six weeks' grades for the report before intervention and the report after intervention, R's grades stayed the same in three subjects, improved one letter in two subjects, and improved two letters in one subject.

In the second general method of contract arrangement, the behavioral steps leading toward the desired terminal behavior were arranged in sequential, programmed fashion. Receipt of the reinforcers was then made contingent on these steps. In the case of S, a "school phobic" child, points were earned for approximations or steps toward full school attendance where she had previously had problems: getting out of bed (5 points); getting dressed (5 points); having breakfast (5 points); no crying before school (5 points); no illness before school (5 points); going to schoolbus (5 points); getting on schoolbus (5 points); going to class (5 points); going into classroom (5 points); staying in class (5 points per 15 min); no crying at school (5 points); no illness at school (5 points); homework started with no reminders (15 points), with one reminder (10 points), with two reminders (5 points), completed (5 additional points). S exchanged points for: TV viewing, renting toys or books, helping mother in kitchen (25 points per 30 min); outside play time (50 points per 30 min); having friends over or going to visit friends (100 points); going out privilege (150 points); overnight visit with friend (200 points); spending money (1 point per penny); plus an additional bonus of one article of new clothing for going to school one full week. The terminal state desired in S's case, full school attendance without resistance, was attained on the eighth school day after the contract was initiated and maintained throughout the rest of that and the next school year.

An essential part of the program was the inclusion of a builtin feedback system. Most of the contracts provided for parents or teachers to mail completed record forms to us weekly. Upon their receipt, blank forms were sent them for another week. Agents were initially given two weeks' worth of forms to allow for one week's transit in the mails. Parents and/or teachers were encouraged to write or call as problems or questions arose. The information gleaned from the obtained record forms was used to initiate telephone conference calls or visits to the agents or to clarify or change the contracts as behavior shifts occurred. This followup was crucial. Even if the contingency change as designed had "hit" upon the right combination of reinforcement schedules, consistent encouragement of the parents or agents of the contract was often necessary in order to maintain the behavior until new patterns of interaction had become more solidified.

In many cases, fading procedures from the contract were instituted at the child's request. A fading procedure was seldom needed to wean the child away from the contract system. In most cases, the children themselves gave agents clues as to when to cease the program or how to ease it back to a more natural set of contingencies. In others, external situations caused a natural change back to more natural behavior management, such as the end of the school year. Parents often indicated a reluctance to terminate the contract before the end of the school year. Only a few resumed use of the contract at the beginning of the subsequent school year.

Parents and school personnel have communicated to the contract writers their enthusiasm about the procedures and results, and have often referred other cases for similar treatment. The fact that the contracts use reinforcers already present in the child's environment, rather than introducing new ones, seems to have appeal to the natural contingency managers with whom we have worked. Training the natural contingency managers inductively through the prescriptive, precise procedures of the contracts seems to result in the principles being learned more completely than when we have attempted to teach the principles of modifying behavior before dealing specifically with the problem behavior at hand.

Optimally, the use of direct observation in the home or the school to ascertain the agent's compliance with the contract, plus the use of multiple baseline procedures to validate the efficacy of the contract on other problem behaviors for the same child, would have provided more data for the validity of the procedures beyond parent and school reportings. Even here, the establishment of a functional relationship between the instigation of the contract and the changes that accrue would be subject to the problems of indeterminacy and changes in expectation (Rosenthal and Jacobson, 1968). Relying on the agent's report of behavior alone also posed difficulties in determining the actual course of the behavior as it was occurring. On the one hand, if the contract was being consistently enforced and still was not working as expected, the possibility existed that the authors of the contract had not eliminated the salient reinforcers maintaining the problem behavior or had not provided strong enough reinforcers to change it to a more adaptive form. In this case, a new combination or revision of the old combination of reinforcers in the old contract was necessary. On the other hand, it appeared to be risky to assume that the system needed changing too soon. Many of the maladaptive behaviors were thought to have been shaped by the child's being able to "wait out" or "outlast" adult contingencies. If this were the case, the problem became one of encouraging the adult agents to maintain the newly initiated contingencies in order to break the control—counter-control cycle being tested by the child. Further studies are now in progress using multiple baseline and independent observation in the home and school to clarify further the processes involved.

A primary concern of professionals often is one of maximum efficiency in meeting the behavioral crises of individual cases while continuing their professional efforts in other endeavors. If experimentally verified, the "contingency contract" method offers one possible avenue to resolve in a clinical setting the perpetual "minimax" conflict of bringing about maximal behavioral change with minimal expenditure of professional time and money. The prospects of the natural contingency managers in the child's situation, teachers and parents, actually administering the new procedures may be one means of closing the gap between the availability of professional staff and the press of public demand for their services.

In summary, the application of reinforcement theory in the form of written contingency contracts as specific directions through which the natural contingency managers can change problem behaviors appears to be a potentially useful tool for professionals dealing with children's problems. The effect of such contracting appears to be largely dependent upon: (1) the capacity of the professionals who prepare the contingencies to derive from verbal information those contingencies that appear to be maintaining the problem behavior and then to change them, and (2) the relative ability of the adults involved to maintain the contingencies spelled out by the contract.

REFERENCES

Bushell, D., Jr., Wrobel, Patricia A., and Michaelis, Mary L. Applying "group" contingencies to the classroom study behavior of preschool children. *Journal of Applied Behavior Analysis,* 1968, 1, 55-62.

Hewett, F. M., Taylor, F. D., and Artuso, A. A. The Santa Monica Project: Evaluation of an engineered classroom design with emotionally disturbed children. *Exceptional Children,* 1969, 35, 523-529.

Homme, L. Human motivation and the environment. In N. Haring and R. Whelan (Eds.) *The learning environment: relationship to behavior modification and implications for special education.* Lawrence: University of Kansas Press, 1966.

McKenzie, H. S., Clark, Marilyn, Wolf, M. M., Kothera, R., and Benson, C. Behavior modification of children with learning disabilities using grades as tokens and allowances as back-up reinforcers. *Exceptional Children,* 1968, 34, 745-752.

Nolen, Patricia A., Kunzelmann, H. P., and Haring, N. G. Behavioral modification in a junior high learning disabilities classroom. *Exceptional Children,* 1967, 33, 163-168.

O'Leary, K. D. and Becker, W. C. Behavior modification of an adjustment class: a token reinforcement program. *Exceptional Children,* 1967, 33, 637-642.

Premack, D. Reinforcement theory. In D. Levine (Ed.), *Nebraska symposium on motivation: 1965.* Lincoln: University of Nebraska Press, 1965. Pp. 123-180.

Rosenthal, R. and Jacobson, Lenore. *Pygmalion in the classroom: teacher expectation and pupils' intellectual development.* New York: Holt, Rinehart & Winston, 1968.

Staats, A. W., Minke, K. A., Finley, J. R., Wolf, M., and Brooks, L. A reinforcer system and experimental procedures for the laboratory study of reading acquisition. *Child Development,* 1964, 35, 209-231.

Ullmann, L. P. and Krasner, L. (Eds.) *Case studies in behavior modification.* New York: Holt, Rinehart & Winston, 1965.

Wolf, M. M., Giles, D. K., and Hall, R. V. Experiments with token reinforcement in a remedial classroom. *Behaviour Research and Therapy,* 1968, 6, 51-64.

III

Procedures for
Decreasing Undesirable Behavior

The majority of the work in behavioral engineering has been concerned with decreasing undesirable behavior. The underlying idea has been that with fewer disruptions there is more time for learning, although possibly this is not always the case. The aim of this section is to illustrate various strategies for decreasing undesirable behavior. Ward and Baker studied the systematic use of attention and praise with no punishment and found that it reliably decreased deviant behavior. McAllister, Stachowiak, Baer, and Conderman worked with both praise and disapproval to reduce inappropriate talking and turning around, and obtained significant results. Zimmerman and Zimmerman eliminated unproductive classroom behavior in two emotionally disturbed boys by removing the social consequences of the behavior (any operant and/or instrumental response may be extinguished by making it ineffective). The use of free time as a reinforcer has been extremely successful in a wide variety of circumstances; Osborne used free time to reduce the frequency of deaf girls leaving their seats. O'Leary, Becker, Evans, and Saudargas present data on the use of a token reinforcement program in a public school, which is representative of the results of this procedure in dealing with disruptive behavior. The application of group contingencies to the behavior of children is explained by Bushell, Wrobel, and Michaelis. Three more articles discuss various applications of teacher attention on behavior manipulation (Schutte and Hopkins; Hall, Lund, and Jackson; and Buell, Stoddard, Harris, and Baer). May and Bongiovanni point out that occasionally the means employed to modify disruptive behavior will also interfere with academic performance.

8

Reinforcement therapy in the classroom

Michael H. Ward and Bruce L. Baker

Teachers were trained in the systematic use of attention and praise to reduce the disruptive classroom behavior of four first-grade children. Observation measures showed a significant improvement from baseline to treatment for these children and no significant changes for same-class controls. While the amount of teacher attention to target children remained the same from baseline to treatment, the proportion of attention to task-relevant behavior of these children increased. Psychological tests revealed no adverse changes after treatment.

Reinforcement techniques have been demonstrated to be quite effective in altering behavior in the laboratory situation (Krasner and Ullmann, 1965), and recently there have been increasing attempts to extend these methods to treatment in "real-life" situations. Of considerable importance is the potential usefulness of reinforcement therapy in the school classroom (e.g., Clarizo and Yelon, 1967; Hall, Lund, and Jackson, 1968; Woody, 1966).

Zimmerman and Zimmerman (1962) eliminated disruptive classroom behavior in two emotionally disturbed boys by removing the social consequences of maladaptive behavior. Quay, Werry, McQueen, and Sprague (1966) reported on the use of conditioning techniques in a small special class with conduct problem children. A program in which public school teachers were trained to

From *Journal of Applied Behavior Analysis*, 1968, 1, 323-328. Copyright 1968 by the Society for the Experimental Analysis of Behavior, Inc. Reprinted by permission.

This research was supported in part by National Institute of Mental Health Grant No. 1-F1-MH-36, 634-01 (MTLH), and Harvard University Faculty Science Research Grant No. 33-493-68-1718. The authors wish to acknowledge the cooperation and assistance of Assistant Superintendent William Cannon of the Boston Public Schools, and Principal Gladys Wood and Assistant Principal Mary Lynch of the Aaron Davis School. Appreciation is expressed to the teachers, Carol Baumgardt, Sandra Napier, and Elaine Schivek, whose collaboration made this study possible. Our sincere thanks to Virginia Worcholick, Susan Hole, and Janet Ward, who served as observers, and to Sally Sanford, who did the testing. Reprints may be obtained from Michael H. Ward, Psychology Services, Menlo Park Division, Palo Alto VAH, Miranda Drive, Palo Alto, California 94204.

manage classroom behavior problems by the contingent use of teacher attention and praise has been described by Becker, Madsen, Arnold, and Thomas (1967).

While these applications of reinforcement methods are certainly encouraging, several legitimate questions are often raised by psychologists and teachers concerned with treating disruptive classroom behavior. One critical area of concern is the generalization of treatment effects. First, when a child's disruptive behavior is successfully reduced, what are the effects on other aspects of his observable behavior and on his psychological test functioning? Second, how are other pupils in the class affected when the teacher concentrates on treating deviant behavior in one or two specific children?

The present study further explored the effectiveness of the teacher as a therapeutic agent, but it also attempted to assess the generalized effects of reinforcement therapy. Thus, teachers were trained to eliminate deviant behavior by differentially reinforcing the target children's desirable and undesirable classroom behavior. Control procedures were instituted to ascertain the effects of the reinforcement therapy procedures on the psychological adjustment of target and nontarget children.

METHOD

Subjects

Twelve first-grade Negro children in an urban public school were assigned to three groups.

The Experimental Group (Group E) consisted of four behavior problem children. Three boys presented a high frequency of disruptive classroom behaviors, such as inappropriate talking and running around; one girl was highly withdrawn and inattentive. These target children were selected from three separate classrooms, on the basis of teachers' referrals and direct observations.

Control Group CI (Group CI) consisted of four children, matched for sex with the Group E children and selected at random from the three teachers' class lists. Thus, for each target child, a control child in the same classroom was also studied.

Control Group CII (Group CII) consisted of three boys and one girl, selected randomly from the classroom of a fourth first-grade teacher. These pupils provided a baseline for test-retest changes in psychological test performance, independent of any experimental manipulations.

Apparatus

All treatment was carried out in the classroom. For two of the experimental subjects, two small (4-in.) electrically operated signal lights were used in six special-treatment sessions (after Patterson, 1965).

Procedure

For five weeks, the frequency of various deviant classroom behaviors of Group E and Group CI children was coded by trained observers. Deviant behavior was calculated as the percentage of 30-sec intervals in which the child exhibited any behavior which was not task-relevant. These observations constituted the baseline measure of deviant behavior.

At week six, the experimental treatment phase was instituted and continued for seven weeks (until the end of the school year). In the treatment phase, teachers systematically ignored deviant behavior and reinforced, with attention and praise, task-relevant productive behavior. Regular classroom observations of the Group E and Group CI children were continued throughout the study; the Group CII children were not observed at any time.

All three groups were administered a battery of psychological tests, both during baseline and at the conclusion of the seven-week experimental treatment phase.

Observers and Observations. Three female undergraduates were trained to observe and record classroom behavior. The observers sat in the rear of the classroom; they did not interact with or respond to the children. Each Group E child was observed for four 15-min periods per week; each Group CI child was observed for two 15-min periods per week. During the observation period, the child was watched for the first 20 sec of each 30-sec interval of time; in the remaining 10 sec, the observers recorded the behaviors that had occurred. The observation periods were randomized throughout the school day to assure an adequate time-sampling. Interobserver reliability checks were made periodically.

Table 1 shows the categories of behavior rated. These included gross and fine motor behaviors, aggression, deviant talking, nonattending, and disobeying, thumbsucking, and relevant appropriate behaviors such as handraising, task-oriented behavior, and so forth. In addition, the teacher's attention to children, as well as the nature of her comments, was coded.

Teachers and Training Sessions. Three female teachers were initially informed that their behavior problem children would be observed for five weeks, at which time the investigators would again meet with them to discuss some techniques for modifying these behavior problems. None of the teachers was given any further information at this time. At no point were the teachers told that the same-class control children were being observed.

After baseline measurements had been completed, the investigators began a series of four weekly seminar-discussions with the three teachers. These sessions were devoted to discussions of behavior modification and the progress of the target children. The seminars included a general introduction to operant conditioning, reinforcement and punishment procedures, schedules of reinforcement, and selected aspects of the experimental literature relating to these and other topics (e.g., Ullmann and Krasner, 1965).

It was first necessary to help teachers identify and specify deviant behaviors. Throughout the treatment phase of the study, the investigators visited the classrooms and pointed out behavior problems. Thus, rather than: "He's always bad," teachers soon learned to define inappropriate behavior in more specific

Table 1. Classroom behavior rating schedule (after Becker et al, 1967).

Motor Behaviors (at seat)

Rocking in chair; moving chair in place; sitting out of position; standing while *touching* chair or desk.

Gross Motor Behaviors (not at desk)

Getting out of seat; running; jumping; skipping; *not touching* desk or chair.

Aggression

Hitting; punching; kicking; slapping; striking with object; throwing object at another person; pulling hair; disturbing another's books, desk, etc.; destroying another's property. Do *not* rate unless act is committed.

Deviant Talking

Carrying on conversation with other children; blurts out answer without being called upon; making comments or remarks; crying; screaming; laughing loudly; coughing loudly, singing, whistling; any vocal noise.

Non-Attending and Disobeying

Does something different from that which he has been directed to do or is supposed to do; includes "daydreaming"; *Note:* the above to be rated *only* when other classes are inappropriate (no other symbol may appear in interval). Note: Ignoring teacher's *direct* question or command may be rated in addition to other categories.

Thumb Sucking (and other objects)

Thumb or finger sucking; sucking such objects as a pencil, etc.

Relevant Behavior

Time-on-task; answering question; listening; following directions. Important: *Must* include *entire* 20-sec interval, except orienting response of less than 4-sec duration.

Hand Raising

Raises hand to ask or answer question; do *not* rate if child blurts out without being acknowledged. *Note:* may be rated with task-relevant behavior.

Teacher Attention

Teacher attends to the Subject *during* the 20-sec interval.

Positive Comments

"Good," "fine," "nice job" are said by teacher to Subject during the 20-sec interval.

General Reprimand

Teacher issues a *general* reprimand to the class or a group of students.

Negative Comments

"Shut up," "sit in your seat," "you're a bad boy," etc. are said by teacher to Subject during the 20-sec interval.

terms: "He is frequently out of his seat and he blurts out without being called on." It was also necessary to indicate to teachers which behaviors were to be reinforced when. Thus, for two of the behavior problem boys, six special 30-min treatment periods were conducted, in which an experimenter-controlled signal light on the child's desk was used as a reinforcer for sustained task-relevant behavior. The main purpose of this procedure was to bring the child's behavior under experimental control and allow the experimenter to indicate to the teacher the types of behaviors to be reinforced.

The principal therapeutic tool was the contingent use of teacher attention. The teachers were instructed to extinguish deviant behaviors by ignoring them, and to strengthen task-relevant behaviors by attending to and praising them. The need for immediacy, consistency, and contingency in reinforcement therapy was stressed. That is, the teacher was instructed to give *immediate* attention in a *consistent* manner, *contingent* upon the child's exhibiting task-relevant behavior.

A fourth female teacher, from whose classroom Group CII was chosen, did not participate in the seminar-discussions; at no time was she informed of the nature of the study.

Tests and Measures. The measure of deviant classroom behavior was the direct observations described above; these included both the target behaviors and other types of deviant behavior.

In the baseline period, and again at the conclusion of the seven-week treatment period, each of the 12 children was tested individually by an independent examiner on the following battery of tests: four subtests of the WISC, the Draw-A-Person Test, and a projective questionnaire designed to measure attitudes toward school and feelings about self.

The Comprehension, Mazes, Digit Span, and Block Design subtests of the WISC were used to reflect the child's ability to pay attention to a task, and his general scholastic functioning. In the DAP Test, the child was asked to draw a picture of a person, using standard art paper and crayons provided by the tester. Such drawings have been used as measures of a child's adjustment, maturity, and self-image. Finally, the child was shown a photograph of a Negro child of the same sex and comparable age; the facial expressions in these pictures were judged by the authors to be "neutral." Twenty questions were asked about this child's feelings toward himself and toward school (e.g., "Is his teacher nice to him?" "Do the other kids in school like him?" "Does he like school?").

All children were given both sets of tests by the same examiner, who was not informed of experimental conditions.

RESULTS

Classroom Behavior

Reliability of Observations. Interobserver reliability of the observation periods was determined by the percentage of intervals in which the observers agreed perfectly as to whether deviant behavior had occurred. The mean percentage perfect agreement of the 31 reliability checks was 81% (SD = 21.6).

Behavior Observations. Figure 1 shows the amount of deviant behavior in the behavior problem children and their same-class controls during baseline and during treatment. In the five-week baseline period, the Group E children showed 74% deviant behavior, while the Group CI children showed 37% deviant behavior, a difference significant at p = 0.002 (t = 5.14; df = 6).* There was no overlap among subjects in the two groups.

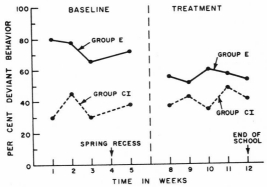

Fig. 1. Deviant behavior of Group E and Group CI.

For the last five weeks of treatment, Group E showed 57% deviant behavior, a decrease from baseline significant at p = 0.03 (t = 3.91; df = 3). During this same period, Group CI showed 41% deviant behavior, a slight, though not significant increase from baseline (t = 0.32; df = 3). The groups no longer differed significantly, although the deviant behavior in the target children was not decreased to the level of their controls by the end of school.

None of the specific categories of deviant behavior showed an increase in either Group E or Group CI, nor did teachers report any new behavior problems. Hence, the reduction in the target disruptive behavior was not followed by an increase in other classroom deviance.

Teacher Attention. The principal therapeutic intervention used in the experiment was teacher attention to task-relevant behavior. However, as shown in Fig. 2, the observed improvement in the experimental children cannot be attributed simply to increased teacher attention, since there was no significant

---

*All statistical tests of significance are two-tailed.

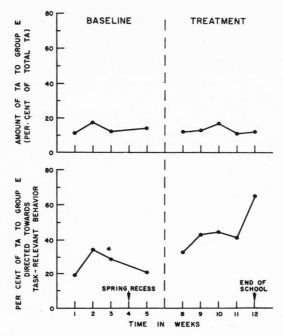

Fig. 2. Teacher attention to Group E: Amount of TA directed towards Group E and per cent of attention to Group E directed towards task-relevant behavior.

change from baseline to treatment in the *amount* of attention to target children (t = 0.07; df = 3). Teachers did increase significantly from baseline to treatment in the *proportion* of their attention to target children that was directed towards task-relevant behavior (t = 3.46; df = 3; p = 0.04).

Nevertheless, it appears that the teachers did not thoroughly master the contingent use of their attention to task-relevant behavior, and that further improvement in the target children might have been possible. For instance, the change in deviant behavior for Group E reported above did not include observations taken during the special treatment sessions with two children. For these two experimental children, the deviant behavior during the special signal-light reinforcement periods decreased dramatically to an average of 18%. Yet there was apparently little generalization to other times.

Although the teachers did not increase their attention to target children, the data suggested that they decreased their attention somewhat to Group CI children; there was a slight, but not significant decrease in the amount of teacher attention from baseline to treatment (t = 2.49; df = 3, p = 0.09). The proportion of teachers' attention directed toward task-relevant behavior did not change from baseline to treatment for Group CI (t = 0.11; df = 3).

Psychological Tests

On the pretreatment WISC, the behavior problem children were significantly lower than the controls on the Mazes subtest (t = 2.71; df = 10; p < 0.03); the groups did not differ on the other subscales. The changes in WISC scores after treatment were minimal and did not significantly differentiate the groups, although Group E tended to decrease on the Comprehension subtest relative to Group CII (t = 2.14; df = 6, p = 0.08).

The pretreatment DAP drawings of the behavior problem children were generally like those of the control children, except that the Group E drawings were significantly smaller in size (t = 2.85; df = 10, p < 0.02). This variable has been considered an indicator of anxiety (Ward, 1963).

The pre- and post-treatment drawings were scored on all those variables considered in the drawing literature to be suggestive of adjustment or maturity. No significant differences between groups in change scores were found on any single variable or on a combination score. Emotional adjustment, rated by two judges uninformed as to the order and conditions in which the drawings were produced, showed no consistent effects. Similarly, changes on the projective questionnaire did not differentiate the groups.

DISCUSSION

One focus of the present study was to ascertain the generalized effects on the target child of treating a specific behavior; especially studied were the deleterious effects on the child's classroom behavior and psychological test functioning. The data provide no evidence for adverse changes in the children as a consequence of teachers' employing reinforcement techniques or as a result of specific deviant behaviors being reduced.

On the other hand, the target children did not show the generalized improvement in psychological test functioning found by Baker (1968) with enuretic children treated by conditioning. Yet, the present treatment did not produce the distinctive cure which results with enuretics. Also, enuresis is usually an "involuntary" behavior, the alleviation of which is a considerable relief for the child. Deviant classroom behavior is in some sense "voluntary"; it is emitted for environmental gains, such as the teacher's attention, and may be more a discomfort to others than to the child himself. If attention is withdrawn from such an operant, the child will attempt other behaviors to regain attention. Whether the end result is new maladaptive behavior or generalized improvement may depend on what the teacher now reinforces.

A second focus was the generalized effects of reinforcement therapy on the class. No support was found for the argument that behavior of other pupils in a class deteriorates when the teacher's attention is somehow diverted from them in treating behavior problem children. Although teachers did slightly decrease the amount of attention given to control children, there was no significant increase in the control children's deviant behavior. This is particularly encouraging since the treatment was carried out in the last weeks of the school year when, according to teachers, disruption in the classroom typically rises. It appears, nonetheless, that in future treatment programs, more stress should be placed on the teacher maintaining normal relations with nontarget children.

The principal reinforcer employed was contingent teacher attention. It is assumed that the decrease in deviant behavior in the target children resulted from the greater proportion of attention that teachers paid to these children's task-relevant behavior. It is recognized that the observed relationship between an increase in the proportion of teacher's attention to task-relevant behavior and an increase in such task-relevant behavior may have been artifactual; that is, if task-relevant behavior increased for some other undetermined reason and amount of teacher attention remained the same, then an increase in proportion of attention to task-relevant behavior would have also been found. Yet, it seems most likely that modified use of teacher attention was primary, especially in view of other reports indicating the functional role of teacher praise in increasing appropriate behavior in the classroom (Madsen, Becker, and Thomas, 1968).

The treatment procedures were not uniformly successful with all target children. Most notably, the withdrawn and inattentive behavior of one child changed very little. This behavior seems less under the control of teacher attention than more acting out behaviors; also, the latter are easier for the teacher to define, to notice, and to respond to correctly. Treating withdrawn behaviors may require better training in behavior shaping. In general it seems possible that more behavioral improvement could have been effected in all of the target children if the teachers had been more thoroughly trained. It is clear from the results of the special treatment sessions, in which the deviant behavior of two of the children dropped to 18%, that the full effectiveness of the reinforcement techniques was not realized at all times. It is likewise possible that a longer treatment period would have provided more time for the teachers' therapeutic skills to take effect.

Yet, the significant decrease in disruptive behavior in the target children, and the absence of adverse changes in these or other pupils, indicate that teachers can be trained as effective "therapists," using reinforcement techniques in the classroom. This finding, consistent with the conclusion reached by Becker et al. (1967), has important implications for in-classroom management of behavior problems. First, the availability to teachers of a set of techniques for controlling the disruptive behavior of students is of obvious advantage in terms of smoother classroom functioning. In addition, being taught to manifest productive task-relevant classroom behavior is worthwhile to the child himself. A child who is hyperactive or otherwise deviant in school necessarily misses many of the learning experiences which normally accrue to an attentive, actively participating pupil. A final consideration is that *in situ* amelioration of maladaptive behavior somewhat obviates the educational and financial disadvantages involved in removing a child from the classroom in order to attempt therapeutic rehabilitation.

While the results of this limited study are themselves encouraging, future research should continue to look beyond the specific behaviors being treated, and consider the generalized effects of reinforcement therapy.

REFERENCES

Baker, B. L. Symptom treatment and symptom substitution in enuresis. *Journal of Abnormal Psychology,* 1969, 74, 42-49.

Becker, W. C., Madsen, C. H. Jr., Arnold, Carol, and Thomas, D. R. The contingent use of teacher attention and praise in reducing classroom behavior problems. *Journal of Special Education,* 1967, 1, 287-307.

Clarizo, H. F. and Yelon, S. L. Learning theory approaches to classroom management: rationale and intervention techniques. *Journal of Special Education,* 1967, 1, 267-274.

Hall, R. V., Lund, Diane, and Jackson, Deloris. Effects of teacher attention on study behavior. *Journal of Applied Behavior Analysis,* 1968, 1, 1-12.

Krasner, L. and Ullmann, L. P. (Eds.). *Research in behavior modification.* New York: Holt, Rinehart & Winston, 1965.

Madsen, C. H. Jr., Becker, W. C., and Thomas, D. R. Rules, praise, and ignoring: elements of elementary classroom control. *Journal of Applied Behavior Analysis,* 1968, 1, 139-150.

Patterson, G. R. An application of conditioning techniques to the control of a hyperactive child. In L. P. .Ullmann and L. Krasner (Eds.), *Case studies in behavior modification.* New York: Holt, Rinehart & Winston, 1965. Pp. 370-375.

Quay, H. C., Werry, J. S., McQueen, Marjorie, and Sprague, R. L. Remediation of the conduct problem child in the special class setting. *Exceptional Children,* 1966, 32, 509-515.

Ullmann, L. P. and Krasner, L. *Case studies in behavior modification.* New York: Holt, Rinehart & Winston, 1965.

Ward, Janet. *Integration and racial identification: a study of Negro children's drawings.* Unpublished bachelor honor's thesis, Radcliffe College, 1968.

Woody, R. H. Behavior therapy and school psychology. *Journal of Social Psychology,* 1966, 4, 1-14.

Zimmerman, Elaine H. and Zimmerman, J. The alteration of behavior in a special classroom situation. *Journal of Experimental Analysis of Behavior,* 1962, 5, 59-60.

9

The application of operant conditioning techniques in a secondary school classroom

Loring W. McAllister, James G. Stachowiak, Donald M. Baer, and Linda Conderman

The effects of teacher praise and disapproval on two target behaviors, inappropriate talking and turning around, were investigated in a high school English class of 25 students. The contingencies were applied to all students in the experimental class utilizing a multiple baseline experimental design in which the contingencies were aimed first at decreasing inappropriate talking behavior and then at decreasing inappropriate turning behavior. Observations were made of both student and teacher behavior. The results demonstrated that the combination of disapproval for the target behaviors and praise for appropriate, incompatible behaviors substantially reduced the incidence of the target behaviors in the experimental class. Observations of these behaviors in a control class of 26 students taught by the same teacher revealed no particular changes. The findings emphasize the importance of teacher-supplied social contingencies at the secondary school level.

Numerous studies have reported the effectiveness of operant conditioning techniques in modifying the behavior of children in various situations. Harris, Wolf, and Baer (1964), in a series of studies on preschool children, described the effectiveness of contingent teacher attention in modifying inappropriate behavior. Hall and Broden (1967), Patterson (1965), Rabb and Hewett (1967), and Zimmerman and Zimmerman (1962) have demonstrated the usefulness of teacher-supplied contingent social reinforcement in reducing problem behaviors and increasing appropriate behaviors of young children in special classrooms.

From *Journal of Applied Behavior Analysis,* 1969, 2, 277-285. Copyright 1969 by the Society for the Experimental Analysis of Behavior, Inc. Reprinted by permission.

This study is based upon a dissertation submitted by the senior author to the Department of Psychology, University of Kansas, in partial fulfillment of the requirements for the degree of doctor of philosophy. The authors express appreciation to Mr. William Medley, Principal, and Mr. Max Stalcup, Head Guidance Counselor, at Lawrence (Kansas) Senior High School for their assistance and cooperation in the conduct of the study. Reprints may be obtained from Loring W. McAllister, Western Mental Health Center, Inc., 438 West Main Street, Marshall, Minnesota 56258.

Becker, Madsen, Arnold, and Thomas (1967); Hall, Lund, and Jackson (1968); and Madsen, Becker, and Thomas (1968) extended these techniques into the regular primary school classroom and demonstrated their effectiveness there. In all of the above studies, only a limited number of children were studied in each situation, usually one or two per classroom.

Thomas, Becker, and Armstrong (1968) studied the effects of varying teachers' social behaviors on the classroom behaviors of an entire elementary school classroom of 28 students. By observing 10 children per session, one at a time, they demonstrated the effectiveness of approving teacher responses in maintaining appropriate classroom behaviors. Bushell, Wrobel, and Michaelis (1968) also applied group contingencies (special events contingent on earning tokens for study behaviors) to an entire class of 12 preschool children.

There has been an effort to extend the study of teacher-supplied consequences to larger groups of preschool and elementary school subjects in regular classrooms, but no systematic research investigating these procedures has yet been undertaken in the secondary school classroom. Cohen, Filipczak, and Bis (1967) reported the application of various nonsocial contingencies (earning points, being "correct," and taking advanced educational courses) in modifying attitudinal and academic behaviors of adolescent inmates in a penal institution. But there is no record of investigations into the effects of teacher-supplied social consequences on the classroom behavior of secondary school students in regular classrooms.

At present, the usefulness of contingent teacher social reinforcement in the management of student classroom behaviors is well documented on the preschool and primary elementary school levels, particularly when the investigation focuses on a limited number of children in the classroom. Systematic replication now requires that these procedures be extended to larger groups of students in the classroom and to students in the upper elementary and secondary grades. The present study sought to investigate the effects of teacher-supplied social consequences on the classroom behaviors of an entire class of secondary school students.

METHOD

Subjects

Students. The experimental group was a low-track, junior-senior English class containing 25 students (12 boys and 13 girls). At the beginning of the study the ages ranged from 16 to 19 yr (mean 17.11 yr); I.Q.s ranged from 77 to 114 (mean 94.43). Approximately 80% of the students were from lower-class families; the remainder were from middle-class families. The control group was also a low-track, junior-senior English class of 26 students (13 boys and 13 girls). The ages ranged from 16 to 19 yr (mean 17.04 yr); I.Q.s ranged from 73 to 111 (mean 91.04). About 76% of these students were from lower-class families, 16% were from middle-class families and 4% were from upper-middle to upper-class families. The experimental class met in the mornings for a 70-min period and the control class met in the afternoons for a 60-min period.

Teacher. The teacher was 23 yr old, female, middle class, and held a Bachelor's degree in education. She had had one year's experience in teaching secondary level students, which included a low-track English class. She taught both the experimental and control classes in the same classroom and utilized the same curriculum content for both. She stated that she had been having some difficulties in controlling classroom behavior in both classes and volunteered to cooperate in the experiment in the interest of improving her teaching-management skills. She stated that she had been able to achieve some rapport with these students during the two months that school had been in session. She described the students, generally, as performing poorly in academic work and ascribed whatever academic behaviors she was able to observe in them as being the result of her rapport with them. She stated that she was afraid that she would destroy this rapport if she attempted to exercise discipline over inappropriate classroom behaviors.

Procedures

The basic design utilized was the common pretest-posttest control group design combined with the use of a multiple baseline technique (Baer, Wolf, and Risley, 1968) in the experimental class.

Target Behaviors. Both classes were observed for two weeks to ascertain general occurrence rates of various problem behaviors that had been described by the teacher. Inappropriate talking and turning around were selected as target behaviors because of their relatively high rate of occurrence. Inappropriate talking was defined as any audible vocal behavior engaged in by a student without the teacher's permission. Students were required to raise their hands to obtain permission to talk, either to the teacher or to other students, except when general classroom discussions were taking place, in which cases a student was not required to obtain permission to talk if his statements were addressed to the class and/or teacher and were made within the context of the discussion. Inappropriate turning was defined as any turning-around behavior engaged in by any student while seated in which he turned more than 90 degrees in either direction from the position of facing the front of the room. Two exceptions to this definition were made: turning behavior observed while in the process of transferring material to or from the book holder in the bottom of the desk was considered appropriate, as was any turning that took place when a student had directly implied permission to turn around. Examples of the latter exception would be when the class was asked to pass papers up or down the rows of desks, or when students turned to look at another student who was talking appropriately in the context of a recitation or discussion.

Observation and Recording. Behavior record forms were made up for recording observed target behaviors in both classes. A portion of the form is illustrated in Fig. 1. The forms for the experimental class contained 70 sequentially numbered boxes for each behavior; the forms for the control class

Minute No.	1	2	3	4	5	6	7	8	9	10	11	12	13	14	15	16	17	18	19	20	21
Talking																					
Turning																					

Fig. 1. Portion of behavior record form used to record incidence of target behavior.

contained 60 sequentially numbered boxes for each behavior (covering the 70- and 60-min class periods, respectively). The occurrence of a target behavior during any minute interval of time (e.g., during the twenty-fifth minute of class time) was recorded by placing a check mark in the appropriate box for that interval (e.g., box 25) beside the behavior listed. Further occurrences of that behavior during that particular interval were not recorded. Thus, each time interval represented a dichotomy with respect to each behavior: the behavior had or had not occurred during that interval of time. A daily quantified measurement of each behavior was obtained by dividing the number of intervals that were checked by the total number of intervals in the class period, yielding a percentage of intervals in which the behavior occurred at least once. Time was kept by referral to a large, easily readable wall clock whose minute hand moved 1 min at a time.

Behaviors were recorded daily during all conditions by the teacher. Reliability of observation was checked by using from one to two additional observers (student teachers and the senior author) who visited the classes twice per week. Students in this particular school were thought to be quite accustomed to observers, due to the large amount of classroom observation done there by student teachers from a nearby university. Except for the senior author and teacher, other observers were not made aware of the changes in experimental conditions. Reliability was assessed by comparing the behavior record forms of the teacher and observers after each class period in which both teacher and observers recorded behavior. A percentage of agreement for each target behavior was computed, based on a ratio of the number of intervals on which all recorders agreed (i.e., that the behavior had or had not occurred) to the total number of intervals in the period. Average reliability for talking behavior was 90.49% in the experimental class (range 74 to 98%) and 89.49% in the control class (range 78 to 96%). Average reliability for turning behavior was 94.27% in the experimental class (range 87 to 98%) and 90.98% in the control class (range 85 to 96%).

In addition, two aspects of the teacher's behavior were recorded during all conditions by the observers when present: (a) the number of inappropriate talking or turning instances that occasioned a verbal reprimand from the teacher, and (b) the number of direct statements of praise dispensed by the teacher for appropriate behaviors. These behaviors were recorded by simply tallying the number of instances in which they were observed on the reverse side of the observer's form. Reliability between observers was checked by computing a percentage of agreement between them on the number of instances of each type of behavior observed. Average reliability for reprimand behavior was 92.78% in the experimental class (range 84 to 100%) and 94.84% in the control class (range 82 to 100%). Average reliability for praise behavior was 98.85% in the experimental class (range 83 to 100%) and 97.65% in the control class (range 81 to 100%).

Baseline Condition. During the Baseline Condition, the two target behaviors and teacher behaviors were recorded in both the experimental and control classes. The teacher was asked to behave in her usual manner in both classrooms and no restrictions were placed on any disciplinary techniques she wished to use. The Baseline Condition in the experimental class was continued for 27 class days (approximately five weeks) to obtain as clear a picture as possible of the student and teacher behaviors occurring.

Experimental Condition I. This first experimental condition began in the experimental class on the twenty-eighth day when the teacher initiated various social consequences contingent on inappropriate talking behavior aimed at lowering the amount of this behavior taking place. The procedures agreed upon with the teacher for the application of social consequences were as follows:

(1) The teacher was to attempt to disapprove of all instances of inappropriate talking behavior whenever they occurred with a direct, verbal, sternly given reproof. Whenever possible, the teacher was to use students' names when correcting them. The teacher was instructed not to mention any other inappropriate behavior (e.g., turning around) that might also be occurring at the time. Examples of reprimands given were: "John, be quiet!", "Jane, stop talking!", "Phil, shut up!", "You people, be quiet!". It was hypothesized that these consequences constituted an aversive social consequence for inappropriate talking.

(2) The teacher was asked not to threaten students with or apply other consequences, such as keeping them after school, exclusion from class, sending them to the Assistant Principal, etc. for inappropriate talking or for any other inappropriate behavior.

(3) The teacher was to praise the entire class in the form of remarks like: "Thank you for being quiet!", "Thank you for not talking!", or "I'm delighted to see you so quiet today!" according to the following contingencies: (a) During the first 2 min of class, praise at the end of approximately each 30-sec period in which there had been no inappropriate talking. (b) During the time in which a lecture, recitation, or class discussion was taking place, praise the class at the end of approximately each 15-min period in which no inappropriate talking had occurred. (c) When silent seatwork had been assigned, do not interrupt the period to praise, but praise the class at the end of the period if no inappropriate talking had occurred during the period. (d) At the end of each class make a summary statement concerning talking behavior, such as: "Thank you all for being so quiet today!", or "There has been entirely too much talking today, I'm disappointed in you!", or, "You have done pretty well in keeping quiet today, let's see if you can do better tomorrow!".

The concentration of praising instances during the first 2-min of class was scheduled because the baseline data revealed inappropriate talking as particularly frequent at this time.

Although the teacher continued to record instances of turning behavior, she was instructed to ignore this behavior in the experimental class during Experimental Condition I. In effect, baseline recording of turning behavior continued during this Condition. No changes were made in the teacher's behavior in the control class.

Experimental Condition II. After Experimental Condition I had been in effect in the experimental class for 26 class days and had markedly reduced talking behavior (see Results), Experimental Condition II was put into effect on the 54th day of the study. In this condition, the contingent social consequences for talking behavior in the experimental class were continued and, in addition, the teacher initiated the same system of contingent social consequences for turning behavior, with the aim of reducing the amount of this behavior occurring. This subsequent provision of similar consequences, first for one behavior and then for another, constitutes the multiple baseline technique.

The procedures agreed upon for providing reprimands for inappropriate turning behavior were the same as those for talking behaviors, except that the teacher referred to "turning" instead of "talking" in her reproofs. She could now also mention both behaviors in her reproof if a student happened to be doing both. The procedures regarding the application of praise contingent on not turning around were also the same as before, except that the higher frequency of praising during the first 2 min of class was not used. Also, the teacher could now combine her positive remarks about not talking and not turning if such were appropriate to existing conditions. Finally, since inappropriate talking behavior had been reduced considerably by this time, the procedure of praising every 30 sec during the first 2-min of class was dropped. As before, no changes were made in the teacher's behavior in the control class.

RESULTS

Because data were not collected on individual students, it is not possible to specify exactly how many students were involved in either inappropriate talking or turning behavior. The observers and teacher agreed that over one-half of the students in both classes were involved in inappropriate talking behavior and that about one-third of the students in both classes were involved in inappropriate turning behavior.

Talking Behavior

Figure 2 indicates the daily percentages of intervals of inappropriate talking behavior in the experimental and control classes throughout the study. During the Baseline Condition in the experimental class and the equivalent period in the control class (Days 1 through 27), the average daily percentage of inappropriate talking intervals was 25.33% in the experimental class and 22.81% in the control class. The two classes were thus approximately equivalent with respect to the amount of inappropriate talking behavior in each before the experimental interventions were made in the experimental class. As can be seen, the introduction

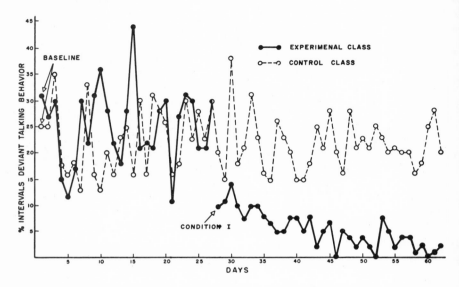

Fig. 2. Daily percentages of intervals of inappropriate talking behavior in experimental and control classes during Baseline and Experimental Condition I periods.

of the contingencies in Experimental Condition I on Day 28 immediately reduced the percentage of intervals of inappropriate talking behavior in the experimental class. From this point on, the amount of inappropriate talking behavior in the experimental class continued to decrease and finally stabilized at a level below 5%. Meanwhile, the control class continued to manifest its previous level of inappropriate talking behavior. In the period from Day 28 through Day 62, when the study was concluded, the average daily percentage of inappropriate talking intervals in the control class was 21.51%, compared with an average of 5.34% in the experimental class.

Turning Behavior

The results obtained with the second target behavior, inappropriate turning around, can be seen in Fig. 3, which indicates the daily percentages of intervals of inappropriate turning behavior in both classes during the study. During the Baseline Condition in the experimental class and the equivalent period in the control class (Days 1 through 53), the level of inappropriate turning behavior was slowly increasing in both classes. The average daily percentage of inappropriate turning intervals during this time was 15.13% in the experimental class and 14.45% in the control class. As with talking behavior, the two classes were

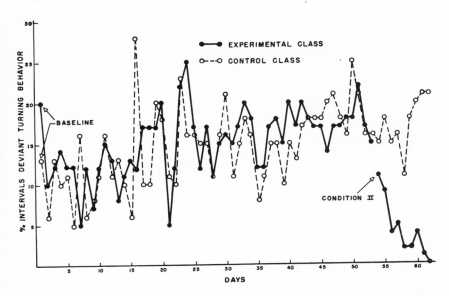

Fig. 3. Daily percentages of intervals of inappropriate turning behavior in experimental and control classes during Baseline and Experimental Condition II periods.

roughly equivalent in the amount of inappropriate turning behavior observed before experimental intervention were made. The introduction of Experimental Condition II contingencies on Day 54 again immediately reduced the percentage of inappropriate turning intervals in the experimental class. This behavior continued to decrease during the remaining days of the study. In the control class, the level of inappropriate turning behavior remained essentially the same. In the period from Day 54 through Day 62, the average daily percentage of inappropriate turning intervals in the control class was 17.22% and in the experimental class was 4.11%.

Teacher Behavior

During the Baseline period on talking behavior, the average number of instances of inappropriate talking per class period that received some type of verbal reprimand from the teacher was 25.76% in the experimental class and 22.23% in the control class. The majority of these verbal responses took the form of saying, "Shhh!". On occasion, observers noted that the teacher corrected students directly, using their names. On several occasions she made general threats, stating that she would keep people after school if talking did not subside; however, she was never observed to carry out this kind of threat. During this period there were no observations of the teacher's dispensing any praise for not talking. During Experimental Condition I, the teacher disapproved of an average of 93.33% of inappropriate talking instances per class period in the experimental class. In the control class during this time, she disapproved of an average of 21.38% of inappropriate talking instances per class period. She also praised on an average of 6.07 occasions per experimental class period, contingent on not talking, during this time. With two exceptions, she was not observed directly to praise not talking in the control class.

During the Baseline period on inappropriate turning behavior, the average percentage of inappropriate turning instances per class period that received verbal reprimands from the teacher was 12.84% in the experimental class and 13.09% in the control class. Most of these were simple instructions, like, "Turn around!", and she used the student's name in most cases. During Experimental Condition II, the average percentage of inappropriate turning instances per class period that occasioned disapproving responses from the teacher was 95.50% in the experimental class and 18.50% in the control class. In addition, she praised on an average of 5.75 occasions per experimental class period, contingent on not turning. In the control class she was not observed to provide any such praise for not turning.

DISCUSSION

The results indicate quite clearly that the statements of praise and disapproval by the teacher had consistent effects on the two target behaviors observed in the experimental class. Both behaviors decreased. That the statements were, in fact, responsible for the observed modifications in behavior was demonstrated through the multiple baseline procedure in which the target behaviors changed maximally only when the statements were applied. The use of the control class data further substantiates this contention. The observations of teacher behavior in the study provide evidence that the program was being carried out as specified in the two classrooms.

The design of the study does not make it possible to isolate the separate effects of the teacher's statements of praise and disapproval on the students' behaviors. It is possible that one or the other of these was more potent in achieving the observed results. In addition to the possibility that statements of praise or disapproval, in themselves, might have differed in their effectiveness in modifying behavior, the different manner in which these two types of statements were delivered may have resulted in differing effects. The design, it will be remembered, called for disapproving statements to be delivered to individual students, while praise was delivered to the class as a whole. This resulted in a sudden onset of numerous disapproving statements delivered to individual students when Experimental Condition I was put into effect. The observers agreed that the students seemed "stunned" when this essentially radical shift in stimulus conditions took place. The immediate and marked decrease in inappropriate talking behavior at this point may have resulted because of this shift. The phenomenon can be compared to the sudden response rate reductions observed in animals when stimulus conditions are shifted suddenly. The decrease in inappropriate turning behavior observed when Experimental Condition II was put into effect, while immediate, was not of the same magnitude as that observed previously. Perhaps some measure of adaptation to this type of stimulus shift had taken place. Regardless of the possible reasons for the immediate effects observed when the experimental conditions were put into effect, it is also true that the direction of these effects was maintained thereafter in both experimental conditions. The combination of praise and disapproval undoubtedly was responsible for this.

Assuming that praise statements were functioning as positive reinforcers for a majority of the experimental class, they may have operated not only directly to reinforce behaviors incompatible with inappropriate talking and turning but also to generate peer-group pressure to reduce inappropriate behavior because such statements were contingent on the entire class' behavior. Further studies are needed to investigate the effects of peer-group contingencies on individual behavior.

Although it appears that the statements of praise and disapproval by the teacher functioned as positive reinforcers and punishers, respectively, an alternative possibility exists. These statements may have been operating primarily as instructions that the students complied with. It is conceivable that had praise statements, for example, been delivered as instructions independent of the occurrence of inappropriate behavior the same results might have been obtained. Also, it should be noted that results obtained in other studies (Lovaas, Freitag, Kinder, Rubenstein, Schaeffer, and Simmons, 1964; Thomas, Becker, and Armstrong, 1968) indicate that disapproving adult behaviors do not have a unitary effect on children's behavior. What would appear to be punishing types of statements are sometimes found to function as positive reinforcers. Informal observations indicated that this seemed to be the case in this study, at least as far as one student was concerned.

Several comments may be made regarding the practical aspects of the present approach. The study further exemplifies the usefulness of the multiple baseline technique, which makes it unnecessary to reverse variables in order to demonstrate the specific effectiveness of the experimental variables. Many teachers and school administrators will undoubtedly find this approach more acceptable in their schools. The notion of reversing variables to reinstitute what is considered to be maladaptive or inappropriate behavior is extremely repugnant to many educators who are more interested in "getting results" than in experimental verification of the results obtained.

The study differs from most previous operant research in classrooms in that the focus was on recording and modifying target behaviors without specific regard to the individual students involved. Most earlier studies have focused on observing the behavior of one student at a time. With this approach, it takes considerable time to extend observations to an entire class and usually this is not done. While observations of an entire class are not always necessary from a practical point of view (i.e., only a few students are involved in inappropriate behaviors), the present approach does seem feasible when the number of students involved in one or more classes of inappropriate behavior is large. From an experimental point of view, this study was deficient in not providing more exact information as to the number of students actually involved in the target behaviors. Once this facet is determined, however, the essential approach seems quite feasible and practical.

It might be argued that a group-oriented approach will not function in the same way with all members of the group. This is potentially possible, if not probable. However, two practical aspects should be considered. In the first place, such an approach could conceivably remediate the total situation enough to allow the teacher to concentrate on those students who either have not responded or who have become worse. Secondly, perhaps a general reduction in inappropriate behavior is all the teacher desires. In this study, for example, the results obtained were, according to the teacher, more than enough to satisfy her. She did not, in other words, set a criterion of eliminating the target behaviors.

A significant practical aspect of this study was the amount of difficulty encountered by the teacher in recording behavior and delivering contingent praise and disapproval. It might be asked how she found time to teach when she was involved in these activities. Perhaps the best judge of the amount of difficulty involved with these techniques is the teacher herself. She reported that, initially, recording behaviors was difficult. The task did take considerable time and did interrupt her on-going teaching. On the other hand, the large amount of talking and other inappropriate behaviors occurring at the beginning of the study also interrupted her teaching. She felt that as the study went on she became more accustomed to recording and it became easier for her to accomplish. She pointed out that the fact that she usually positioned herself at her desk or rostrum also made recording somewhat easier because the forms were readily available. This was her usual position in the classroom; she did not change to make recording easier. Considerable time was required to deliver contingent praise and disapproval at the beginning of the experimental conditions. This also tended to interrupt teaching tasks as far as the teacher was concerned. However, she felt that this state of affairs did not last long because the target behaviors declined so immediately and rapidly. The overall judgment of the teacher was that the procedures of recording and dispensing contingent consequences did, indeed, interfere with her teaching but that the results obtained more than compensated for this. When the levels of inappropriate behavior had been lowered she felt she could carry out her teaching responsibilities much more efficiently and effectively than before. She felt strongly enough about the practicality and effectiveness of the techniques to present information and data on the study to her fellow teachers and to offer her services as a consultant to those who wanted to try similar approaches in their classrooms.

The senior author held frequent conferences with the teacher after class periods. The aim was to provide her with feedback regarding her performance in class. She was actively praised for appropriate modifications in her classroom behavior and for record-keeping behavior. Likewise, she was criticized for mistakes in her application of program contingencies.

Finally, the data of this experiment are considered significant by reason of the strong implication that teacher praise and disapproval can function to modify the behavior of high-school level students. This potentially extends the implications of earlier research accomplished on the preschool and elementary levels.

REFERENCES

Baer, D. M., Wolf, M. M., and Risley, T. R. Some current dimensions of applied behavior analysis. *Journal of Applied Behavior Analysis,* 1968, 1, 91-97.

Becker, W. C., Madsen, C. H., Jr., Arnold, C. R., and Thomas, D. R. The contingent use of teacher attention and praise in reducing classroom behavior problems. *Journal of Special Education,* 1967, 1, 287-307.

Bushell, D., Jr., Wrobel, P. A., and Michaelis, M. L. Applying "group" contingencies to the classroom study behavior of preschool children. *Journal of Applied Behavior Analysis,* 1968, 1, 55-61.

Cohen, H. L., Filipczak, J., and Bis, J. S. *Case I: an initial study of contingencies applicable to special education.* Silver Spring, Md.: Educational Facility Press—Institute for Behavioral Research, 1967.

Hall, R. V. and Broden, M. Behavior changes in brain-injured children through social reinforcement. *Journal of Experimental Child Psychology,* 1967, 5, 463-479.

Hall, R. V., Lund, D., and Jackson, D. Effects of teacher attention on study behavior. *Journal of Applied Behavior Analysis,* 1968, 1, 1-12.

Harris, F. R., Wolf, M. M., and Baer, D. M. Effects of adult social reinforcement on child behavior. *Young Children,* 1964, 20, 8-17.

Lövaas, O. I., Freitag, G., Kinder, M. I., Rubenstein, D. B., Schaeffer, B., and Simmons, J. B. *Experimental studies in childhood schizophrenia—establishment of social reinforcers.* Paper read at Western Psychological Assn., Portland, April, 1964.

Madsen, C. H., Becker, W. C., and Thomas, D. R. Rules, praise and ignoring: elements of elementary classroom control. *Journal of Applied Behavior Analysis,* 1968, 1, 139-150.

Patterson, G. R. An application of conditioning techniques to the control of a hyperactive child. In L. P. Ullmann and L. Krasner (Eds.), *Case studies in behavior modification.* New York: Holt, Rinehart & Winston, 1966. Pp. 370-375.

Rabb, E. and Hewett, F. M. Developing appropriate classroom behaviors in a severely disturbed group of institutionalized kindergarten-primary children utilizing a behavior modification model. *American Journal of Orthopsychiatry,* 1967, 37, 313-314.

Thomas, D. R., Becker, W. C., and Armstrong, M. Production and elimination of disruptive classroom behavior by systematically varying teacher's behavior. *Journal of Applied Behavior Analysis,* 1968, 1, 35-45.

Zimmerman, E. H. and Zimmerman, J. The alteration of behavior in a special classroom situation. *Journal of the Experimental Analysis of Behavior,* 1962, 5, 59-60.

10

The alteration of behavior in a special classroom situation

Elaine H. Zimmerman and J. Zimmerman

Unproductive classroom behavior was eliminated in two emotionally disturbed boys by removing social consequences of the behavior. Behavior which was more adequate and efficient with respect to social and scholastic adjustment was shaped and maintained with social reinforcers.

The classroom behavior of two emotionally disturbed boys was altered by arranging and manipulating its consequences.

The boys, in-patients in a residential treatment center (LaRue D. Carter Memorial Hospital), attended the first author's English class daily for 1 hr as part of an educational therapy program. There were three boys in the class, each receiving individual attention.

CASE I

Subject 1 (S-1) was 11 years old. He appeared to have no organic disorder and was of normal intelligence. In early class sessions, whenever S-1 was called upon to spell a word which had previously been studied and drilled, he would pause for several seconds, screw up his face, and mutter letters unrelated to the word. Following this, the instructor (E) consistently asked him to sound out the word, often giving him the first letter and other cues, encouraging him to spell the word correctly. Only after E had spent considerable time and attention would the boy emit a correct response. The procedure was inefficient and profitless for improving the boy's spelling behavior. In fact, it may have been maintaining the undesirable pattern, since over the first 10 or 15 class sessions, consistently more time and attention were required of E to obtain a correct spelling response.

While "studying" in class, S-1 would obtain sheets of paper, wrinkle them, and throw them away, laughing as he caught E's eye or that of one of the other students.

The Change in Approach

After several weeks in class, S-1 was quizzed via paper-and-pencil test on a lesson based on 10 spelling words, with time allotted for study and review. He handed in a paper with a muddled combination of barely legible letters. Immediately, E asked him to go to the blackboard. Her instructions were simply: "We will now have a quiz. I will read a word and you will spell it correctly on the board." She read the first word, and the subject misspelled it 10 or more times on the board. During this time, E sat at her desk, ignoring S-1, apparently busy reading or writing. Each time S-1 misspelled the word, he glanced at E; but she did not respond. The boy erased the word and tried again, several times repeating "I can't spell it," or "I can't remember how," etc. Although ignored, the boy made no effort to sit down or leave the room. After approximately 10 min. he spelled the word correctly: E looked up at him immediately, smiled, and said, "Good, now we can go on." She read a second word, and after a similar series of errors and verbal responses, S-1 spelled the word (through 10 words), the number of inappropriate (unreinforced) responses decreased, as did the latency of the correct response. At the end of the quiz, E took the boy's spelling chart, wrote an "A" on it, and praised him. She then asked the subject to help her color some Easter baskets. They sat down together, and chatted and worked.

Thereafter, attention in the form of smiling, chatting, and physical proximity was given only immediately after the emission of desired classroom behavior or some approximation of it in the desired direction. Undesirable behavior was consistently ignored. As a result of a month of this treatment, the frequency of bizarre spelling responses and other undesirable responses declined to a level close to zero per class session. At the conclusion of this study, the boy was working more efficiently, and was making adequate academic progress.

CASE II

Subject S-2 was an 11-year old boy, who, like S-1, had no apparent organic disorder and was also of normal intelligence. In initial class Sessions, S-2 emitted behavior considered undesirable in the classroom context with high frequency. He displayed temper tantrums (kicking, screaming, etc.) spoke baby-talk, and incessantly made irrelevant comments or posed irrelevant questions.

Several times a week, attendants dragged this boy down the hall to one of his classes as the boy screamed and buckled his knees. On several of these occasions, the boy threw himself on the floor in front of a clasroom door. A crowd of staff members inevitably gathered around him. The group usually watched and commented as the boy sat or lay on the floor, kicking and screaming. Some members of the group hypothesized that such behavior seemed to appear after the boy was teased or frustrated in some way. However, only observable in the situation was the consistent consequence of the behavior in terms of the formation of a group of staff members around the boy.

Observing one such situation which occurred before E's class, E asked the attendent to put the boy in the classroom at his desk and to leave the room. Then E closed the door. The boy sat at his desk, kicking and screaming; E proceeded to her desk and worked there, ignoring S-2. After 2 or 3 min. the boy, crying softly, looked up at E. Then E announced that she would be ready to work with him as soon as he indicated that he was ready to work. He continued to cry and scream with diminishing loudness for the next 4 or 5 min. Finally, he lifted his head and stated that he was ready. Immediately, E looked up at him, smiled, went to his desk, and said, "Good, now let's get to work." The boy worked quietly and cooperatively with E for the remainder of the class period.

The Handling of Tantrums, Irrelevant
Verbal Behavior, and Baby-talk

Each time a tantrum occurred, E consistently ignored S-2. When tantrum behavior was terminated, E conversed with the boy, placed herself in his proximity, or initiated an activity which was appealing to him. After several weeks, class tantrums disappeared entirely. Because the consequence of tantrum behavior varied in other situations, no generalization to situations outside the classroom has been observed.

Furthermore the frequency of irrelevant verbal behavior and of baby-talk declined almost to the point of elimination following the procedure of withholding attention after the emission of such behavior. On the other hand, when S-2 worked quietly or emitted desirable classroom behavior, E addressed him cordially and permitted some verbal interchange for several seconds. When a lesson was being presented to the class at large and S-2 listened attentively, E reinforced him by asking him a question he could answer or by looking at him, smiling at him, etc. The reinforcement was delivered intermittently rather than continuously because: (a) reinforcing every desired response of one student was impossible since E's time was parcelled out among several students; and (b) intermittent reinforcement would probably be more effective than continuous reinforcement in terms of later resistance of the desired behavior to extinction. Like S-1, at the conclusion of the study this boy was working more efficiently in class and was making good progress. His speech was more generally characterized by relevancy and maturity.

11

Free-time as a reinforcer in the management of classroom behavior

J. Greyson Osborne

Six subjects, comprising one class at a school for the deaf, were given reinforcement consisting of time free from school work for remaining seated in the classroom. As a result, the frequency of leaving their chairs was sharply reduced. A second procedure presented free-time not contingent on remaining seated. Little change was seen in the already lowered response rate. An extension of the time required to be seated with corresponding reduction in the number of daily free-time periods did not reduce the effectiveness of the procedure. A one-day observation after six weeks indicated that the procedure was still effective. A one-day contingency reversal, requiring subjects to leave their chairs at least once during each seated period in order to receive free-time, substantially raised the frequency of out-of-seat responses.

Recent studies have indicated that classroom behavior of humans can be successfully manipulated given proper application of the controlling environmental contingencies. Homme, C. de Baca, Devine, Steinhorst, and Rickert (1963) reported that preschool nursery children would engage in the low-probability behaviors of sitting quietly and looking at a blackboard if those behaviors were intermittently followed by the opportunity to engage in higher-probability behaviors such as running or shouting. Thomas, Becker, and Armstrong (1968) showed that disruptive behavior in the classroom can be manipulated as a function of teacher's behavior. They further suggested that one important classroom management device is the use of approval for appropriate behavior.

The usefulness of the token economy has also been proven in the classroom. Wolf, Giles, and Hall (1968) demonstrated that overall achievement gains could be nearly doubled in a remedial classroom, using a token reinforcement system, over what was achieved in the regular classroom without the token system. Wolf

From *Journal of Applied Behavior Analysis*, 1969, 2, 113-118. Copyright 1969 by the Society for the Experimental Analysis of Behavior, Inc. Reprinted by permission.

Reprints may be obtained from the author, New Mexico School for the Deaf, 1060 Cerrillos Road, Santa Fe, New Mexico 87501.

et al. (1968) estimated the average cost of their token system at $250 for each of the 16 students for a year. Other investigators have produced gains in specific academic areas utilizing token systems. For example, Staats and Butterfield (1965) produced a large number of reading responses in a nonreading juvenile delinquent. The cost for that subject was $20.31 over 40 hr of work. Staats, Minke, Goodwin, and Landeen (1968) extended Staats' earlier work to 18 junior-high aged subjects. Reading responses were strengthened over 38.2 hr of training at a cost of approximately $22 per subject. In both studies, significant achievement gains in reading resulted.

Birnbrauer, Bijou, Wolf, and Kidder (1965) in their work with institutionalized retardates showed that the token economy need not be expensive to be effective. Extrapolation from their data, which indicate an average payoff of 5¢ per week per student for a regular school year, would suggest a financial cost of less than $20 for backup reinforcers. In an extension of their earlier work, these same investigators were able to strengthen academic behavior within a similar token system. The costs averaged approximately $7 per student for the 15 students in the class over 1 yr (Birnbrauer, Wolf, Kidder, and Tague, 1965).

Studies utilizing the token economy have demonstrated its usefulness in education. However, in many cases the cost of providing backup reinforcers is outside the financial ability of most institutions without special funding. In addition, most school administrations oppose paying their students for learning. The classroom management techniques propounded by Homme and Becker indicate that much behavior can be modified in the classroom without a token economy and its cost.

The present study illustrates a behavior management technique that can be used to control behavior in the classroom with no financial cost to the institution involved.

METHOD

A teacher approached the experimenter regarding her class's behavior. She was experiencing problems in maintaining students' attention. Discussion indicated that a major difficulty was the occurrence of behavior incompatible with academic behavior: students were often out of their chairs while the teacher was teaching. The teacher reported that this was disruptive to the entire class. Attempts to reseat students meant interruption of the teacher's presentation until calm was restored. The strong possibility existed that the behavior of students leaving their seats was being maintained by the time away from school work it provided.

Subjects

Six girls at the New Mexico School for the Deaf ranged in age from 11 yr 8 months to 13 yr 8 months; they were grouped in one class because of poor school achievement and less than average intelligence.

Table 1

Subjects	Age	Achieve-ment*	I.Q.**	Hearing Loss
1	12-10	2.1	74***	Severe
2	13-8	2.0	63	Severe-Profound
3	13-3	2.5	62	Severe-Profound
4	11-8	2.4	65	Profound
5	13-4	2.1	53	Profound
6	12-10	2.1	53	Severe

*Stanford Achievement Test (Elementary).
**Leiter International Performance Scale (1948 revision) except as noted.
***Wechsler Intelligence Scale for Children (Performance Scale).

Table 1 contains a complete description of the subjects. None of the girls was described by the staff as a behavior problem.

The class was in session in the same room from 8:05 A.M. until 12:10 P.M. Monday through Friday with no scheduled recess. A once-weekly session in the school library provided the only regular occasion on which a scholastic activity took place outside the classroom. Physical education, home economics, and other activities took place in the afternoon elsewhere on campus.

Procedures

Baseline Measurement. The overall procedure followed the standard single-organism, ABA design where each subject was her own control. Before instituting modification procedures, the frequency of occurrence of students leaving their seats was measured over five days. All data were recorded by the teacher on special data sheets, divided by subject, into sucessive time periods from 8:05 A.M. to 12:00 noon. The length of these periods was arbitrarily established at 15 min with each period separated from the former one by 5 min.

Response Definition. The response was easily defined. A subject attaining an upright position without teacher permission constituted an out-of-seat response. Construction of the one-piece chair-desks made it impossible to assume this position within the plane of the chair-desk. Hence, a subject was literally out of her seat before the response criterion was met. (Without the help of elaborate timing apparatus, it was not feasible to measure the time spent seated; hence, the use of an easily definable response, the converse of remaining seated.) In "emergencies," an out-of-seat response was allowed with teacher permission. Sharpening pencils, getting a drink of water, going to the restroom and the like were allowed only on "free" time.

The teacher continued her usual policy with respect to all other negative behavior throughout the study. Generally, this involved verbal reprimands, turning a student's chair-desk toward the wall, or taking the student to the principal's office. These consequences generally followed severe disobedience, foul language, or temper outbursts.

Reliability. Responses were also recorded by the experimenter and a supervising teacher on separate occasions. The supervisor was largely unaware of the nature of the project. She was given a chart identical to the teacher's, told how the response was defined, and asked to note instances of the behavior when she visited the classroom during her regular observation periods. Generally, the length of the supervisor's stay was for one or two of the seated segments. The experimenter also occasionally recorded response occurrences. A total of 15 seated segments over the course of the study was observed by the supervisor or the experimenter in which the six subjects were present. Over these 90 observations the teacher's record was compared with the supervisor's or the experimenter's. Reliability was computed by dividing the sum of agreements and disagreements between teacher and observer into total agreements. In this way, reliability was checked in each phase of the study on approximately 18% of the days the study was in effect. On none of the 90 observations did the teacher's record differ from that of the supervisor or the experimenter.

First Free-time Contingent Period. To begin the modification, the teacher presented the following instructions to the class at 8:05 A.M.: "From now on we will be doing something new. I want you all to sit in your chairs. You must not leave them without asking me. If you can do that, you will be given five minutes of your own time at 8:20."

The teacher announced each successive free-time period as it occurred. If the teacher was engaging in a formal presentation to the class, this presentation was halted during the free-time period. If a student left her seat during a seated segment, the teacher said: "You forgot, no break." Otherwise, her presentation of the ongoing seat work was continued.

Free-time was restricted to the interior of the classroom with the exception of trips to the restroom or water fountain. The subjects were not forced to get up during free-time periods if they did not want to. Those who had not earned the free-time were required to remain seated and working and not allowed to interact with their peers during that period. At the end of a free-time period, the teacher indicated that it was time to begin again and when the next free-time period would come. Five days were completed under this condition.

Free-time Noncontingent Period. To start this period the teacher presented the following instructions at 8:05 A.M. of the eleventh day: "I want you all to sit in your chairs. You must not leave them without asking me; but if you forget, you will still be given your break." In this section of the study if a student left her seat during a seated segment, the response was noted but the teacher said nothing and the class activity continued.

Five days were allowed under this condition.

Second Free-time Contingent Period. The second modification period began immediately after the noncontingent free-time condition was terminated. To reinstate modification conditions the teacher repeated the set of instructions delivered in the first modification period. Thirty-five days were recorded under these conditions.

Pursuant to another modification in the class, a point system for completion of academic work was introduced on Day 28. Within this system, the subjects could earn check marks and gummed stars on a chart, and were occasionally given a field trip outside of school time. In all other respects the class was conducted as usual.

Third Free-time Contingent Period. The teacher noted that the students did not always use all of their free-time periods. That is, for one or two of these periods each day some students would remain seated and perhaps working. Thus, it was thought likely that an increase in seated time and a corresponding decrease in number of free-time periods would not lessen the effectiveness of the procedure. Beginning on the fifty-first day of the study at 8:05 A.M., the teacher presented the following instructions to the class: "Starting today we will work until 8:30 before we take our break. Remember you must not leave your chairs without asking me. If you can do that, you will be given five minutes of your own time at 8:30."

For the remainder of the study seated segments were 25 min in length. Free-time periods remained 5-min long; however, lengthening each seated segment by 10 min reduced the number of free-time periods per morning from 12 to 8.

Post-check. Approximately six weeks after the termination of data collection, a single day's post-check was made. The contingencies of the third free-time contingent period had been left in effect by the teacher throughout the intervening time.

Contingency Reversal. In the week following the post-check the teacher was asked to reverse the response requirement for a single day. At 8:05 A.M. that day she presented the following instructions to the class: "Today we will do something different. If you remain seated, you will not be allowed to take your break. You must get out of your seat at least once each period in order to have your break."

RESULTS

Figure 1 shows the rate of out-of-seat responses for each subject under the different procedures. The different procedures are separated by the vertical dashed lines. Omitted data points comprise days when a given subject was absent.

Before the reinforcement contingency was introduced (Days 1 to 5) the students engaged in slightly more than one out-of-seat response per 15-min segment. After the modification procedure was introduced, responding decreased sharply (Days 6 to 10). During the first free-time contingent period, only 0.08 responses took place per student in the average 15-min period. That is, a response occurred approximately once each 30 min. The difference between baseline and first modification periods was highly significant (t=47.35; p < 0.001 one-tailed).

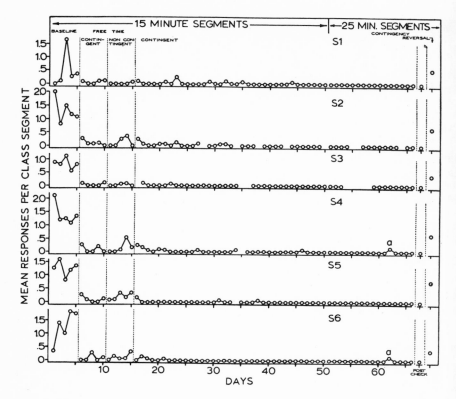

Fig. 1. The average number of out-of-seat responses for each subject per class segment for each day of the study.

While the shapes of premodification baselines were dissimilar for the six subjects, Fig. 1 shows that the effect of the procedure, a sharply reduced response rate, was similar for all.

When free-time periods were awarded noncontingently (Days 11 to 15), little change was noted in the lowered response rate (Fig. 1).

Making free-time periods again contingent on remaining seated produced another decrease in the frequency of the response. The difference between the free-time noncontingent period and the second free-time contingent period was significant ($t=1.86$; $p < 0.05$ one-tailed).

Free-time periods contingent on remaining seated for 15-min segments were left in effect through Day 50. Inspection of the individual performances (Fig. 1) indicates that fewer responses occurred as that point was approached.

On Day 51 the seated segments were lengthened to 25 min. It can be seen that no responses occurred on 15 of the 16 days recorded under this procedure. On Day 62 (points "a" in Fig. 1), one student told two others that it was time for a break, when in fact it was not. These two responses were the only instances of out-of-seat behavior during this condition.

On the day of the post-check six weeks later, no responses were observed during the entire morning.

Approximately one week after the post-check the contingency was reversed. On that day, 25 responses occurred. This was a rate of one response approximately every 8 min, as compared to no responses for the entire morning during the post-check.

DISCUSSION

Reinforcing behavior that is compatible with learning would seem possible by offering brief periods of free-time from the learning environment. In this study, the amount of in-seat behavior was increased by making time away from school work contingent on remaining seated for specified periods of time.

Several alternative explanations could account for the effectiveness of the free-time periods as reinforcers in this study. No experimental manipulations were made which would favor one explanation over another.

If the aversiveness of the regular classroom environment is granted (Skinner, 1968), the presentation of free-time may have constituted an escape conditioning procedure. That is, by remaining seated for a given period of time, the subjects could escape seat work and the teacher's formal presentation for a 5-min period, while those who had been out of their seats in the preceding segment had to continue working.

On the other hand, the free-time periods afforded the subjects the opportunity to engage in positively reinforcing activities such as obtaining a drink of water, talking with classmates, or talking with the teacher about favored subjects; the free-time periods may, therefore, have been positive reinforcers. If that was in fact the case, the present procedure constituted operant conditioning of desirable classroom behavior by positive reinforcement.

Finally, the present results can be explained in terms of the Premack reinforcement principle. That principle states that one event is capable of reinforcing another event if the reinforcing event has a higher probability of occurrence and its occurrence is made contingent upon emission of a lower-probability behavior (Premack, 1959). In the present study, the high-probability behavior (i.e., reinforcing event) was nonacademic behavior which could be emitted during the free-time period contingent upon prior emission of the lower-probability behavior of remaining seated for a given time.

The possibility exists that the students came under instructional control when procedural changes were instituted. This is unlikely, however, in view of the fact that instructions were presented only once at the beginning of each procedural change. Hence, long-term maintenance of the behavior was probably due to the modification procedures.

The lack of clear change in the response rate when free-time (i.e., reinforcement) was presented noncontingently may have been due to "adventitious" reinforcement. At the start of that procedure (Day 11), all subjects had attained nearly perfect performances in remaining seated to obtain free-time That is, more in-seat behavior was occurring than its converse, out-of-sea behavior. Hence, at free-time presentation the behavior most likely to be occur ring was in-seat behavior and, therefore, remaining seated may have been adven titiously maintained in strength by the subsequent presentation of the non contingent free-time. The literature presents a similar case with pigeon (Herrnstein, 1966).

The use of the point system to increase academic output that began on Day 28 may have contributed to keeping the subjects seated. However, inspection o Fig. 1 shows that in the 10 days before Day 28, nearly 80% of the 60 subject days in that period contained no out-of-seat responses.

In terms of financial outlay, the study provided a "cost-free" technique fo managing classroom behavior available to most teachers. At the end of the study total free-time per day equalled 40 min—a time approximately double a standar recess in the public school—but seemingly a reasonable payment to maintain th behavior of a special population. Although not attempted in the present study, i is conceivable that a further lengthening of the time required to be seated, an consequent reduction in the number and total daily duration of free-tim periods, could have been successfully implemented.

REFERENCES

Birnbrauer, J. S., Wolf, M. M., Kidder, J. D., and Tague, C. E. Classroor behavior of retarded pupils with token reinforcement. *Journal of Experi mental Child Psychology*, 1965, 2, 219-235.

Birnbrauer, J. S., Bijou, S. W., Wolf, M. M., and Kidder, J. D. Programme instruction in the classroom. In L. Ullmann and L. Krasner (Eds.), *Cas studies in behavior modification.* New York: Holt, Rinehart & Winston, 1965 Pp. 358-363.

Herrnstein, R. J. Superstition: a corollary of the principles of operant condi tioning. In W. K. Honig (Ed.), *Operant behavior: areas of research and appli cation.* New York: Appleton-Century-Crofts, 1966. Pp. 33-51.

Homme, L. E., C. de Baca, P., Devine, J. V., Steinhorst, R., and Rickert, E. J Use of the Premack principle in controlling the behavior of nursery schoc children. *Journal of the Experimental Analysis of Behavior,* 1963, 6, 544.

Premack, D. Toward empirical behavior laws: I. Positive reinforcement. *Psycho logical Review,* 1959, 66, 219-233.

Skinner, B. F. *The technology of teaching.* New York: Appleton-Century-Crofts 1968.

Staats, A. W. and Butterfield, W. H. Treatment of non-reading in a cultural) deprived juvenile delinquent: an application of reinforcement principles *Child Development,* 1965, 36, 925-942.

Staats, A. W., Minke, K. A., Goodwin, W., and Landeen, J. Cognitive behavio modification: 'motivated learning' reading treatment with subprofessiona therapy-technicians. *Behaviour Research and Therapy,* 1965, 5, 283-299.

Thomas, D. R., Becker, W. C., and Armstrong, M. Production and elimination o disruptive classroom behavior by systematically varying teacher's behavio *Journal of Applied Behavior Analysis,* 1968, 1, 35-45.

Wolf, M. M., Giles, D. K., and Hall, R. V. Experiments with token reinforcement in a remedial classroom. *Behavior Research and Therapy*, 1968, 6, 51-64.

12

A token reinforcement program
in a public school:
a replication and systematic analysis

K. D. O'Leary, W. C. Becker,
M. B. Evans, and R. A. Saudargas

A base rate of disruptive behavior was obtained for seven children in a second-grade class of 21 children. Rules, Educational Structure, and Praising Appropriate Behavior while Ignoring Disruptive Behavior were introduced successively; none of these procedures consistently reduced disruptive behavior. However, a combination of Rules, Educational Structure, and Praise and Ignoring nearly eliminated disruptive behavior of one child. When the Token Reinforcement Program was introduced, the frequency of disruptive behavior declined in five of the six remaining children. Withdrawal of the Token Reinforcement Program increased disruptive behavior in these five children, and reinstatement of the Token Reinforcement Program reduced disruptive behavior in four of these five. Followup data indicated that the teacher was able to transfer control from the token and backup reinforcers to the reinforcers existing within the educational setting, such as stars and occasional pieces of candy. Improvements in academic achievement during the year may have been related to the Token Program, and attendance records appeared to be enhanced during the Token phases. The

From *Journal of Applied Behavior Analysis,* 1969, 2, 3-13. Copyright 1969 by the Society for the Experimental Analysis of Behavior, Inc. Reprinted by permission.

Portions of this paper were presented to the American Psychological Association, September, 1968, San Francisco, California. This research was supported primarily by Research Grant HD 00881-05 to Wesley C. Becker from the National Institutes of Health and secondarily by a Biomedical Science Grant 31-8200 to K. Daniel O'Leary from the State University of New York at Stony Brook. The authors are grateful to Nancy Brown, Connie Dockterman, Pearl Dorfmann, Jeanne Kappauf, Margery Lewy, Stanley Madsen, and Darlene Zientarski who were the major observers in this study. Appreciation for support of this study is expressed to Dr. Lowell Johnson, Director of Instruction, Urbana Public Schools, and to Mr. Richard Sturgeon, elementary school principal. The greatest thanks goes to Mrs. Linda Alsberg, the teacher who executed the Token Reinforcement Program and tolerated the presence of observers both morning and afternoon for eight months. Her patience and self-control during the Praise and Withdrawal Phases of the program were especially appreciated. Reprints may be obtained from K. Daniel O'Leary, Dept. of Psychology, State University of New York at Stony Brook, Stony Brook, N.Y. 11790.

Token Program was utilized only in the afternoon, and the data did not indicate any generalization of appropriate behavior from the afternoon to the morning.

Praise and other social stimuli connected with the teacher's behavior have been established as effective controllers of children's behavior (Allen, Hart, Buell, Harris, and Wolf, 1964; Becker, Madsen, Arnold, and Thomas, 1967; Brown and Elliot, 1965; Hall, Lund, and Jackson, 1968; Harris, Johnston, Kelley, and Wolf, 1964; Harris, Wolf, and Baer, 1964; Scott, Burton, and Yarrow, 1967; Zimmerman and Zimmerman, 1962). When the teacher's use of praise and social censure is not effective, token reinforcement programs are often successful in controlling children (Birnbrauer, Wolf, Kidder, and Tague, 1965; Kuypers, Becker, and O'Leary, 1968; O'Leary and Becker, 1967; Quay, Werry, McQueen, and Sprague, 1966; Wolf, Giles, and Hall, 1968).

The token reinforcement program utilized by O'Leary and Becker (1967) in a third-grade adjustment class dramatically reduced disruptive behavior. In order to maximize the possibility of reducing the disruptive behavior of the children, O'Leary and Becker used several major variables simultaneously. The first objective of the present study was to analyze the separate effects of some of the variables utilized in the former study. More specifically, the aim was to examine the separate effects of Classroom Rules, Educational Structure, Teacher Praise, and a Token Reinforcement Program on children's disruptive behavior. Rules consisted of a list of appropriate behaviors that were reviewed daily. Educational Structure was the organization of an academic program into specified 30-min lessons such as spelling and arithmetic. The second objective was to assess whether a Token Reinforcement Program used only in the afternoon had any effect on the children's behavior in the morning. Third, the present study sought to examine the extent to which the effects of the Token Reinforcement Program persisted when the Token Program was discontinued.

METHOD

Subjects

Seven members of a second-grade class of 21 children from lower-middle class homes served. At the beginning of the school year, the class had a mean age of 7 yr, 5 months, a mean IQ score of 95 (range 80 to 115) on the California Test of Mental Maturity, and a mean grade level of 1.5 on the California Achievement Test. The class was very heterogeneous with regard to social behaviors. According to the teacher, three of the children were quite well behaved but at least eight exhibited a great deal of undesirable behavior. The teacher, Mrs. A., had a master's degree in counseling but had only student teaching experience. She was invited to participate in a research project involving her class and received four graduate credits for participating in the project.

Observation

Children. Mrs. A. selected seven children for observation. All seven children were observed in the afternoon and four of the seven (S1, S2, S4, and S6) were also observed in the morning. Morning observations were made by a regular observer and a reliability checker from 9:30 to 11:30 every Monday, Wednesday, and Friday. Afternoon observations were made by two regular observers and a reliability checker from 12:30 to 2:30 every Monday, Wednesday, and Friday. Observations were made by undergraduate students who were instructed never to talk to the children or to make any differential responses to them in order to minimize the effect of the observers on the children's behavior. Before Base Period data were collected, the undergraduates were trained to observe the children over a three-week period in the classroom, and attention-seeking behaviors of the children directed at the observers were effectively eliminated before the Base Period.

Each child was observed for 20 min each day. The observers watched the children in a random order. Observations were made on a 20-sec observe, 10-sec record basis; i.e., the observer would watch the child for 20 sec and then take 10 sec to record the disruptive behaviors which had occurred during that 20-sec period. The categories of behavior selected for observation were identical to those used by O'Leary and Becker (1967). Briefly, the seven general categories of disruptive behavior were as follows: (1) *motor behaviors:* wandering around the room; (2) *aggressive behaviors:* hitting, kicking, striking another child with an object; (3) *disturbing another's property:* grabbing another's body, tearing up another's paper; (4) *disruptive noise:* clapping, stamping feet; (5) *turning around:* turning to the person behind or looking to the rear of the room when Mrs. A. was in the front of the class; (6) *verbalization:* talking to others when not permitted by teacher, blurting out answers, name-calling; and (7) *inappropriate tasks:* doing arithmetic during the spelling lesson.

The present study was a systematic replication of O'Leary and Becker (1967). To facilitate comparison of the two studies, the dependent measure reported is the percentage of intervals in which one or more disruptive behaviors was recorded. Percentages rather than frequencies were used because the length of the observations varied due to unavoidable circumstances such as assemblies and snow storms. Nonetheless, most observations lasted the full 20 min, and no observation lasting less than 15 min was included.

Teacher. In order to estimate the degree to which the teacher followed the experimental instructions, Mrs. A. was observed by two undergraduates for 90 min on Tuesday and Thursday afternoons. Teacher behavior was not observed on Monday, Wednesday, and Friday when the children were observed because Mrs. A. understandably did not wish to have as many as five observers in the room at one time. Furthermore, because Mrs. A. was somewhat reluctant to have three regular observers and one or two graduate students in the room at most times, she was informed of the need for this observational intrusion and the mechanics thereof. This explanation made it impossible to assess the teacher's behavior without her knowledge, but it was felt that deception about teacher observation could have been harmful both to this project and future projects in the school. Nonetheless, frequent teacher observations by two graduate students who were often in the room the entire week ensured some uniformity of her behavior throughout the week. The graduate students frequently met with Mrs. A. to alert her to any deviations from the experimental instructions, and equally important, to reinforce her "appropriate" behavior. Observations of the teacher's behavior were made on a 20-sec observe, 10-sec record basis. The categories of teacher behavior selected for observation were as follows:

I. Comments *preceding* responses.
   A. *Academic instruction:* "Now we will do arithmetic"; "Put everything in your desk"; "Sound out the words."
   B. *Social instruction:* "I'd like you to say 'please' and 'thank you' "; "Let me see a quiet hand"; "Let's sit up."

II. Comments *following* responses.
   A. *Praise:* "Good"; "Fine"; "You're right"; "I like the way I have your attention."
   B. *Criticism:* "Don't do that"; "Be quiet"; "Sit in your seat!"
   C. *Threats:* "If you're not quiet by the time I count to three . . . ."; "If you don't get to work you will stay after school"; "Do you want to stay in this group?"

The teacher's praise, criticism, and threats to individual children were differentiated from praise, criticism, and threats to the class as a whole. For example, "Johnny, be quiet!" was differentiated from "Class, be quiet!". Thus, eight different classes of teacher behavior were recorded: two classes of comments preceding responses and six classes following responses.

Procedure

The eight phases of the study were as follows: (1) Base Period, (2) Classroom Rules, (3) Educational Structure, (4) Praising Appropriate Behavior and Ignoring Disruptive Behavior, (5) Tokens and Back-up Reinforcement, (6) Praising Appropriate Behavior and Ignoring Disruptive Behavior (Withdrawal), (7) Tokens and Backup Reinforcement, and (8) Followup. Three procedures, Educational Structure and both of the Token Reinforcement Phases, were instituted for a 2-hr period during the afternoon. The remainder of the procedures were in effect for the entire day. The eight procedures were in effect for all 21 children. The first four conditions were instituted in the order of hypothesized increasing effectiveness. For example, it was thought that Rules would have less effect on the children's behavior than the use of Praise. In addition, it was thought that the combination of Rules and Praise would have less effect than the Tokens and Backup Reinforcers.

Base Period. After the initial three-week observer training period, the children were observed on eight days over a six-week Base Period to estimate the frequency of disruptive pupil behavior under usual classroom conditions.[1] The teacher was asked to handle the children in whatever way she felt appropriate. During the Base Period, Mrs. A. instructed all the children in subjects like science and arithmetic or took several students to small reading groups in the back of the room while the rest of the class engaged in independent work at their seats. Neither the particular type of activity nor the duration was the same each day. Stars and various forms of peer pressure were sporadically used as classroom control techniques, but they usually had little effect and were discontinued until experimentally reintroduced during the Followup Phase.

Classroom Rules. There were seven observations over a three-week period during the second phase of the study. The following rules or instructions were placed on the blackboard by the teacher: "We sit in our seats; we raise our hands to talk; we do not talk out of turn; we keep our desks clear; we face the front of the room; we will work very hard; we do not talk in the hall; we do not run; and, we do not disturb reading groups." Mrs. A. was asked to review the rules at least once every morning and afternoon, and frequent observations and discussions with Mrs. A. guaranteed that this was done on most occasions. The classroom activities again consisted of reading groups and independent seat work.

Educational Structure. It has been stated that a great deal of the success in token reinforcement programs may be a function of the highly structured regimen of the program and not a function of reinforcement contingencies. Since the Token Phase of the program was designed to be used during structured activities that the teacher directed, Mrs. A. was asked to reorganize her program into four 30-min sessions in the afternoon in which the whole class participated, e.g., spelling, reading, arithmetic, and science. Thus, the purpose of the Educational Structure Phase was to assess the importance of structure *per se.* Mrs. A. continued to review the rules twice a day during this phase and all succeeding phases. During this phase there were five observations over a two-week period.

Praise and Ignore. In addition to Rules and Educational Structure, Mrs. A. was asked to praise appropriate behavior and to ignore disruptive behavior as much as possible. For example, she was asked to ignore children who did not raise their hands before answering questions and to praise children who raised their hands before speaking. In addition, she was asked to discontinue her use of threats. During this phase there were five observations over a two-week period.

Token I. Classroom Rules, Educational Structure, and Praise and Ignoring remained in effect. The experimenter told the children that they would receive points or ratings four times each afternoon. The points which the children received on these four occasions ranged from 1 to 10, and the children were told that the points would reflect the extent to which they followed the rules placed on the blackboard by Mrs. A. Where possible, these points also reflected the

---

[1] Ten of the 18 observations during the Base Period were eliminated because movies were shown on those days, and disruptive behavior on those days was significantly less than on days when movies were not shown. Although movies were seldom used after Base Period, the seven subsequent observations when movies occurred were eliminated.

quality of the children's participation in class discussion and the accuracy of their arithmetic or spelling. The children's behavior in the morning did not influence their ratings in the afternoon. If a child was absent, he received no points. The points or tokens were placed in small booklets on each child's desk. The points were exchangeable for backup reinforcers such as candy, pennants, dolls, comics, barrettes, and toy trucks, ranging in value from 2 to 30 cents. The variety of prizes made it likely that at least one of the items would be a reinforcer for each child. The prizes were on display every afternoon, and the teacher asked each child to select the prize he wished to earn before the rating period started.

During the initial four days, the children were eligible for prizes just after their fourth rating at approximately 2:30. Thereafter, all prizes were distributed at the end of the day. For the first 10 school days the children could receive prizes each day. There were always two levels of prizes. During the first 10 days, a child had to receive at least 25 points to receive a 2 to 5¢ prize (level one prize) or 35 points to receive a 10¢ prize (level two prize). For the next six days, points were accumulated for two days and exchanged at the end of the second day. When children saved their points for two days, a child had to receive 55 points to receive a 10¢ prize or 70 points to receive a 20¢ prize. Then, a six-day period occurred in which points were accumulated for three days and exchanged at the end of the third day. During this period, a child had to receive 85 points to receive a 20¢ prize or 105 points to receive a 30¢ prize. Whenever the prizes were distributed, the children relinquished all their points. During Token I, there were 13 observations over a five-week period.

For the first week, the experimenter repeated the instructions to the class at the beginning of each afternoon session. Both the experimenter and Mrs. A. rated the children each day for the first week in order to teach Mrs. A. how to rate the children. The experimenter sat in the back of the room and handed his ratings to Mrs. A. in a surreptitious manner after each rating period. Mrs. A. utilized both ratings in arriving at a final rating which she put in the children's booklets at the end of each lesson period. The method of arriving at a number or rating to be placed in the child's booklet was to be based on the child's improvement in behavior. That is, if a child showed any daily improvement he could receive a rating of approximately 5 to 7 so that he could usually earn at least a small prize. Marked improvement in behavior or repeated displays of relatively good behavior usually warranted ratings from 8 to 10. Ratings from 1 to 5 were given when a child was disruptive and did not evidence any daily improvement. Although such a rating system involves much subjective judgment on the part of the teacher, it is relatively easy to implement, and a subsidiary aim of the study was to assess whether a token system could be implemented by one teacher in a class of average size. After the first week, the teacher administered the Token Program herself, and the experimenter was never present when the children were being observed. If the experimenter had been present during the Token Phases but not during Withdrawal, any effects of the Token Program would have been confounded by the experimenter's presence.

Withdrawal. To demonstrate that the token and backup reinforcers and not other factors, such as the changes that ordinarily occur during the school year, accounted for the observed reduction in disruptive behavior, the token and backup reinforcers were withdrawn during this phase. There were seven observations over a five-week period. When the prizes and the booklets were removed from the room, Mrs. A. told the children that she still hoped that they would behave as well as they had during the Token Period and emphasized how happy she was with their recent improvement. Rules, Educational Structure, and Praise and Ignoring remained in effect.

Token II. When the tokens and backup reinforcers were reinstated, the children obtained a prize on the first day if they received 25 to 35 points. For the next four days there was a one-day delay between token and backup reinforcement; the remainder of the Token Reinstatement Period involved a two-day delay of reinforcement. The prize and point system was identical to that during Token I. During this phase, there were five observations over a two-week period.

Followup. The token and backup reinforcers were again withdrawn in order to see if the appropriate behavior could be maintained under more normal classroom conditions. In addition to the continued use of Praise, Rules, and Educational Structure, it was suggested that Mrs. A. initiate the use of a systematic star system. Children could receive from one to three stars for good behavior twice during the morning and once during the afternoon. In addition, the children received extra stars for better behavior during the morning restroom break and for displaying appropriate behavior upon entering the room at 9:15 and 12:30. At times, extra stars were given to the best behaved row of children. The children counted their stars at the end of the day; if they had 10 or more stars, they received a gold star that was placed on a permanent wall chart. If a child received 7 to 9 stars, he received a green star that was placed on the chart. The boys' gold stars and the girls' gold stars were counted each day; and each member of the group with the greater number of gold stars at the end of the week received a piece of candy. In addition, any child who received an entire week of gold stars received a piece of candy. All children began the day without stars so that, with the exception of the stars placed on the wall chart, everyone entered the program at the same level.

Such a procedure was a form of a token reinforcement program, but there were important procedural differences between the experimental phases designated Token and Followup. The backup reinforcers used during the Token Phases were more expensive than the two pieces of candy a child could earn each week during the Followup Phase. In addition, four daily ratings occurred at half-hour intervals in the afternoons during the Token Phases but not during Follow-up. On the other hand, stars, peer pressure, and a very small amount of candy were used in the Followup Phase. As mentioned previously, both stars and peer pressure had been used sporadically in the Base Period with little effect. Most importantly, it was felt that the procedures used in the Followup Phase could be implemented by any teacher. During this phase there were six observations over a four-week period.

Reliability of Observations

The reliabilities of child observations were calculated according to the following procedure: an agreement was scored if both observers recorded one or more disruptive behaviors within the same 20-sec interval; a disagreement was scored if one observer recorded a disruptive behavior and the other observer recorded none. The reliability of the measure of disruptive behavior was calculated for each child each day by dividing the number of intervals in which there was agreement that one or more disruptive behaviors occurred by the total number of agreements plus disagreements. An agreement was scored if both observers recorded the same behavior within the same 20-sec interval. A disagreement was scored if one observer recorded the behavior and the other did not. The reliability of a particular class of teacher behavior on any one day was calculated by dividing the total number of agreements for that class of behaviors by the total number of agreements plus disagreements for that class of behaviors. Reliabilities were calculated differently for child behaviors and teacher behaviors because different types of dependent measures were utilized for children and the teacher, and it was felt that reliability measures should be reported for the specific dependent measures used.

At least one reliability check was made during the afternoon on every child during the Base Period, and one child had three.[2] The average reliability of the measure of disruptive behavior during the afternoons of the Base Period for each of the seven children ranged from 88 to 100%. The following figures represent the number of reliability checks and the average of those reliability checks after the Base Period through the first Token Period for each child: S1: 6, 86%; S2: 7, 94%; S3: 6, 94%; S4: 6, 93%; S5: 6, 87%; S6: 6, 84%; S7: 6, 97%. Because of the repeated high reliabilities, reliability checks were discontinued when the token and backup reinforcers were reinstated; i.e., no reliability checks were made during or after the Withdrawal Phase.

Adequate morning reliabilites were not obtained until the Rules Phase of the study. The following figures represent the number of reliability checks and the average of those reliability checks during the Rules Phase: S1: 3, 93%; S2: 4, 68%; S4: 3, 91%; S6: 3, 88%. Morning reliability checks after the Rules Phase were made approximately every three observations (approximately seven occasions) through the first Token Period. Average reliabilities of the four children during the Rules, Educational Structure, Praise and Ignore, and Token I Phases ranged from 92 to 99%.

Eleven reliability checks for the various classes of teacher behavior before the Praise and Ignore Phase was introduced yielded average reliabilities as follows: academic instruction, 75%; social instruction, 77%; praise to individuals, 77%; praise to the class, 94%; criticism to individuals, 73%; criticism to the class, 72%; threats to individuals, 83%; and threats to the class, 83%.

---

[2] Before 10 of the 18 observation days during the Base Period were eliminated because movies were shown on those days, at least three reliability checks had been made during the afternoon on each child.

RESULTS

Child Behavior

Figures 1 and 2 present morning and afternoon data; some of the variability within conditions can be seen. Figure 3 presents data of individual children as well as an average of seven children across afternoon conditions. An analysis of variance was performed on the percentages of combined disruptive behavior, averaged within the eight afternoon experimental conditions, for the seven subjects (See Fig. 3). The analysis of variance for repeated measures (Winer, 1962, p. 111) indicated differences among the eight experimental conditions ($F=7.3$; $df=7, 42$; $p < 0.001$). On the other hand, the percentages of combined disruptive behavior of the four children observed in the morning, averaged within conditions, did not change during Rules, Educational Structure, Praise and Ignore, or Token I ($F=1.0$; $df=4, 12$). Differences among afternoon conditions were assessed by t-tests. Significant and nonsignificant differences are grouped individually in Table 1.[3]

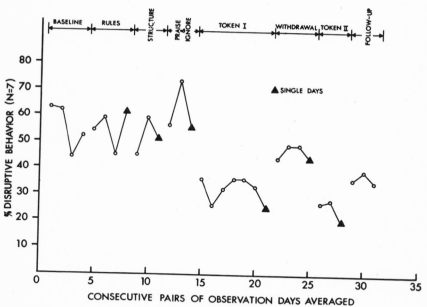

Fig. 1. Average percentage of combined disruptive behavior of seven children during the afternoon over the eight conditions: Base, Rules, Educational Structure, Praise and Ignore, Token I, Withdrawal, Token II, Followup.

---

[3] Two-tailed tests.

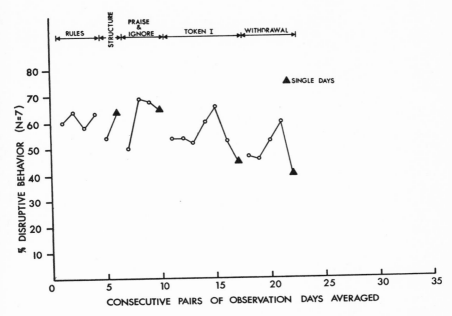

Fig. 2. Average percentage of combined disruptive behavior of four children during the morning over five conditions: Base, Rules, Educational Structure, Praise and Ignore, Token I, Withdrawal, Token II, Followup.

It should be emphasized that comparisons between Followup and Praise and Ignore are more meaningful than comparisons between Followup and Base, Rules, or Educational Structure. Praise and Followup were similar procedures; both included Rules, Educational Structure, and Praise and Ignore. The Base Period did not include any of these. Furthermore, after Rules and Educational Structure were initiated, Mrs. A. stated that she required more academic work from the children than during Base Period. A statistical analysis of the group data suggests that a token reinforcement program can reduce disruptive behavior and that a token reinforcement program can be replaced with a variant of a token program without an increase in disruptive behavior. However, a more detailed analysis of the data for individual children indicated that the Token Reinforcement Program was more effective for some children than others.

The introduction of Rules, Educational Structure, and Praise and Ignore did not have any consistent effects on behavior (see Fig. 3). Praising Appropriate Behavior and Ignoring Disruptive Behavior deserve special mention. Although Mrs. A. used criticism occasionally during the Praise and Ignore Phase, she generally ignored disruptive behavior and used praise frequently. Initially, a number of children responded well to Mrs. A.'s praise, but two boys (S2 and S4) who had been disruptive all year became progressively more unruly during the

Praise and Ignore Phase. Other children appeared to observe these boys being disruptive, with little or no aversive consequences, and soon became disruptive themselves. Relay races and hiding under a table contributed to the pandemonium. Several children were so disruptive that the academic pursuits of the rest of the class became impossible. The situation became intolerable, and the Praise and Ignore Phase had to be discontinued much earlier than had been planned.

The disruptive behavior of S7 was reduced to a very low level of 15% by a combination of Rules, Educational Structure, and Praise and Ignore. In the previous token program (O'Leary and Becker, 1967), in which a number of variables including rules, praise, educational structure, and a token program were simultaneously introduced, disruptive behavior during the token period was reduced to a level of 10%. Thus, the present Token Reinforcement Program probably would not be expected further to reduce disruptive behavior in this child.

During Token I, there was a marked reduction ($\cong 18\%$) in the disruptive behavior of five children (S1, S2, S3, S4, and S6) and a reduction of 3% in S5. Withdrawal of the Token Program increased disruptive behavior from 5% to 45% in these six children. Reinstatement of the Token Program led to a decrease in five of these six children (S1, S2, S3, S4, S5). The disruptive behavior of five children (S1, S2, S4, S5, and S6) ranged from 8% to 39% lower during the Followup than during the Praise and Ignore Phase of the study. Since on no occasion did the Followup procedures precede Token I and/or Token II, this study did not demonstrate that Token I and/or Token II were necessary conditions for the success of the Followup procedures.

Table 1

Significant		Non-Significant	
Token I *vs.* Withdrawal	$t=3.3**$	Rules *vs.* Educational Structure	$t=0.8$
Token II *vs.* Withdrawal	$t=2.9*$	Educational Structure *vs.* Praise	$t=1.0$
Token I *vs.* Praise	$t=3.4**$	Base *vs.* Withdrawal	$t=1.2$
Token II *vs.* Praise	$t=3.0*$	Token I *vs.* Followup	$t=1.1$
Base *vs.* Followup	$t=3.2**$	Token II *vs.* Followup	$t=1.5$
Praise *vs.* Followup	$t=3.3**$		
Withdrawal *vs.* Followup	$t=3.2**$		

$**p < 0.02, df=6$
$*p < 0.05, df=6$

In summary, Token I and Token II were definitely associated with a reduction of disruptive behavior, and the Followup procedure was effective with three of the six children (S1, S2, and S4) who had more than 15% disruptive behavior during the Praise and Ignore Phase (S7 had 15% disruptive behavior during the Praise and Ignore Phase). Token I and Token II were associated with marked reductions of disruptive behavior of S3, but the frequency of disruptive behavior during the Followup was not substantially lower than during the Praise and Ignore Phase. Definitive conclusions concerning the effects of the Token Program cannot be drawn for S5 and S6, although some reduction of disruptive behavior was associated with either Token I and Token II for both of these children. In addition, the disruptive behavior of S5 and S6 was 8% and 20% less respectively during Followup than during the Praise and Ignore Phase.

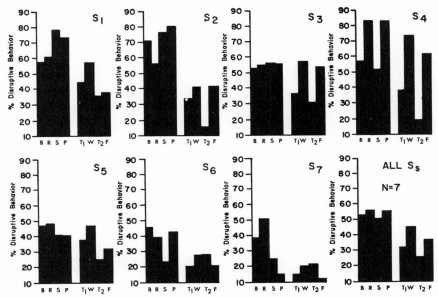

Fig. 3. Percentage of combined disruptive behavior for each of seven children during the eight conditions: Base, Rules, Educational Structure, Praise and Ignore, Token I, Withdrawal, Token II, Followup.

Teacher Behavior

On any one day, the percentage of each of the eight classes of teacher behavior was calculated by dividing the number of intervals in which a particular class of behavior occurred by the total number of intervals observed on that day. Percentages rather than frequencies were used because of slight variations from the usual 90-min time base.

The percentages of different classes of teacher behavior were averaged within two major conditions: (1) data before Praise and Ignore Phase, and (2) data in the Praise and Ignore and succeeding Phases. The data in Fig. 4 show that in the Praise and Ignore Phase, Mrs. A. increased use of praise to individual children from 12% to 31% and decreased use of criticism to individuals from 22% to 10%. Mrs. A. also increased use of praise to the class from 1% to 7% and decreased

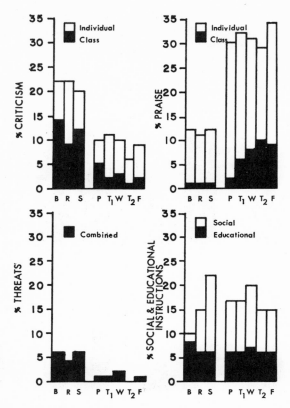

Fig. 4. Percentage of various teacher behaviors to individuals and to the class during the eight conditions: Base, Rules, Educational Structure, Praise and Ignore, Token I, Withdrawal, Token II, Followup.

criticism directed to the class from 11% to 3%. Because the frequency of threats was quite low, threats to individuals and threats to the class were combined in one measure. Using this combined measure, Mrs. A.'s use of threats decreased from 5% to 1%. There were no differences in Mrs. A.'s use of academic or social instruction. Consequently, the changes in the children's disruptive behavior can probably be attributed to contingencies and not to Mrs. A.'s use of cues concerning the desired behaviors.

DISCUSSION

Although a Token Reinforcement Program was a significant variable in reducing disruptive behavior in the present study, the results are less dramatic than those obtained by O'Leary and Becker (1967). A number of factors probably contributed to the difference in effectiveness of the programs. The average of disruptive behavior during the Base Period in the 1967 study was 76%; in the present study it was 53%. The gradual introduction of the various phases of the program was probably less effective than a simultaneous introduction of all the procedures, as in the previous study. In the earlier study, the children received more frequent ratings. Five ratings were made each day at the introduction of the 1.5-hr token program, and they were gradually reduced to three ratings per day. In the present study, the children received four ratings per day during a 2-hr period. In the 1967 study, the class could earn points for popsicles by being quiet while the teacher placed ratings in the children's booklets; in the present study, group points were not incorporated into the general reinforcement program. In the 1967 study, the teacher attended a weekly psychology seminar where teachers discussed various applications of learning principles to classroom management. An *esprit de corps* was generated from that seminar that probably increased the teacher's commitment to change the children's behavior. Although Mrs. A. received graduate credits for her extensive participation in the project, she did not attend a seminar in classroom management. A number of children in the present study had an abundance of toys at home and it was difficult to obtain inexpensive prizes which would serve as reinforcers; in the earlier study, selection of reinforcers was not a difficult problem, since the children were from disadvantaged homes.

Related Gains

Academic. The 14 children for whom there were both pre- and post-measures on the California Achievement Test (including S1, S4, S5, S6, and S7) gained an average of 1.5 yr from October to June. The mean CAT score in October was 1.5 while the mean score in June was 3.0. Although there was no matched control group, such gains are greater than those usually obtained (Tiegs and Clark, 1963). While such gains are promising, conclusions about the effects of a token system on academic performance must await a more systematic analysis.

Attendance. Comparisons of the attendance records of the seven children during the observational days of the token and nontoken phases yielded the following results: the average attendance percentage during the 45 observation days of Base, Rules, Educational Structure, Praise and Ignore, and Withdrawal was 86%. The average attendance percentage during the 20 observation days of Token I and Token II was 98%; the average attendance percentage during the 26 observation days of Token I, Token II, and Followup (a variant of a token program) was 99%. These attendance records are very encouraging, but because of the usual seasonal variations in attendance and the small sample of children, more definitive evidence is needed before conclusions about the effects of a token program on attendance can be made.

Cost of Program

The cost of the reinforcers in the present study was approximately $125.00. It is estimated that 3 hr of consulting time per week would be essential to operate a token reinforcement program effectively for one class in a public school. The cost of such a program and the amount of consulting time seem relatively small when compared to the hours psychologists spend in therapy with children, often without producing significant behavioral changes (Levitt, 1963). Furthermore, as evidenced in the present study, control of behavior may be shifted from reinforcers, such as toys, to reinforcers existing within the natural educational setting, such as stars and peer prestige.

Generalization

During the morning, the majority of the children were engaged in independent seat work, while four or five children were in a reading group with the teacher in the back of the room. Although there were rules and frequent instructions during the morning, there was little reinforcement for appropriate behavior, since Mrs. A. felt that it would be disruptive to the rest of the class to interrupt reading groups to praise children who were doing independent work at their seats. Ayllon and Azrin (1964) found that instructions without reinforcement had little effect on the behavior of mental patients. Similarly, Rules (instructions) without reinforcement did not influence the behavior of the children in this study.

Mrs. A. was instructed to praise appropriate behavior and ignore disruptive behavior in the morning as well as the afternoon. However, Mrs. A.'s criteria of appropriate behavior in the morning differed from her criteria in the afternoon. For example, in the morning she often answered questions when a child failed to raise his hand before speaking. In the afternoon, on the other hand, she generally ignored a child unless he raised his hand. In order to achieve "generalization" of appropriate behavior in a Token Program such as this one, the teacher's response to disruptive behavior must remain constant throughout the day. The percentage of disruptive behavior was reduced during the morning of the first few days of Token I, but the children presumably learned to discriminate that their appropriate behavior was reinforced only in the afternoon. The differences in the children's behavior between the morning and the afternoon help to stress the point that "generalization" is no magical process, but rather a behavioral change which must be engineered like any other change.

REFERENCES

Allen, K. Eileen, Hart, Betty M., Buell, Joan S., Harris, Florence R., and Wolf, M. M. Effects of social reinforcement on isolate behavior of a nursery school child. *Child Development,* 1964, 35, 511-518.

Ayllon, T. and Azrin, N. H. Reinforcement and instructions with mental patients. *Journal of the Experimental Analysis of Behavior* 1964, 7, 327-331.

Becker, W. C., Madsen, C. H., Arnold, Carole R., and Thomas, D. R. The contingent use of teacher attention and praise in reducing classroom behavior problems. *Journal of Special Education,* 1967, I (3), 287-307.

Birnbrauer, J. S., Wolf, M. M., Kidder, J. D., and Tague, Celia. Classroom behavior of retarded pupils with token reinforcement. *Journal of Experimental Child Psychology,* 1965, 2, 219-235.

Brown, P. and Elliot, R. Control of aggression in a nursery school class. *Journal of Experimental Child Psychology,* 1965, 2, 103-107.

Hall, R. V., Lund, Diane, and Jackson, Deloris. Effects of teacher attention on study behavior. *Journal of Applied Behavior Analysis,* 1968, I, 1-12.

Harris, Florence R., Johnston, Margaret K., Kelley, C. Susan, and Wolf, M. M. Effects of positive social reinforcement on regressed crawling of a nursery school child. *Journal of Educational Psychology,* 1964, 55, 35-41.

Harris, Florence R., Wolf, M. M., and Baer, D. M. Effects of social reinforcement on child behavior. *Young Children,* 1964, 20, 8-17.

Kuypers, D. S., Becker, W. C., and O'Leary, K. D. How to make a token system fail. *Exceptional Children,* 1968, 35, 101-109.

Levitt, E. E. Psychotherapy with children: A further evaluation. *Behaviour Research and Therapy,* 1963, I, 45-51.

O'Leary, K. D. and Becker, W. C. Behavior modification of an adjustment class: A token reinforcement program. *Exceptional Children,* 1967, 33, 637-642.

Quay, H. C., Werry, J. S., McQueen, Marjorie, and Sprague, R. L. Remediation of the conduct problem child in a special class setting. *Exceptional Children,* 1966, 32, 509-515.

Scott, Phyllis M., Burton, R. V., and Yarrow, Marian R. Social reinforcement under natural conditions. *Child Development,* 1967, 38, 53-63.

Tiegs, E. V. and Clark, W. W. Manual, California Achievement Tests, Complete Battery. 1963 Norms. California Test Bureau, Monterey, California.

Winer, B. J. *Statistical principles in experimental design.* New York: McGraw-Hill, 1962.

Wolf, M. M., Giles, D. K., and Hall R. V. Experiments with token reinforcement in a remedial classroom. *Behaviour Research and Therapy,* 1968, 6, 51-64.

Zimmerman, Elaine H. and Zimmerman, J. The alteration of behavior in a special classroom situation. *Journal of the Experimental Analysis of Behavior,* 1962, 5, 59-60.

13

Applying "group" contingencies to the classroom study behavior of preschool children

D. Bushell, Jr., Patricia A. Wrobel, and Mary L. Michaelis

A group of 12 children were enrolled in a preschool class. During the first experimental stage they participated in special events contingent on token earning. Tokens were acquired by engaging in a variety of study behaviors. After a level of study behavior was established under this contingency, the special events were provided noncontingently. Study behavior declined throughout the noncontingent stage. Reestablishing the original contingencies produced an immediate return to the initial level of study behavior. Noncontingent special events reduced the amount of independent study, group participation, and cooperative study. The study behavior of each child was altered in the same direction, though differences in the magnitude of effects from child to child were observed.

The experimental analysis of behavior has concentrated on the examination of responses emitted by a single subject. Recently, extensions of this research have begun to deal with groups of individuals. Behavioral research with adult psychiatric patients (Ayllon and Azrin, 1965), and retarted children (Birnbrauer, Wolf, Kidder, and Tague, 1965) has indicated that certain operant techniques can be applied effectively well beyond the "artificial" conditions of the experimentally isolated subject.

From *Journal of Applied Behavior Analysis,* 1968, 1, 55-61. Copyright 1968 by the Society for the Experimental Analysis of Behavior, Inc. Reprinted by permission.

This study was carried out as a part of the program of the Webster College Student Behavior Laboratory, and preparation of the report was supported in part by the Institute for Sociological Research, The University of Washington. The authors gratefully acknowledge the able assistance of the observers who made this study possible: Alice Adcock, Sandra Albright, Sister Eleanor Marie Craig, S. L., Jim Felling, and Cleta Pouppart. We are particularly indebted to Donald M. Baer who encouraged us to commit this study to paper and subsequently gave thoughtful criticism to the manuscript. Reprints may be obtained from Don Bushell, Jr., Dept. of Human Development, University of Kansas, Lawrence, Kansas 66044.

138

In most group situations it is not practical to program individually special contingencies for the responses of each group member. Uniform criteria must be designed according to which a number of individuals are to be rewarded or punished. Schools, prisons, hospitals, business, and military organizations all maintain systems of response contingencies which are quite similar for all the individuals of a certain category within the organization. The objective of this research was to determine whether operant techniques may be applied to a group of individuals with effects similar to those expected when a single subject is under study. The specific behavior under analysis was the study behavior of a group of preschool children.

The dependent variables were behaviors such as attending quietly to instructions, working independently or in cooperation with others as appropriate, remaining with and attending to assigned tasks, and reciting after assignments had been completed. Counter examples are behaviors such as disrupting others who are at work, changing an activity before its completion, and engaging in "escape" behaviors such as trips to the bathroom or drinking fountain, or gazing out the window. To the extent that the first constellation of behaviors is present and the second is absent, a student might be classified as industrious, highly motivated, or conscientious; in short, he has good study habits.

METHOD

Children and Setting

The subjects were 12 children enrolled in a summer session. Three other children were not considered in this report because they did not attend at least half of the sessions due to illness and family vacations. Four of the 12 children were 3-yr old, two were 4-yr old, five were 5-yr old, and one was 6-yr old. These 10 girls and two boys would be described as middle class; all had been enrolled in the preschool the preceding spring semester, all scored above average on standardized intelligence tests, and all had experienced some form of token system during the previous semester.

Classes were conducted from 12:45 to 3:30 p.m., five days a week for seven weeks. A large room adjoining the classroom afforded one-way sight and sound monitoring of the class. The program was directed by two head teachers who were assisted for 25 min each day by a specialist who conducted the Spanish lesson. All of the teachers were undergraduates.

Daily Program

Data were collected in three phases during the first 75 min of each of the last 20 class days of the summer session. During the first 20 min, individual activities were made available to the children for independent study, and the amount of social interaction, student-student or student-teacher, was very slight. The next 25 min were devoted to Spanish instruction. The interaction pattern during this period was much like that of a typical classroom, with the teacher at the front of the assembled children sometimes addressing a specific individual but more often talking to the entire group. The remaining 30 min were given over to "study teams," with the children paired so the one more skilled at a particular task would teach the less skilled. Composition of the groups and their tasks varied from day to day according to the developing skills of the children.

Following this 75 min, a special event was made available to the children. Special events included: a short movie, a trip to a nearby park, a local theater group rehearsal, an art project, a story, or a gym class. The special event was always 30 min long and was always conducted outside the regular classroom. The children were not told what the activity would be for the day until immediately before it occurred.

Token Reinforcement

The tokens, colored plastic washers about 1.5-in. in diameter, served as a monetary exchange unit within the classroom. As the children engaged in individual activities, Spanish, and study teams, the teachers moved about the room giving tokens to those who appeared to be actively working at their various tasks, but not to those who were not judged to be attending to the assignment at the moment.

To minimize unproductive talking about the tokens, the teachers avoided mentioning them. Tokens were never given when requested. If a child presented a piece of work and then asked for a token, the request was ignored and additional work was provided if needed. Similarly, the presentation of tasks was never accompanied by any mention of tokens, such as, "If you do thus and so, I will give you a token." The tokens were simply given out as the children worked and, where possible, the presentation was accompanied by such verbal statements as "good," "you're doing fine, keep it up," "that's right," etc. The teachers avoided a set pattern in dispensing the tokens so that their approach would not become discriminative for studying. They would watch for appropriate behavior, move to that child, present a token and encouragement, then look for another instance not too nearby. During Spanish, the two teachers were able to present tokens for appropriate responding to the children who were assembled in front of the Spanish teacher. During study teams the teachers presented tokens as they circulated from group to group, and also at a checking session at the end of the period. Here, the student-learner recited what had been learned and both children were given tokens according to the performance of the learner. Each teacher distributed from 110 to 120 tokens during the 75 min.

The tokens could be used to purchase the special-event ticket. The price varied from 12 to 20 tokens around an average of 15 each day so the children would not leave their study activities as soon as they acquired the necessary amount. Children who did not earn enough to purchase the special-event ticket remained in the classroom when the others left with the teachers. There were no recriminations or admonishments by either the teachers or the students, and the one or two children left behind typically found some toy or book to occupy themselves until the rest of the class returned. After the special event, additional activities enabled the children to earn tokens for a 3:00 p.m. snack of cookies, ice cream, milk, or lemonade, and a chair to sit on while eating. Tokens could be accumulated from day to day.

As tokens became more valuable, theft, borrowing, lending (sometimes at interest), hiring of services and a variety of other economic activities were observed. No attempt was made to control any of these except theft, which was eliminated simply by providing the children with aprons which had pockets for the tokens.

Observation and Recording Procedures

The four principal observers were seated in an observation room. Each wore earphones which enabled audio monitoring of the class and also prevented inter-observer communication. On a signal at the beginning of each 5-min period, each observer looked for the first child listed on the roster and noted that child's behavior on the data sheet, then looked for the second child on the list and noted its behavior; and so on for each child. All observers were able to complete the total observational cycle in less than 3 min. During the 75 min of observation, the children's behavior was described by noting what the child was looking at, to whom he was talking, and what he was doing with his hands. Fourteen daily observations of each child by each observer produced 672 items of data each day.

Criteria were established by which each behavioral description on the data sheets could be coded as either "S," indicating study behavior, or "NS," indicating nonstudy behavior. Behaviors such as writing, putting a piece in a puzzle, reciting to a teacher, singing a Spanish song with the class, and tracing around a pattern with a pencil were classified as "S," if they were observed in the appropriate setting. Descriptions of behaviors such as counting tokens, putting away materials, walking around the room, drinking at the fountain, looking out the window, rolling on the floor and attending to another child, were classified as "NS." Singing a Spanish song was scored "S" if it occurred during the Spanish period when called for, but "NS" if it occurred during an earlier or later period. Similarly, if one child was interacting with another over instructional materials during the study teams period, the behavior was labeled "S," but the same behavior during another period was classified "NS."

If a given child's behavior was described 14 times and eight of these descriptions were coded "S," then the amount of study time for that child was 8/14 for that day. The amount of study behavior for the entire class on a given day was the sum of the 12 individual scores.

Time-Sampling Validity Check

Time-sampling assumes that, in a given situation, the behavior observed at fixed spacings in time adequately represents the behavior occurring during the total interval. To check the validity of this assumption, a fifth observer described the behavior of only three children much more frequently. At the beginning of each 15-sec interval an automatic timing device beside the fifth observer emitted a click and flashed a small light. The observer then described the ongoing behavior of the first of the three target children of the day, noting essentially the child's looking, talking, and hand behaviors. The procedure was repeated for the second child, then the third. At the onset of the next 15-sec interval, the sequence was repeated. The tape ran continuously. Consequently, during the same interval when the principal observers made 14 observations, the fifth made slightly more than 300 observations of each of the three children. This procedure was used during nine of the 20 experimental sessions, and the three children chosen for this type of observation varied.

The data sheets completed by the four regular observers and the tapes recorded by the fifth observer were coded each day by the four principal observers who assigned either an "S" or "NS" to each description. Coding was accomplished independently by each observer without consultation. The fifth observer did not participate in classifying any of the tape descriptions.

Design

The study, a within-group design, consisted of three stages. During the first stage, participation in the special event was contingent upon the purchase of the necessary ticket with tokens. After nine days under these conditions, participation in the special event was made noncontingent. During the seven days of the noncontingent stage, the children were presented with special-event tickets and snack tickets as they arrived for school. Tokens and verbal statements of praise and encouragement were still given for the same behaviors as during the first phase, but the tokens no longer had any purchasing power. All the privileges of the classroom were available to every child regardless of how much or how little study behavior he or she displayed.

The decision to continue dispensing tokens but devalue them by providing everything free was made in order to retain all of the original procedures except the contingent special event. Had the tokens been given on a noncontingent basis at the beginning of each session, or eliminated entirely, this might have altered the behavior of the teachers toward the children throughout the remainder of the session.

After the sixteenth day of the study, the aprons containing the accumulated tokens were "sent to the cleaners" and all of the tokens were removed. As the children arrived the next day and asked where their tickets were, they were told they would have to buy them. When the children noted that they couldn't because they had no tokens, the teachers responded by saying: "Perhaps you can earn some. Your (activity—name) is over there." Thus, for the final four days, the last days of the summer session, the initial conditions were restored with special-event and snack tickets again being made contingent upon tokens acquired by the students for study behavior.

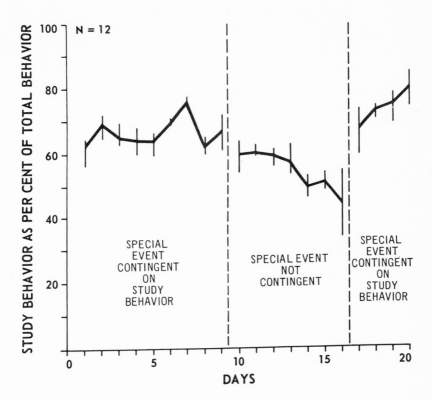

Fig. 1. Mean per cent of 12 children's study behavior over 20 school days. Vertical lines indicate the range of scores obtained by the four observers each day.

RESULTS

Figure 1 shows that study behavior was influenced by whether or not the special event was contingent upon it. During the first nine-day stage, offering the special event contingent on study behavior resulted in an average score for the class as a whole of 67%. During the noncontingent stage, the observed study behavior declined 25 percentage points over seven days to a low of 42%. Restoring the original contingencies on Day 17 was associated with a 22% increase in study behavior over that of the previous day.

Because the study behavior data were derived from observational measures, a number of checks were made to establish the reliability of the procedures. First, the total class score obtained by each observer for each day was compared to the scores of the other three observers. The vertical lines at each point in Fig. 1

describe the range of group scores obtained by the four observers each day. Inspection of these lines indicated that the same pattern was described even if the summary class score for any given day was drawn at random from the four available scores. Indeed, the data of any one, or any combination, of the four observers presented the same pattern with respect to the effects of contingent reinforcement upon study behavior.

The fact that the behavior descriptions of each day were coded within a few hours after they were obtained might have been an additional source of error. A description might have been coded "NS" on Day 15 and "S" on Day 19 simply because the observer expected study behavior to increase during the final contingent stage. To check for such effects, four new coders were empaneled nine months after the study was completed. These new coders had no knowledge of the details of the original investigation. They were trained to read behavioral descriptions like those appearing on the original data sheets and assign an "S" or "NS" to each according to the criteria outlined in the previous section. Once they agreed within 5% on the independent scoring of a given data sheet, they were each given nine of the original sheets.

The data sheets given to the new coders were in scrambled order with all dates and other identifying marks obscured so they had no way of determining which stage a sheet came from even if they understood the significance of the experimental conditions. Sheets from Days 3, 4, 5, 12, 13, 14, 18, 19, and 20 (three from each stage) were recoded in this fashion. The procedure guaranteed that the expectations of the coder would not influence the scores obtained. The comparison of the original scores and those obtained by the new coders are shown in Fig. 2.

As a further check on coding bias, two of the original observers were recalled after a nine-month interval to recode one set of four data sheets from each of the three stages of the study, 12 sheets in all, also presented in random order. These two observers each recoded the descriptions of one of the other observers and their own data sheets completed at the time of the original study. The results are also shown in Fig. 2 for Days 2, 11, and 17. These points, marked △, indicate that the results obtained by having the original observers recode their own and someone else's data do not differ from those obtained when newly trained coders score the original data. In all cases the scores obtained described the effects of contingent and noncontingent reinforcement in the same way.

The comparison of the total score for the three target children obtained by the regular method and the tapes is shown in Fig. 3 and supports the validity of the 5-min time-sampling technique.

The data describing the effects of the different contingencies upon each of the three instructional styles (individual activities, group instruction, teams), failed to demonstrate that this was an important dimension in the present study. Day-to-day variability was greater for these smaller periods than for the entire session, but in all cases the proportion of study behavior dropped similarly in the absence of the contingent special event and rose during the final four days.

Just as the day-to-day variability increased as the analysis moved from the whole class to periods within each day's class, individual study behavior was

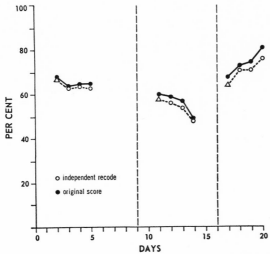

Fig. 2. Mean study behavior scores obtained by original observers compared with scores obtained by a panel of coders nine months after the completion of the study. Δ indicates scores obtained by two of the original observers who recoded the original data sheets nine months after the completion of the study.

more variable than the aggregate data for all 12 children. It is to be expected that students of different age, sex, and educational background will perform differently in comparable settings, but all 12 records shown in Fig. 4 indicate that noncontingent reinforcement was less effective in sustaining study behavior than contingent reinforcement. There was no case in which an individual student displayed more study behavior during the second stage of the study than was displayed during the first and third stages.

DISCUSSION

The results indicate that the contingent special event controlled much of the study behavior. In the time available it was not possible to continue the noncontingent stage until study behavior stabilized. With such an extension, study behavior might have gone lower.

A token system has much to recommend it from a practical standpoint, for there are many school activities (recess, early dismissal, extra-curricular events) which might be employed to develop and maintain higher levels of study behavior. Further, the classroom teacher responsible for the behavior of many students can manage a token system, but faces some difficulty in relying solely on verbal praise and attention as reinforcers. Behavior modification with social reinforcement requires constant monitoring of the subject's responding (Baer and Wolf, 1967). This can be done only on a very limited scale in a classroom by a single teacher.

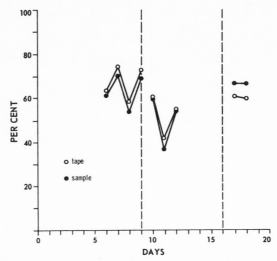

Fig. 3. Mean study behavior of various trios of children based on taped observations each day compared with written time-samples during the same period.

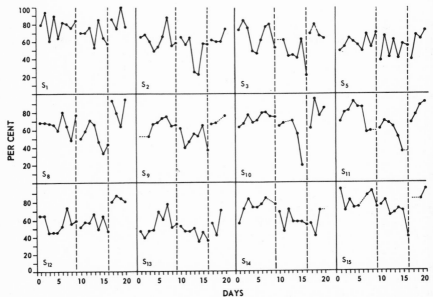

Fig. 4. Per cent of each individual child's behavior classified as study behavior under all conditions. Dotted lines without points indicate absence.

The day-to-day variability in individual records requires further study. At first glance it would appear that the individual fluctuations could indict the smoother curve of the group as resulting from the canceling effect of numerous measurement errors at the individual level. However, the several measurement checks suggest that other factors may have been more important in explaining the variability. For example, the practice of allowing the children to accumulate tokens from day to day may have produced some variability. It allowed the children to work hard and lend one day, and loaf and borrow the next; work hard and save one day, loaf and spend their savings the next. This would tend to produce a smooth curve for the group, since not everyone could lend at the same time nor could all borrow at once. The present practice in the preschool is to remove all tokens from the children's pockets after each day's session.

The next approximation toward a useful classroom observational technique will require additional measures to determine the effects of the students' changing behavior on the attending and helping behavior of the teachers. This work is now in progress.

It may be concluded that: (1) practical reinforcement contingencies can be established in a classroom; (2) the effects of various contingencies can be ascertained by direct observational techniques where the use of automated recording equipment is not practicable.

REFERENCES

Ayllon, T. and Azrin, N. H. The measurement and reinforcement of behavior of psychotics. *Journal of the Experimental Analysis of Behavior,* 1965, 8, 357-383.

Baer, D. M. and Wolf, M. M. The reinforcement contingency in preschool and remedial education. In Robert D. Hess and Roberta Meyer Baer (Eds.), *Early education: current theory, research, and practice.* Chicago: Aldine, 1968.

Birnbrauer, J. S., Wolf, M. M., Kidder, J. D., and Tague, C. E. Classroom behavior of retarded pupils with token reinforcement. *Journal of Experimental Child Psychology.* 1965, 2, 219-235.

14

The effects of teacher attention on following instructions in a kindergarten class

R. C. Schutte and B. L. Hopkins

A kindergarten class, composed of five girls ages 4.8 to 6 yr, participated in the study. In each of 20 daily sessions a sequence of 10 simple instructions was given to the class. In baseline sessions, the teacher did not interact with the students, other than to give instructions. During these sessions, the children followed the teacher's instructions 60% of the time. When the teacher began attending to each child if she followed an instruction, the mean percentage of instructions followed increased to 78%. Subsequently, the teacher again employed the baseline procedures and the percentage of instructions followed decreased to 68.7%. When the teacher again provided attention dependent on the children's following the instructions, the percentage of instructions followed increased to 83.7%. The results are consistent with research that has treated instructions as discriminative stimuli. The general findings are that consequences of instructed behavior determine the extent to which the instructions are followed.

Elementary school teachers often try to develop academic skills and appropriate general classroom behaviors by verbal suggestions and instructions. If the students do not reliably follow the teacher's instructions their behaviors are likely to be labeled as discipline or achievement problems. Many forms of advice have been proffered to teachers in attempts to help them develop better instructional control over their students. For example, Peckenpaugh (1958) suggested that teachers follow general commandments, such as be sincere, consistent, firm and friendly.

From *Journal of Applied Behavior Analysis,* 1970, 3, 117-122. Copyright 1970 by the Society for the Experimental Analysis of Behavior, Inc. Reprinted by permission.

This report is based on an MA thesis by the senior author, Behavior Modification Program, Rehabilitation Institute, Southern Illinois University. This research was made possible by the support and cooperation of the staff and school board of the Alto Pass Elementary School, Alto Pass, Illinois. The authors are particularly indebted to Mr. Robert W. MacVicar, Chancellor, Southern Illinois University for his encouragement and support. Reprints may be obtained from B. L. Hopkins, Rehabilitation Institute, Southern Illinois University, Carbondale, Illinois 62901.

A more precise approach to an analysis of instructional control problems results from the operant conditioning literature (Terrace, 1966; Skinner, 1957). This approach views instructions as discriminative stimuli that set the occasion for the occurrence of certain behaviors. Consequently, it is possible to analyze the functional relationship that exists between verbal instructional stimuli and the listener's response to determine what environmental variables control responding to instructions. Findley (1966) found a very rapid weakening of instructed behaviors for which there were no explicit consequences. Ayllon and Azrin (1964) observed that instructions had no lasting effects on simple behaviors of mental patients unless the behaviors were followed by reinforcement. Hopkins (1968), while working with a retarded subject, found that instructing the subject increased the frequency of desired behavior but that instructions then became progressively more ineffective unless followed by reinforcement. Zeilberger, Sampen, and Sloane (1968) showed that obedience will increase when differential reinforcement is employed as a consequence of instruction following behaviors.

Little experimentation has been devoted to instructional control in the classroom. Madsen, Becker, Thomas, Koser, and Plazer (1968) studied the reinforcing properties of the individual instruction, "Sit down!" Their data indicated that the instruction reinforced students' standing behaviors. However, they suggested that most children temporarily sat down when told to do so. Zimmerman, Zimmerman, and Russell (1969) found that tokens would maintain a higher rate of instruction-following behavior than would praise. Their study was one of the first to expose all students in a classroom to a single, specific set of differential reinforcement contingencies when verbal instructions were given to the class as a whole.

Recently reported studies have shown adult social attention to function as a reinforcer for a pre-school child's talking (Reynolds and Risley, 1968); smiling by retarded subjects (Hopkins, 1968); and outdoor play of a pre-school child (Buell, Stoddard, Harris, and Baer, 1968). Other studies have shown that differential teacher attention can be used to control typical classroom behaviors (Hall, Lund, and Jackson, 1968; Thomas, Becker, and Armstrong, 1968; Madsen, Becker, and Thomas, 1968; and Ward and Baker, 1968).

The present research suggests at least one practical solution to the problem of developing appropriate classroom instructional control. This solution would be to combine the findings that the effects of instructions are determined by the consequences of the instructed behaviors and that teacher attention is a suitable and convenient reinforcer for the behavior of school children. Therefore, this experiment examined the effects of teacher attention on students' following the teacher's instructions.

METHOD

Subjects

Five girls, 4.8 to 6 yr of age, who were enrolled in the afternoon kindergarten at the Alto Pass Grade School in Alto Pass, Illinois, served.

Setting

The study was conducted in the school's kindergarten classroom. The room contained a teacher's desk and chair, a low rectangular table, eight student chairs, toys stacked against one wall, and a steel cabinet used to store sleeping mats and educational materials.

Instructions and Response Criteria

An arbitrary list of 10 instructions, which were frequently given by the teachers, was selected for use in this experiment. The 10 instructions and the behavioral criteria for each instruction are listed below. In every case except those noted, the indicated behaviors had to occur within 15 sec of the time the teacher spoke the instructions to be considered as meeting the criterion.

1. "Pick up the toys." This referred to any toys not in the appropriate containers against the wall. A child would pick up at least one toy or piece of a toy and place it in the container.

2. "Sit down." A child would be seated in her chair with the chair within 3 ft of the table.

3. "Come and get a pencil and paper." The child was to walk to the teacher's desk and pick up a pencil and paper or be in line to get the pencil and paper within the 15-sec time limit.

4. "Write your name on the paper." The child would print her complete first name in any location on the paper she had obtained from the teacher's desk.

5. "Fold your paper." The child would fold the piece of paper with her name written on it so that it covered approximately one-half the area it did before being folded.

6. "Bring the pencil and paper to my desk." The child was to place the pencil and piece of paper on the teacher's desk or be in line to place them on the desk within the 15-sec time limit.

7. "Put your chair on the table." The child would pick up her chair from the floor, turn it upside down, and place the seat of the chair on top the table with the back hanging off the table so that the chair would remain on the table when it was no longer supported by her.

8. "Get your mat out." The child would lift her mat from the shelf of the steel cabinet and remove it to any location outside of the cabinet.

9. "Lie down." The child was to be in a horizontal position any place on the floor of the room.

10. "Be quiet." There were to be no voice or throat sounds or any sounds made with the hands or feet for 15 sec after the instructions.

Procedures

The students were brought into the classroom at 12:30 p.m. each day after the noon recess. They were first told that they could play for 5 or 10 min. At the end of this period of free-play the teacher began giving the instructions in the order listed. Generally, each instruction was given only once for the entire group of children with a 2-min interval between successive instructions.

The sequence in which the instructions were given and the timing of instructions approximated a normal classroom procedure. The children got out sufficient toys during free play that there was always a a toy for every child to pick up. The free play and the picking up of toys insured that none of the children were sitting when they were told to sit down. Once a child had a pencil and piece of paper, she would generally draw some simple picture or print letters during the time she had the paper, etc.

These general procedures were maintained for 20 daily sessions with each session lasting for about 20 min. After the tenth session, the teacher volunteered that an occasional exception to the general procedures had been made. This exception was a repetition of certain instructions when, in the teacher's opinion, the children may have been making so much noise that they could not hear the instruction. The teacher was not sure but thought that she had made this exception for three individual instructions. She did not remember on which days she had repeated the instructions or which instructions were involved. The possibility that this exception could have an effect on the children's responses was explained and the teacher was asked to avoid repeating instructions even if they might not have been heard by the children. On frequent subsequent checks, the teacher indicated that all instructions were presented exactly once each day.

Recording

For each session of the experiment, the teacher was equipped with a stopwatch and a score sheet that listed the 10 instructions and each student's name. The stopwatch was used to time the interval beginning with the presentation of an instruction and ending 15 sec later and the interval beginning with an instruction and ending 2 min later when the next instruction was presented. The teacher recorded an "X" on the score sheet for a student if the student emitted the appropriate response within 15 sec after an instruction. If the appropriate behavior did not occur, or occurred later than 15 sec after the instruction, an "O" was recorded.

To determine the extent to which the data could be reliably recorded, an observer, who had been familiarized with the instructions and the response criteria, sat in the classroom during three separate sessions and independently scored each student's responses for each instruction. This observer was similarly equipped with a stopwatch and score sheet. One reliability check was taken during the condition named below as Contingent Teacher Attention I, another during Baseline II, and the third during Contingent Teacher Attention II. Percent agreement was computed as number of agreements divided by the total number of possible agreements. The per cent of agreement for these three sessions was 97.5, 94, and 100 respectively. The total number of possible agreements was 40 50, and 40 respectively.

Experimental Conditions

Two different experimental conditions were employed during the experiment and each condition was scheduled twice. The only difference between the two conditions was the extent to which the teacher interacted with the children and the circumstances under which these interactions occurred.

Baseline I

Throughout the sessions under this condition, the teacher, except for giving the instructions, spoke to the children only if asked a direct question; she in no way responded differentially to the children when they followed or failed to follow an instruction. This condition was in effect for the first five sessions o the experiment.

Contingent Teacher Attention I

During this condition, the teacher differentially attended to each student in the class who emitted the appropriate criterion response within 15 sec after an instruction. This attention consisted of the teacher's emitting some natural verbal response such as: "My, aren't you good today, Lidia?", "That's nice!" or "Thank you for doing what I asked, Rhoda!" Occasionally, the teacher would touch or pat the child on the head while talking to her. In all cases, the teacher tried to attend to or praise the children while the criterion responses were occurring or as soon after the response occurred as was practical. This condition was in effect from Session 6 through Session 11.

Baseline II

During Sessions 12 through 16, conditions identical to those employed during Baseline I were in effect.

Contingent Teacher Attention II

Attention was again given each child whenever she followed one of the teacher's instructions. This condition was in effect for the last four sessions.

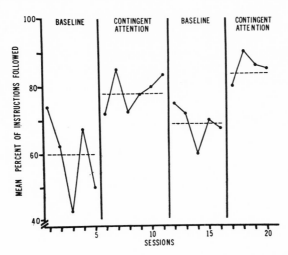

Fig. 1. The daily mean per cent of instructions followed by all subjects for each session. The horizontal dashed line under each condition shows the mean per cent of instructions followed for all observations within that condition.

RESULTS

Figure 1 displays the mean per cent of instructions followed by the children present on a given day. Each data point was obtained by dividing the total number of instructions followed by the children on that day by the total number of opportunities to follow instructions. For example, during Session 1, the five children followed instructions 37 times out of the 50 possibilities; a mean of 74% of instructions followed.

During Baseline I, the daily mean per cent of instructions followed varied between 42.5 and 74. The mean of these daily means was 60%. There were no obvious trends present in the data during this condition.

When the teacher began attending to the children whenever they followed an instruction, Sessions 6 through 11, the mean per cent of instructions followed on each day increased abruptly. The mean over sessions during this condition was 78%. The daily means varied from 72 to 85%. The average mean percentage of instructions followed during this condition was 30% greater than the average mean percentage during the first baseline condition.

When the teacher no longer attended to the student's instruction-following behaviors, from Sessions 12 through 16, the mean per cent of instructions followed decreased to 68.7. The daily means varied between 60 and 70%. There is a slight suggestion of a downward trend in the percentage of instructions followed for the five days during Baseline II.

When the teacher again began attending to the children when they followed instructions, the daily mean per cent of instructions followed varied between 80 and 90. The average mean percentage for this condition was 83.7. This was 39.5% greater than in Baseline I and 21.9% greater than in Baseline II.

The mean percentage of instructions followed by the individual students during the four experimental conditions is shown in Fig. 2. One of these data points represents the total number of instructions followed by the indicated student during that particular condition, divided by the number of opportunities to follow instructions.

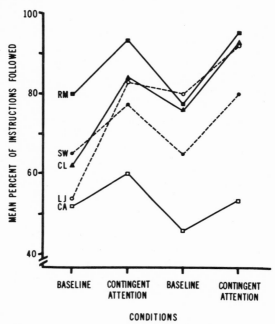

Fig. 2. The mean per cent of instructions followed in each condition for each of the five subjects, C.L., C.A., L.J., S.W., and R.M.

These individual data are generally qualitatively consistent with the group data displayed in Fig. 1. For four of the subjects, R.M., S.W., C.L., and C.A., the mean percentage of instructions followed during the two conditions in which the teacher attended to the children when they followed instructions is clearly higher than the percentage during the two baseline conditions. For the fifth student, L.J., this relationship also holds, but the difference in the percentage of instructions followed during the first contingent attention condition is only slightly greater than the percentage during the second baseline condition.

Student absences from school were not differentially correlated with changes in the experimental conditions. C.L. was absent from Session 11, C.A. from Session 19, L.J. from Session 20, S.W. from Sessions 4, 7, 8, 16, and 18, and R.M. from Sessions 2, 3, 5, 9, 10, 11, and 12. Therefore, the group data could not be deceptively biased by the differential presence during contingent attention conditions of children who followed a large percentage of the instructions given by the teacher.

DISCUSSION

This research repeated the frequent finding that teacher attention is an effective positive reinforcer for the behaviors of preschool and elementary school children (Hall et al. 1968; Thomas et al. 1968; Madsen et al. 1968; and Ward and Baker, 1968). More importantly, contingent teacher attention reliably increased the probability that every child in this study followed the teacher's instructions.

The practical importance of these findings is potentially great. A teacher faced with students who are difficult to manage or who fail to follow instructions related to academic work may substantially improve her instructional control by simply attending to the students at appropriate times.

Some limitations to the application of the present study should be noted. The present study used normal, preschool children as subjects and generalization to classrooms with older or non-normal subjects should be done cautiously pending further study. For some children, social attention may not be reinforcing. Lövaas, Freitag, Rubenstein, Schaffer, and Simmons (1966) observed this to be true of some autistic children.

It is also possible that peers can exert considerable control over the behaviors of individual students. It was casually observed in the present study that students would urge a slower student to hurry even though there was no apparent reinforcement for doing so. Such interactions could exert control over the instructed behaviors. At this time it is not clear whether such peer interaction would serve as aversive stimuli, which a student might escape by following instructions, or reinforcing stimuli, which would strengthen a student's not following the instructions. Therefore, it is possible that peer interactions could either support or hinder a teacher's instructional control.

The instructions in the present study were employed as discriminative stimuli to occasion desired behaviors. Madsen, Becker, Thomas, Koser, and Plazer (1968), however, showed that instructions also have reinforcing properties and could cause an increase rather than a decrease in undesirable behaviors, which they frequently follow. Thus, it is possible that instructions should not be given when undesirable or competing behaviors are occurring.

Previous research has similarly substantiated the casual observation that instructions may exert some control over the behaviors of a variety of human subjects (Zimmerman et al., 1969; Ayllon and Azrin, 1964; Hopkins, 1968; and Findley, 1966). However, in all of these studies, and in the present research, the permanence and magnitude of the control is dependent on the extent to which appropriate consequences follow the instructed behaviors.

REFERENCES

Ayllon, T. and Azrin, N. H. Reinforcement and instructions with mental patients. *Journal of the Experimental Analysis of Behavior,* 1964, 7, 327-331.

Buell, Joan, Stoddard, Patricia, Harris, Florence, R., and Baer, D. M. Collateral social development accompanying reinforcement of outdoor play in a preschool child. *Journal of Applied Behavior Analysis,* 1968, 1, 167-173.

Findley, J. D. Programmed environments for the experimental analysis of human behavior. In W. K. Honig (Ed.), *Operant behavior: areas of research and application.* New York: Appleton-Century-Crofts, 1966. Pp. 827-848.

Hall, R. V., Lund, Diane, and Jackson, Deloris. Effects of teacher attention on study behavior. *Journal of Applied Behavior Analysis,* 1968, 1, 1-12.

Hopkins, B. L. Effects of candy and social reinforcement, instructions, and reinforcement schedule leaning on the modification and maintenance of smiling. *Journal of Applied Behavior Analysis,* 1968, 1, 121-278.

Madsen, C. H., Becker, W. C., and Thomas, D. R. Rules, praise, and ignoring: elements of elementary classroom control. *Journal of Applied Behavior Analysis,* 1968, 1, 139-150.

Peckenpaugh, Adah. The teacher and preventive discipline. *NEA Journal,* 1958, 47, 372-373.

Reynolds, Nancy J. and Risley, T. R. The role of social and material reinforcers in increasing talking of a disadvantaged preschool child. *Journal of Applied Behavior Analysis,* 1968, 1, 253-262.

Madsen, C. H., Becker, W. C., Thomas, D. R., Koser, Linda, and Plager, Elaine. An analysis of the reinforcing function of "sit-down" commands. In R. K. Parker (Ed.), *Readings in educational psychology.* Boston: Allyn and Bacon, 1968. Pp. 265-278.

Skinner, B. F. *Verbal behavior.* New York: Appleton-Century-Crofts, 1957.

Terrace, H. S. Stimulus control. In W. K. Honig (Ed.), *Operant behavior: areas of research and application.* New York: Appleton-Century-Crofts, 1966. Pp. 271-344.

Thomas, D. R., Becker, W. C., and Armstrong, Marianne. Production and elimination of disruptive classroom behavior by systematically varying teacher's behavior. *Journal of Applied Behavior Analysis,* 1968, I, 35-45.

Ward, M. H. and Baker, B. L. Reinforcement therapy in the classroom. *Journal of Applied Behavior Analysis,* 1968, 1, 323-328.

Zeilberger, Jane, Sampen, Sue E., and Sloane, H. N. Modification of a child's problem behaviors in the home with the mother as therapist. *Journal of Applied Behavior Analysis,* 1968, 1, 47-53.

Zimmerman, Elaine H., Zimmerman, J., and Russell, C. D. Differential effects of token reinforcement on instruction-following behavior in retarded students instructed as a group. *Journal of Applied Behavior Analysis,* 1969, 2, 101-112.

15

Effects of teacher attention on study behavior

R. Vance Hall, Diane Lund, and Deloris Jackson

The effects of contingent teacher attention on study behavior were investigated. Individual rates of study were recorded for one first-grade and five third-grade pupils who had high rates of disruptive or dawdling behavior. A reinforcement period (in which teacher attention followed study behavior and non-study behaviors were ignored) resulted in sharply increased study rates. A brief reversal of the contingency (attention occurred only after periods of non-study behavior) again produced low rates of study. Reinstatement of teacher attention as reinforcement for study once again markedly increased study behavior. Follow-up observations indicated that the higher study rates were maintained after the formal program terminated.

A series of studies carried out in preschools by Harris, Wolf, and Baer (1964) and their colleagues demonstrated the effectiveness of contingent teacher atten-

From *Journal of Applied Behavior Analysis,* 1968, 1, 1-12. Copyright 1968 by the Society for the Experimental Analysis of Behavior, Inc. Reprinted by permission.

The authors wish to express appreciation to Dr. O. L. Plucker, Ted Gray, Alonzo Plough, Clarence Glasse, Carl Bruce, Natalie Barge, Lawrence Franklin, and Audrey Jackson of the Kansas City, Kansas, Public Schools and Wallace Henning, University of Kansas, without whose cooperation and active participation these studies would not have been possible. Special tribute is due to Dr. Montrose M. Wolf and Dr. Todd R. Risley for their many contributions in developing research strategy and for their continuing encouragement. We are also indebted to Dr. R. L. Schiefelbusch, Director of the Bureau of Child Research, and administrative director of the project, who provided essential administrative support and counsel. Reprints may be obtained from R. Vance Hall, 2021 North Third St., Kansas City, Kansas 66101.

The research was carried out as part of the Juniper Gardens Children's Project, a program of research on the development of culturally deprived children and was partially supported by the Office of Economic Opportunity: (OEO KAN CAP 694/1, Bureau of Child Research, Kansas University Medical Center) and the National Institute of Child Health and Human Development: (HD-00870-(04) and HD 03144-01, Bureau of Child Research, University of Kansas).

tion in modifying behavior problems of preschool children. In these studies inappropriate and/or undesirable rates of isolate play (Allen, Hart, Buell, Harris, and Wolf, 1964), crying (Hart, Allen, Buell, Harris, and Wolf, 1964), crawling (Harris, Johnston, Kelley, and Wolf, 1964), and a number of other problem behaviors were modified by systematically manipulating teacher-attention consequences of the behaviors. Similarly, teacher and peer attention were manipulated by Zimmerman and Zimmerman (1962), Patterson (1965), and Hall and Broden (1967) to reduce problem behaviors and increase appropriate responses of children enrolled in special classrooms.

To date, however, there has been little systematic research in the application of social reinforcement by teachers in the regular school classroom beyond the successful case studies reported by Becker, Madsen, Arnold, and Thomas (1967) in which no attempt was made to evaluate the reliability of these procedures through experimental reversals.

The present studies analyzed experimentally the reliability with which teachers could modify the study behavior of children of poverty-area classrooms by systematic manipulation of contingent attention.

GENERAL PROCEDURES

Subjects and Setting

The studies were carried out in classrooms of two elementary schools located in the most economically deprived area of Kansas City, Kansas. Teachers who participated were recommended by their principals. The teachers nominated pupils who were disruptive or dawdled. They were told that one or two observers would come regularly to their classrooms to record behavior rates of these pupils.

Observation

The observers used recording sheets lined with triple rows of squares, as shown in Fig. 1. Each square represented an interval of 10 sec. The first row was used to record the behavior of the student. (The definition of study behavior was somewhat different for each student and depended on the subject matter taught. Generally, study behavior was defined as orientation toward the appropriate object or person: assigned course materials, lecturing teacher, or reciting classmates, as well as class participation by the student when requested by the teacher. Since each pupil was observed during the same class period, however, the response definition was consistent for each student throughout the course of an experiment.) Teacher verbalizations to the student were recorded in the second row. The third row was used to record occasions when the teacher was within a 3-ft proximity to the student.

These observations were made during each 10-sec interval of each session. The observers sat at the rear or the side of the classroom, and avoided eye contact or any other interaction with pupils during observation sessions.

Inter-observer agreement was analyzed by having a second observer periodically make a simultaneous observation record. Agreement of the two records was checked interval by interval. The percentage of agreement of the records [no. agreements x 100 ÷ (no. agreements + no. disagreements)] yielded the percentage of inter-observer agreement.

EXPERIMENTAL CONDITIONS

Baseline

Rates of study were obtained for the selected pupils. Thirty-minute observations were scheduled at a time each day when the pupils were to be working in their seats. In most cases observations were made two to four times per week. After obtaining a minimum of two weeks of baseline, the students' study rates were presented graphically to the teachers. Then, selected studies (Hart et al., 1964; Allen et al., 1964; Hall and Broden, 1967) were presented to the teachers, the fundamentals of social reinforcement were discussed, and a pupil was selected for systematic study.

SECONDS   ONE MINUTE

10 20 30 40 50 60

N	N	N	N	N	N	N	S	S	S	N	N	S	S	S	S	N	N	N	N	N	N	N	N
		T	T	T							T											T	T
			/	/					/		/												

ROW 1   N   Non-Study Behavior.   S   Study Behavior.

ROW 2   T   Teacher Verbalization directed toward pupil.

ROW 3   /   Teacher Proximity (Teacher within three feet).

Fig. 1. Observer recording sheet and symbol key.

Reinforcement[1]

During reinforcement sessions the observer held up a small square of colored paper in a manner not likely to be noticed by the pupil whenever the pupil was engaged in study. Upon this signal, the teacher attended to the child, moved to his desk, made some verbal comment, gave him a pat on the shoulder, or the like. During weekly after-school sessions, experimenters and teachers discussed the rate of study achieved by the pupil and the effectiveness of attention provided by the teacher, and made occasional adjustments in instructions as required.

Reversal

When a satisfactory rate of study had been achieved, the observer discontinued signaling and (as much as possible) the teacher returned to her former pattern, which typically consisted of attending to nonstudy behavior.

Reinforcement$_2$

When the effect of the reversal condition had been observed, social reinforcement of study was reinstituted. When high study rates were achieved again, the teacher continued reinforcement of study behavior without the observer's signals.

Post Checks

Whenever possible, periodic post-checks were made through the remainder of the year to determine whether the new levels of study were being maintained.

Correlated Behavioral Changes

Where possible, other behavioral changes, including teacher reports, grades, and other records of academic achievement were recorded. Because such data are difficult to evaluate, their importance should not be unduly stressed.

INDIVIDUAL EXPERIMENTS

Robbie

Robbie was chosen because he was considered a particularly disruptive pupil who studied very little. Figure 2 presents a record of Robbie's study behavior, defined as having pencil on paper during 5 sec or more of the 10-sec interval. During baseline, study behavior occurred in 25% of the intervals observed during the class spelling period. The behaviors which occupied the other 75% of his time included snapping rubber bands, playing with toys from his pocket, talking and laughing with peers, slowly drinking the halfpint of milk served earlier in the morning, and subsequently playing with the empty carton.

During the baseline period the teacher would often urge Robbie to work, put his milk carton away, etc. In fact, 55% of the teacher attention he received followed nonstudy behavior. Robbie engaged in continuous study for 60 sec or more only two or three times during a 30-min observation.

Following baseline determination, whenever Robbie had engaged in 1 min of continuous study the observer signaled his teacher. On this cue, the teacher approached Robbie, saying, "Very good work, Robbie," "I see you are studying," or some similar remark. She discontinued giving attention for nonstudy behaviors including those which were disruptive to the class.

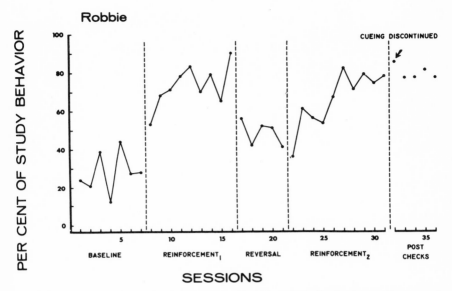

Fig. 2. A record of study behavior for Robbie. Post-check observations were made during the fourth, sixth, seventh, twelfth, and fourteenth weeks after the completion of Reinforcement₂ condition.

Figure 2 shows an increased study rate during the first day of the first reinforcement period. The study rate continued to rise thereafter and was recorded in 71% of the intervals during this period.

During the brief reversal period, when reinforcement of study was discontinued, the study rate dropped to a mean of 50%. However, when reinforcement for study was reinstituted, Robbie's study rate again increased, stabilizing at a rate ranging between 70% and 80% of the observation sessions. Subsequent followup checks made during the 14 weeks that followed (after signaling of the teacher was discontinued) indicated that study was being maintained at a mean rate of 79%. Periodic checks made during each condition of the experiment revealed that agreement of observation ranged from 89% to 93%.

Robbie's teacher reported behavior changes correlated with his increased rate of study. During Baseline, she reported that Robbie did not complete written assignments. He missed 2 of 10, 5 of 10, and 6 of 10 words on three spelling tests given during Baseline. By the final week of Reinforcement₂ she reported that he typically finished his initial assignment and then continued on to other assigned work without prompting. Disruptive behavior had diminished and it was noted that he continued to study while he drank his milk and did not play with the carton when finished. He missed 1 of 10 words on his weekly spelling test.

Rose

Rose was a classmate of Robbie's. Baseline observations were made during the math and/or spelling study periods. The mean rate of study during Baseline was 30%, fluctuating from 0% to 71%. Her nonstudy behaviors included laying her head on the desk, taking off her shoes, talking, and being out of her seat.

On the day her teacher was first to reinforce Rose's study behavior, Rose did not study at all, and the teacher was thus unable to provide reinforcement. Therefore, beginning with the second reinforcement session, the teacher attended to behavior that approximated study (e.g., getting out pencil or paper, or opening her book to the correct page). Once these behaviors were reinforced, study behavior quickly followed, was in turn reinforced, and had risen to 57% by the third reinforcement session.

During the fourth session, however, study dropped to 25%. An analysis of the data indicated Rose had increased in out-of-seat behavior, to have her papers checked and to ask questions. Consequently her teacher thereafter ignored Rose when she approached but attended to her immediately if she raised her hand while seated. There was an immediate drop in out-of-seat behavior and a concurrent increase in study behavior. As can be seen in Fig. 3, during the last 10 sessions of Reinforcement$_1$ study behavior ranged between 74% and 92%, the mean rate for the entire period being approximately 71%. A high rate of study was maintained after the observer discontinued signaling after the thirteenth reinforcement session.

During the four reversal sessions, study was recorded in only 29% of the intervals. However, a return to attention for study immediately increased study behavior and during the second reinforcement period study was recorded in 72% of the observed intervals. Observer agreement measured under each condition ranged from 90% to 95%.

An analysis of the attention provided Rose by her teacher demonstrated that it was not the amount of attention, but its delivery contingent on study which produced the changes in this behavior. Figure 4 shows these amounts, and the general lack of relationship between amount of attention and experimental procedures.

In fact these data show that when teacher attention occurred primarily during nonstudy intervals there was a low rate of study. When teacher attention occurred primarily during study intervals there was a higher rate of study. Figure 4 also shows that the mean rate of total teacher attention remained relatively stable throughout the various experimental phases, rising somewhat in the Reinforcement$_1$ and Reversal phases and declining to baseline levels in the Reinforcement$_2$ phase.

Rose's grades at the end of the baseline phase were D in arithmetic and D in spelling. Her grades for the reinforcement phase of the experiment were C− in arithmetic and B in spelling.

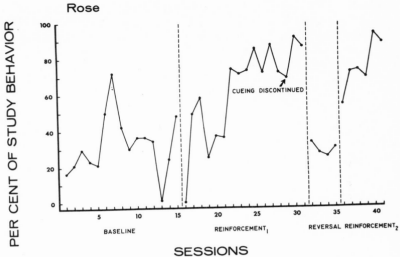

Fig. 3. A record of study behavior for Rose.

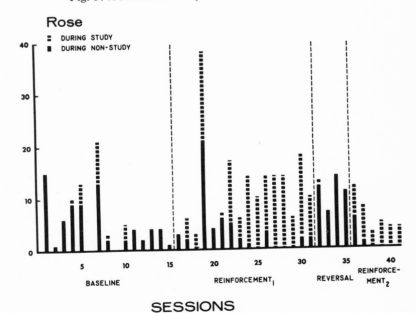

Fig. 4. A record of teacher attention for Rose.

Ken

Ken was one of the other 41 pupils in Rose's class. He had a wide range of disruptive behaviors including playing with toys from his pockets, rolling pencils on the floor and desk, and jiggling and wiggling in his seat. His teacher had tried isolating him from his peers, reprimanding by the principal, and spanking to control his behavior. These efforts apparently had been ineffective. Study behavior ranged from 10% to 60%, with a mean rate of 37%, as seen in Fig. 5.

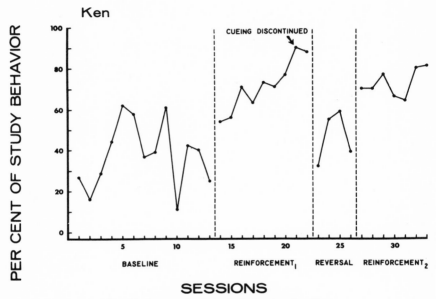

Fig. 5. A record of study behavior for Ken.

Reinforcement of study behavior was begun at the same time for both Ken and Rose. The observer used different colored cards to signal when the behavior of each pupil was to be reinforced. Ken's study increased to a mean rate of 71% under reinforcement conditions. However, during his brief reversal, Ken's rate of study was again about 37%. The re-introduction of the reinforcement for study recovered study behavior in 70% of the observed intervals. Agreement between observers measured during each of the conditions ranged from 90% to 92%.

Ken's teacher reported several correlated behavior changes. Before the experiment she had stated that he rarely, if ever, finished an assignment. His grades for the baseline period included D in math, D in spelling and U (unsatisfactory) in conduct. After reinforcement was instituted his teacher reported a marked decrease in disruptive behavior and stated, "He's getting his work done on time now." Ken's report card grades subsequently were C in spelling, C in arithmetic and S (satisfactory) in conduct.

Gary

Gary, a third-grade boy in another classroom of 39 pupils, was chosen as a subject because he failed to complete assignments. The course of Gary's program is shown in Fig. 5. Observations made during the 30-min morning math period indicated that Gary engaged in study during 43% of the 10-sec intervals observed. Nonstudy behaviors included beating his desk with a pencil, chewing and licking pages of books, moving his chair back and forth in unison with a classmate, banging his chair on the floor, blowing bubbles and making noises while drinking his milk, and punching holes in the carton so that milk flowed onto the desk. He would also gaze out the window or around the room and would say "This is too hard," "Shoot, I can't do this," and "How did you say to work it?"

Gary had been observed to engage in appropriate study for 60 sec or more at least one to three times during most study periods. The observer thus signaled the teacher whenever Gary had engaged in study for six consecutive 10-sec intervals, and he was attended to by the teacher only on those occasions.

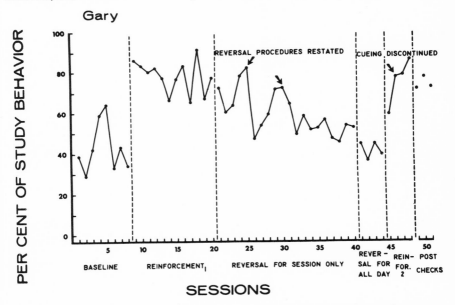

Fig. 6. A record of study behavior for Gary. Post-check observations were made during the first, fourth, and tenth weeks after completion of Reinforcement₂ condition.

As shown in Fig. 6, reinforcement produced a marked increase in studying. With the rise, almost all disruptive behavior disappeared. He still talked out of turn in class but typically to say "I know how to do it," "He's wrong," "Can I do it, teacher?", "Oh, this is easy." Gary engaged in study during approximately 77% of the 10-sec intervals observed during Reinforcement$_1$.

After the twentieth session a reversal was programmed, and the teacher was signaled whenever Gary engaged in nonstudy behavior for 30 sec. When this occurred, the teacher gave Gary a reminder to get back to work. No attention was given for study behavior.

As can be seen, this resulted in a fluctuating but declining rate of study during the 30-min math period. At this point it was noted that Gary's rate of study was again rising, and that the teacher was in fact providing intermittent reinforcement for study. Therefore, on two occasions the procedures for reversal were gone over once again in conference with the teacher and a subsequent slow but steady decline in study rate was achieved. There also appeared to be an increase in disruptive behavior. The mean rate of study at this point of Reversal was about 60%.

It was then noted that a more rapid reversal effect had been brought about in the previous studies, probably because that teacher had carried out reversal procedures for the entire day whereas Gary's teacher practiced reversal only during the 30-min observation period. Reversal of reinforcement conditions was, therefore, extended to the entire day. The mean rate for these sessions was approximately 42%. However, resumption of reinforcement immediately recovered a study rate of 60% which increased as reinforcement continued. After the first day of this reinforcement phase the teacher expressed confidence in being able to work without cues from the observer. Signaling was therefore discontinued without loss of effect. Periodic checks made during subsequent weeks indicated study behavior was being maintained at a level higher than 70%. The reliability of observation measured during each condition ranged from 92% to 96%.

Joan

Joan, one of Gary's classmates, did not disrupt the class or bother other pupils but was selected because she dawdled. Typically, during arithmetic study period, she would lay her head on her desk and stare toward the windows or her classmates. At other times she would pull at or straighten her clothing, dig in her desk, pick or pull at her hair, nose or fingernails, draw on the desk top or play with her purse. During baseline her study rate was approximately 35%.

During the Reinforcement$_1$ phase, after the observer signaled that 60 sec of continuous study had occurred, the teacher made comments such as, "That's a good girl", and often tugged lightly at Joan's hair or patted her shoulder. As can be seen in Fig. 7 this resulted in an immediate increase in study behavior. The observer discontinued signaling after Session 20 when the teacher stated it was no longer necessary. Though the study rate fluctuated in subsequent sessions it generally remained higher than in Baseline. The lowest rate of study came in Session 26 when Joan was without a pencil through the first part of the session. Study was observed in 73% of the intervals of the Reinforcement$_1$ phase.

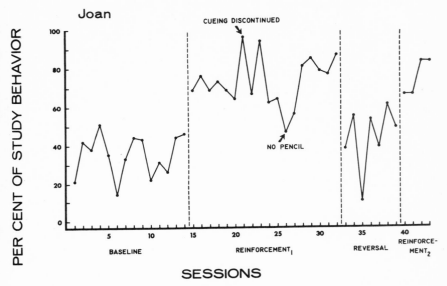

Fig. 7. A record of study behavior for Joan.

During Reversal, Joan's study rate declined markedly and play with clothes, pencils, and head on desk behaviors appeared to increase. The mean study rate for the reversal sessions was approximately 43%. Reinstatement of reinforcement for study, however, resulted in a rapid return to a study rate of approximately 73%. No post-checks were obtained because of the close of school. Observer agreement ranged from 93% to 97%.

Joan's arithmetic-paper grades provided interesting correlated data. During Baseline a sampling of her arithmetic papers showed an average grade of F. During Reinforcement₁ they averaged C. All her arithmetic papers graded during Reversal were graded F. In Reinforcement₂ the average grade on arithmetic papers was C−.

Levi

Levi was a first-grade boy who was selected because of his disruptive behaviors. Although he achieved at a fairly high level, he often disturbed the class by making loud noises, by getting out of his seat, and by talking to other students. The school counselor suggested using reinforcement techniques after counselling with the pupil and teacher brought about no apparent improvement in Levi's behavior.

The counselor was trained in the observation procedures and he obtained baseline rates of Levi's study and disruptive behaviors during seatwork time. A second observer was used to supplement data gathering. During Baseline, Levi's rate of study was approximately 68%, ranging from 34% to 79%. An analysis of teacher attention during baseline showed that although Levi had a relatively high rate of study, he received almost no teacher attention except when he was disruptive (i.e., made noise or other behaviors which overtly disturbed his neighbors and/or the teacher).

During Reinforcement$_1$ the teacher provided social reinforcement for study and, as much as possible, ignored all disruptive behavior. No signals were used since Levi had a relatively high study rate and the teacher was confident she could carry out reinforcement without cues. Figure 8 shows that study occurred in approximately 88% of the intervals of Reinforcement$_1$ and at no time went below that of the highest baseline rate. A brief reversal produced a marked decrease in study to a mean rate of 60%. However, when reinforcement for study was reinstated study again rose to above the baseline rate (approximately 85%).

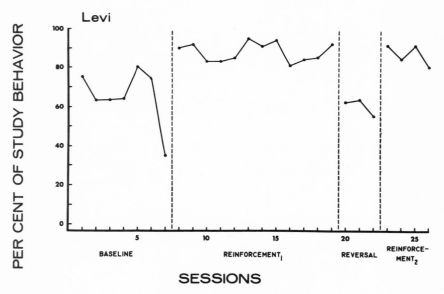

Fig. 8. A record of study behavior for Levi.

Figure 9 presents the disruptive behavior data for the four periods of the experiment. Disruptive behavior was defined to occur when Levi made noises, got out of his seat or talked to other students and the response appeared to be noticed by the teacher or another student. During Baseline the mean rate of disruptive behavior was 7%. During Reinforcement$_1$ the mean rate declined to 2.2%. During the brief Reversal phase the mean rate rose to 3.2%. In Reinforcement$_2$ the rate declined to an almost negligible 0.25%. No followup data were obtained because of the close of the school year. Observer agreement measured under each condition was consistently over 80%.

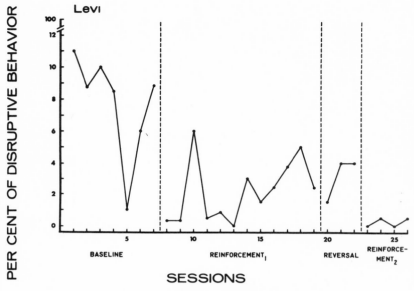

Fig. 9. A record of disruptive behavior for Levi.

The teacher and the school counselor reported at the conclusion of the experiment that in their opinion Levi was no longer a disruptive pupil.

DISCUSSION

These studies indicate clearly that the contingent use of teacher attention can be a quick and effective means of developing desirable classroom behavior. Effective teachers have long known that casually praising desired behaviors and generally ignoring disruptive ones can be useful procedures for helping maintain good classroom discipline. What may appear surprising to school personnel, however, is the degree to which student behavior responds to thoroughly systematic teacher attention.

One purpose of these studies was to determine whether the procedures could be carried out by teachers in public school classrooms. Although these teachers were initially unfamiliar with reinforcement principles and had had no prior experience with the procedures, they were clearly able to carry them out with important effect. The fact that they were carried out in crowded classrooms of schools of an urban poverty area underscores this point. In such areas one would expect a high incidence of disruptive behaviors and low interest in academic achievement, conditions generally conceded to make teaching and motivation for study difficult. Yet, with relatively slight adjustment of the social environment, it was possible to increase rates of study with comparative ease.

The teachers in these studies did not have poor general control of their classrooms. Most of their pupils seemed to apply themselves fairly well, although a few did not. When their baseline data were analyzed, it became clear that these pupils were in effet being motivated not to study. It became apparent that for these pupils, most teacher attention was received during nonstudy intervals rather than when they were studying. This was not surprising since many of the nonstudy behaviors were disruptive and thus seemed to the teacher to require some reprimand.

Several aspects of the teacher training program appear worthy of mention. During baseline, as far as the teacher was concerned, the primary purpose was to determine study rates. After baseline, a simple procedure designed to increase those study rates was emphasized (rather than the fact that the teacher had in all probability been reinforcing the very behaviors which were causing concern).

The teacher was constantly informed of the results of each day's sessions and its graphed outcome. These daily contacts, plus weekly conferences in which the procedures were discussed and the teacher was praised for bringing about the desired behavioral changes, may have been central to the process of a successful study.

The teachers readily accepted the advisability of carrying out a brief reversal when it was presented as a means of testing for a causal relationship between teacher attention and pupil behavior. All, however, felt reversal sessions were aversive and were glad when they were terminated.

These procedures did not seem to interfere greatly with ongoing teaching duties. For one thing they did not necessarily result in more total teacher attention for a pupil. In fact, the teachers had more time for constructive teaching of all pupils because of the decrease in disruptive behaviors in the classroom.

Two teachers reported they were able to utilize systematic attention to increase appropriate study of other pupils in their classrooms who were not included in these studies. No corroborative data were collected to verify their reports. Investigation of the degree to which this kind of generalization occurs should be a goal of further research, however, since such a result would be highly desirable.

In the first five subjects, cueing of the teacher was initially used to make certain that the teacher could discriminate when study behavior was occurring. Later, cueing was discontinued without loss of effectiveness. In the case of Levi, cueing was never used. Further research will be needed to determine how often cueing contributes to the efficiency of the procedures.

In one classroom, a teacher was unable to carry out the procedures in spite of the fact that the same orientation and training processes were used which had previously proved successful. Although the teacher seemed sincere in her efforts to reinforce study, she observably continued to give a high rate of attention for non-study behaviors. Observations indicated that the teacher gave almost no praise or positive attention to any member of the class. Virtually her entire verbal repertoire consisted of commands, reprimands, and admonitions. Consequently the teacher was instructed to provide positive verbal reinforcement for appropriate behavior of all class members. This did result in a measurable increase in the number of positive statements made to individuals and to the class. According to both the teacher and the observers, this greatly improved general classroom behavior. Only slight increases in study were recorded for the two pupils for whom data were available, however, and the close of the school year prevented further manipulations.

This failure prompted the authors to begin developing a system for recording appropriate behavior rates for an entire class. It also indicates that there may be certain teachers who need different or more intensive training to carry out these procedures effectively.

Finally, it should be noted that the pupils of this study did have at least a minimal level of proficiency in performing the academic tasks and thus seemed to profit from the increased time they spent in study. The teachers apparently assigned study tasks within the range of the pupils' skills, and correlated gains in academic achievement were noted. If teachers were to use the procedures but failed to provide materials within the range of the pupil's level of skill, it is unlikely that much gain in achievement would result.

REFERENCES

Allen, K. E., Hart, B. M., Buell, J. S., Harris, F. R., and Wolf, M. M. Effects of social reinforcement on isolate behavior of a nursery school child. *Child Development,* 1964, 35, 511-518.

Becker, W. C., Madsen, C. H., Jr., Arnold, R., and Thomas, D. R. The contingent use of teacher attention and praise in reducing classroom behavior problems. *Journal of Special Education,* 1967, 1, 287-307.

Hall, R. V. and Broden, M. Behavior changes in brain-injured children through social reinforcement. *Journal of Experimental Child Psychology,* 1967, 5, 463-479.

Harris, F. R., Johnston, M. K., Kelley, C. S., and Wolf, M. M. Effects of positive social reinforcement on regressed crawling of a nursery school child. *Journal of Educational Psychology,* 1964, 55, 35-41.

Harris, F. R., Wolf, M. M., and Baer, D. M. Effects of adult social reinforcement on child behavior. *Young Children,* 1964, 20, 8-17.

Hart, Betty M., Allen, K. Eileen, Buell, Joan S., Harris, Florence R., and Wolf, M. M. Effects of social reinforcement on operant crying. *Journal of Experimental Child Psychology,* 1964, 1, 145-153.

Patterson, G. R. An application of conditioning techniques to the control of a hyperactive child, Ullmann, L. P., and Krasner, L. (Eds.), *Case studies in behavior modification.* New York: Holt, Rinehart and Winston, Inc., 1966. Pp. 370-375.

Zimmerman, Elaine H. and Zimmerman, J. The alteration of behavior in a special classroom situation. *Journal of the Experimental Analysis of Behavior,* 1962, 5, 59-60.

16

Collateral social development accompanying reinforcement of outdoor play in a preschool child

Joan Buell, Patricia Stoddard,
Florence R. Harris, and Donald M. Baer

A 3-yr-old preschool girl with deficits in both motor and social repertoires was socially reinforced by teachers for use of outdoor play equipment, as a contribution to her motor skills and as a tactic to produce increased social contact with other children. Her use of outdoor play equipment, and various examples of her social interaction with both teachers and children were scored in the course of experimental development and analysis of her rate of equipment use. Equipment use increased greatly under the social reinforcement contingency; certain desirable examples of social interaction with other children showed a collateral development; other examples of adult-oriented development remained constant; and one class of undesirable baby-like behavior decreased markedly. Thus, the study provided a picture of what other behavior changes may take place in the course of behavior modification aimed at a single response class.

That the preschool teacher should be a notable source of social reinforcement for the children in her class has rarely been doubted. That she can effectively wield this reinforcement as a technique of behavior modification in the service of those children has now been demonstrated in numerous instances (see Harris, Wolf, and Baer, 1964; Allen, Henke, Harris, Baer, and Reynolds, 1967; Baer and Wolf, 1968; Hart, Reynolds, Baer, Brawley, and Harris, 1968). These demonstrations uniformly single out a specific class of behavior (a behavior problem for the child studied) and demonstrate that remediation can be produced experimentally. The changes produced are clearly desirable in such cases, and are rarely questioned. However, a persistent question has concerned the possibility of

From *Journal of Applied Behavior Analysis,* 1968, 1, 167-173. Copyright 1968 by the Society for the Experimental Analysis of Behavior, Inc. Reprinted by permission.

This research was supported in part by a grant to Donald M. Baer by the National Institute of Mental Health, MH-02208-entitled An Experimental Analysis of Social Motivation. The research was conducted while the authors were staff members of the Institute of Child Development, University of Washington. Reprints may be obtained from Donald M. Baer, Department of Human Development, University of Kansas, Lawrence, Kansas 66044.

allied behavioral changes in the course of the study. These allied changes are often pointed to as desirable in themselves. Sometimes they are more far-reaching than the behavior originally treated (Baer and Wolf, 1967), and thereby could be seen as the more valuable target of the remediation effort. By contrast, it is sometimes suspected that the allied behavioral changes will represent undesirable developments, due to a surface rather than basic suppression of the child's "real" problem. That is, the new behaviors could represent merely new expressions of the old problem (such that crying, once reduced, might be replaced by, say, thumbsucking).

In the past, little data concerning the actual nature of such allied behavioral changes have been collected objectively. Global observations and impressions have usually testified to the generally desirable character of whatever behavior changes took place, but nothing more specific or precise has been available for close inspection. The present study was designed to provide more objective data, of a reasonably comprehensive nature, concerning the variety and amount of behavioral change that might result, in the course of a behavior modification program aimed at a single specific class of problem behavior. The problem behavior in this case was a lack of both motor play and social repertoires in a 3-yr-old girl; the behavioral setting for remediation was the pre-school; and the basic technique applied was social reinforcement.

Procedure

The subject was a strong, attractive 3-yr-old girl, called Polly for this report. Her parents were not native speakers of English, and Polly had spent all of her second year living abroad with them. Presumably as a consequence, her language skills in English, although technically well developed for her age, nevertheless were distinctively strange, by the standards of the usual American audience, and especially so for 3-yr-olds. Thus, it was not particularly surprising to find that Polly participated very little in her preschool program, where she was one of 12 children, the other 11 being normal speakers for their age. In particular, her teachers noted that she showed no cooperative play with the children, never used their names, infrequently touched or spoke to them, and showed only a certain rate of parallel play as her major form of social interaction. She rarely used the outdoor play equipment of the schoolyard. Her behaviors with teachers were frequent, but equally discouraging: she would most often hang on a teacher's coattail and engage in a type of stylized monosyllabic prattling which was clearly a bright imitation of her infant brother's babytalk. No improvement was reported by the teachers after a full month of preschool attendance, and consequently a systematic program of behavior modification was planned.

The essence of this program was to explore a tactic, simple in its basic dimensions but possibly effective in contributing to the totality of Polly's behavior problems. The tactic chosen was to develop Polly's use of outdoor play equipment. It was assumed that if her rate of using such equipment could be increased and maintained, she would very likely be thrown into a steady variety of interactions with her peers, and that from such interactions many useful contributions to her behavioral repertoire could result. To evaluate the extent to which this happened, it was necessary to observe a representative sample of these interactions. A set of behaviors reflecting child-oriented and teacher-oriented social behaviors, and equipment used, was defined, as listed in Table 1.

Table 1. Definitions of responses under study.

Object of Response	Type of Response	Criteria of Response
Teacher	Touching	Polly and teacher in contact, no matter who originated the contact; or both touching the same object, such as holding the same toy.
Child	Touching	Same as for touching teacher, but involving another child instead of teacher.
Teacher	Verbalization	Verbalization within 3 ft of a teacher, either using her name or facing the teacher directly.
Child	Verbalization	Verbalization within 3 ft of a child or within 3 ft of a child and teacher, but not also using teacher's name or facing her directly.
Child	Using Child's Name	Speaking the proximate child's name, or saying "you" to the child directly.
Child	Parallel Play	Playing within 3 ft of another child or at the same recognizable location (e.g., sandbox, table, easel) but not sharing material (such as same piece of clay, same jar of paint, etc.)
Child	Cooperative Play	Shared play, such as building same structure, taking objects from same container, talking together to coordinate activity, following rules of game, sharing roles in activity such as playing store, etc.
Teacher	Baby Behavior	Monosyllabic, repetitive babytalk, babylike hand flapping, hopping from one foot to the other and back repetitively, and speaking incomplete sentences.
Equipment	Play on Outdoor Equipment	Appropriate use of swing, trike, boat, tunnel, log, rocking board, jumping board, ladder box, rocking boat, and climbing frames, with or without another child present on the same equipment.

These categories of response were scored by time-sampling. An observer, watching Polly constantly throughout each outdoor preschool session, recorded every 10 sec which of these behaviors, if any, Polly had shown during that 10-sec interval. The observer also recorded teacher response to Polly, whether contingent on these behaviors or offered at other times. Thus, Polly's rate in any behavioral category could be computed as the percentage of 10-sec intervals during which she was observed that she displayed the behavior in question. These rates, expressed as percentages, comprised the basic data of the study.

Observer reliability was checked frequently, mainly because of the unusually large number of categories to be recorded. On three of every five days of each school week, two observers worked as a pair. At the end of each day, their records were compared and a percent-agreement score calculated. Agreement meant that for a given interval of the day, both observers had scored the same behavior as occurring. (Instances in which both observers agreed that nothing had occurred were not counted.) Percent-agreement was calculated as the number of agreements divided by the number of agreements and disagreements combined. Percent-agreement was never less than 85%, and typically exceeded 90%, for each behavior category defined in Table 1. It was thus concluded that observation was adequate to the demands of the study, which then proceeded according to the following design.

The experimental design consisted of a baseline period, followed first by reinforcement coupled with an auxiliary technique of "priming," and then by reinforcement without priming. This subsequent period of reinforcement without priming was probed twice, briefly, by periods of noncontingent reinforcement to examine the role of reinforcement in maintaining any behavioral changes that had appeared so far.

Baseline. The baseline period lasted five days, sufficient to demonstrate that the observational categories and techniques of the study were adequate to produce reliable data, and to confirm the teachers' estimate of Polly's behavioral characteristics. During this time, teachers gave Polly random, noncontingent attention as usual. Polly asked to use play equipment only once, requesting that the seesaw be set up. When it was, she then refused to use it. She did show a low rate of spontaneous use of the outdoor play equipment, but never in response to a teacher's invitation, which she invariably answered with "No, I don't want to."

Reinforcement With Priming. Starting on Day 6, teachers began creating an instance of using play equipment outdoors each day, and then reinforcing the behavior created. Referred to here as priming, this technique consisted simply of lifting Polly bodily onto a piece of play equipment once each outdoor session, and holding her there at least 30 sec if necessary. A different piece of equipment was used each successive day. Teachers chose their occasions for doing this by taking advantage of Polly's normal shifts of locale, selecting a piece she had happened to come near at the moment (so long as that piece had not been used for priming on a previous day). Polly was put on equipment whether or not another child was using that equipment, and whether or not she protested (which she did the first three times it occurred). As long as Polly stayed on the equipment, on these as well as on any unprimed occasions, the teacher remained close (within 3 ft or less), watching, touching her as seemed appropriate, smiling and talking about her play, and generally displaying interest, approval, and delight in Polly's activity.

The period of reinforcement with priming lasted nine days (Day 6 to 14), when teachers judged it had served its purpose; it was then supplanted by a period of reinforcement without priming. During this period, in addition to the consistent, continuous reinforcement offered for all forms of equipment play, primed or not, teachers continued their usual practice of giving random, intermittent reinforcement for Polly's other behaviors.

Reinforcement Without Priming. Beginning on Day 15, teachers discontinued their daily priming technique. Polly's behavior was reinforced as before if she showed any use of the outdoor play equipment, but she was never lifted or placed on any piece unless she first requested it. Teachers continued to suggest occasionally that she might like to use the equipment ("Polly, would you like a trike?") but urged no further if the invitation were refused. (This had been their standard practice throughout Polly's stay at preschool.) Starting with the fifth day of this period (Day 19), teachers began gradually to make their reinforcement of equipment play more intermittent, stepping a few feet away from Polly between comments (which averaged every 30 sec), and then a few feet more, etc. Then, they began staying away longer than 30 sec, gradually lengthening this interval over the days of this and succeeding reinforcement periods of the study. Reinforcement without priming was continued for 27 days, interrupted twice by probes of noncontingent reinforcement.

First Probe. After eight days of reinforcement without priming, a five-day probe of noncontingent reinforcement was instituted (Days 23 to 27). During this time, teachers continued (as always) their patterns of intermittent, random reinforcement of various of Polly's activities, as these happened to attract the teachers' attention. Reinforcement for play on outdoor equipment, however, was almost but not quite zero. A five-day probe was judged adequate to show the dependence of the behavior on reinforcement, which accordingly was resumed.

Second Probe. Another nine days of reinforcement (Days 28 to 36) followed the first probe. Thereafter, a second four-day probe was initiated (Days 37 to 40), which again was judged sufficiently long to demonstrate the continuing reliance on teacher reinforcement of Polly's outdoor equipment use. Procedures during the second probe were essentially identical to those during the first, with the following exceptions:

Use of outdoor play equipment was never reinforced: if Polly asked to use the equipment, she was simply told that it was all right to do so if she wanted; and teachers consistently reinforced Polly within 20 sec of her leaving any piece of outdoor play equipment.

After the second probe had ended, reinforcement was resumed for a final 10 days (Day 41 to 50) when the study ended as the teachers judged that Polly's total pattern of behavior had improved sufficiently.

RESULTS

Use of Outdoor Play Equipment

Figure 1 shows Polly's rate of using outdoor play equipment, as defined in Table 1. It is clear that the initially low rate of equipment used was markedly increased by reinforcement, changing from approximately 2% during baseline to a near-70% rate by the end of the study. These percentages reflect the time that this equipment was available to Polly, not her total day at preschool. (During indoor times, she of course would not be able to use any of the equipment located in the play yard.)

Figure 1 also displays an effect attributable to the priming technique. When on Day 15 priming was discontinued, Polly's rate of equipment use dropped from its previous rate near 50% of the time available to a notably lower rate approximating 30%. This was apparently a transitory loss, her rate soon recovering its previous near-50% level by the fifth day of this period. Nevertheless, it indicates that a certain amount of Polly's use of equipment was dependent on the one instance which the teachers prompted each day of the preceding period. The teachers' technique guaranteed only 30 sec of such activity each day. The gradual rise of equipment use during the reinforcement with priming period, coupled with initial loss of rate and its subsequent recovery under reinforcement alone, suggests that the two techniques interacted to produce the initial results, but that reinforcement was certainly basic to the development produced. This is further supported by the clear collapse of Polly's rate of equipment use during the later probes of noncontingent reinforcement.

An interesting observation made by the teachers and confirmed by the observers was that during the reinforcement with priming period, Polly never spontaneously used a piece of play equipment on which she had not previously been primed. Indeed, it was not until the final period of the study that she used a piece of equipment not involved in the priming of the first reinforcement period.

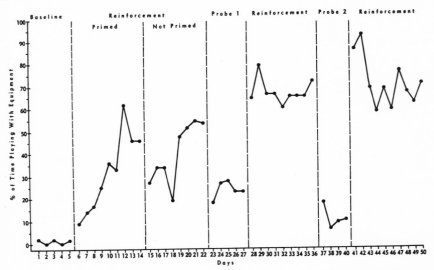

Fig. 1. The development of outdoor equipment use by priming and reinforcement procedures, probed by noncontingent reinforcement.

Collateral Social Development

Of the behaviors listed in Table 1, some showed no change in the course of the study, some increased, and one decreased. These changes are shown in Fig. 2. Those behaviors which remained constant were primarily teacher-oriented behaviors, specifically touching a teacher or verbalizing to her. However, parallel play remained consistently unstable during the study, too, and this was assumed to be a child-oriented behavior, although one of only rudimentary social significance.

The behaviors which did increase were primarily child-oriented. Specifically, touching or verbalizing to other children, using their names, and engaging in cooperative play with them showed various patterns of increase. Touching children was most prompt in its increase from zero baseline, and was followed closely by a fairly steadily increasing tendency to verbalize to the children touched. Cooperative play also emerged from its near-zero baseline relatively early after reinforcement of equipment play started, and developed slowly but adequately (for 3-yr-old standards) in the course of the next few weeks. The use of other children's names appeared late in the study, but developed to more than adequate levels within a few more days (again, by preschool standards, as exemplified by other children judged quite normal in their social development in such settings).

The one behavior which decreased following reinforcement of equipment use was baby behavior. This category consisted of baby talk, hand-flapping, and hopping responses, appreciated by the teachers as highly accurate imitations of Polly's infant brother, and also of incompleted simple sentences. As the study progressed, baby talk, hopping, and flapping disappeared, leaving an increased frequency of incomplete sentences; presently, however, these too disappeared, leaving a near-zero level of the total response class by the end of the study.

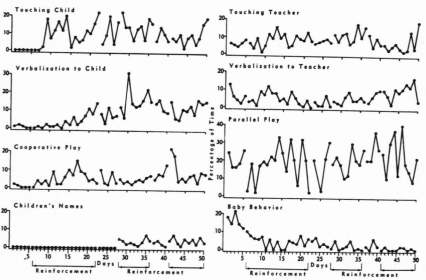

Fig. 2. Collateral patterns of behavior change accompanying the development of outdoor equipment use.

DISCUSSION

The study shows again the clear and powerful role which teacher-supplied social reinforcement can have in developing a selected response class in a preschool child. In this regard, it adds one more behavior class to those already shown sensitive to such analysis. This study also shows, quantitatively and in some breadth, the kinds of behavior changes which may accompany such behavior modification, especially if the behavior chosen for direct modification is a sound tactical choice, in view of the child's total range of behavioral deficit. In this case, the child's basic problems were considered both motor and social. A reasonable tactic, on the face of it, would be to contribute directly to improving the child's motor skill in a sphere—use of outdoor play equipment—where the resulting behavior would tend automatically to create increased social contact with other children. This social contact in itself, if it contained any effective reinforcers for Polly, could be adequate to shape a wide variety of social skills suitable for child-child interaction. The results of this study generally conform with this expectation. Desirable patterns of child-oriented behavior did appear shortly after reinforcement of equipment use was successfully applied, and did continue to develop throughout the periods of the study of equipment use. The developmental curves of these behaviors in general conform only to the initiation of reinforcement at the outset of the study, rather than to its continuing pattern of application in contingent and noncontingent schedules. That appears reasonable, in that this programmed teacher-reinforcement was applied directly only to equipment use, not to the other behaviors under study. Thus, they would have met teacher-reinforcement in the usual way during all phases of the study. More probably, the increasing contact of these behaviors with the demanding contingencies of reinforcement supplied by Polly's peers, now that she was sharing their much-used outdoor play equipment, brought about the desired developments.

Finally, it is encouraging to note that the behavior under study, which might be taken to connote emotional disturbance, autism, regression, or the like, specifically Polly's babylike repertoire, decreased steadily as the study progressed. Babylike behavior may have been under more effective extinction during experimental conditions than it had been during the baseline period. The teaching staff, aware of how easy it would be to maintain that behavior by intermittent reinforcement, had from the outset of Polly's year at preschool attempted to ignore it. Unfortunately, they found themselves failing to do exactly that, from time to time. However, during reinforcement of equipment use, the teachers noted that Polly was most likely to begin her baby performance just when she had stopped playing on equipment; it was of course at exactly these moments that teachers turned away from her, as their assignment was to reinforce equipment play, not its cessation. Thus, a side benefit of the reinforcement procedure may have been an increased efficiency of extinction for the babylike behaviors.

The priming technique used in this study deserves comment. It was designed to hasten the emergence of equipment use, so that more and more examples of that behavior class would be available for reinforcement. Clearly, it accomplished that. The teachers had wondered whether the use of priming would handicap Polly when priming was later discontinued: would she be able to initiate her own use of the play equipment without teacher assistance? The results show clearly that she was able to do that, with only transitory partial loss of her new rate when priming was discontinued. However, the teachers also noted that not until quite late in the study did Polly show any spontaneous use of a piece of play equipment on which she had not been primed earlier. Thus, priming appears in one sense to have hastened generalization, if it is to be assumed that Polly would not have used any equipment which she was not first acquainted with by teachers. But in another sense, it seems that priming may have restricted generalization, in that Polly would not approach any apparatus she had not previously been primed to use. It is, of course, the same fact of observation which can be interpreted in these two ways. A thorough evaluation of the role of priming in contributing to generalization must remain for future study. In this case, it is clear only that priming can hasten the process of reinforcement, by making available behaviors suitable for reinforcement faster than they would have appeared without priming (according to baseline performance).

REFERENCES

Allen, K. E., Henke, L. B., Harris, F. R., Baer, D. M., and Reynolds, N. J. Control of hyperactivity by social reinforcement of attending behavior. *Journal of Educational Psychology,* 1967, 58, 231-237.

Baer, D. M. and Wolf, M. M. The entry into natural communities of reinforcement. Paper read at American Psychological Association convention, Washington, 1967.

Baer, D. M.. and Wolf, M. M. The reinforcement contingency in preschool and remedial education. In R. D. Hess and Roberta M. Bear (Eds.), *Early education: current theory, research, and practice.* Chicago: Aldine, 1968. Pp. 119-130.

Harris, F. R., Wolf, M. M., and Baer, D. M. Effects of adult social reinforcement on child behavior. *Young Children,* 1964, 20, 8-17.

Hart, D. M., Reynolds, N. J., Baer, D. M., Brawley, E. R., and Harris, F. R. Effect of contingent and noncontingent social reinforcement on the cooperative play of a preschool child. *Journal of Applied Behavior Analysis,* 1968, 1, 73-76.

17

The control of disruptive behavior in an elementary classroom: peer ratings, token reinforcement, and a negative side-effect

James G. May and Sandra J. Bongiovanni

A token reinforcement procedure based on peer ratings was employed to control disruptive behavior in an elementary remedial math class. Observations before, during, and after a period in which reinforcement was for behavior other than disruptive activity revealed a significant decrement in such misbehavior during the token reinforcement period. Subjects with low overall levels of disruptive responses exhibited only a slight decrease, while subjects with moderate and high overall disruptive behavior were markedly affected. Disruptive responses in the latter group increased observably during the final extinction phase. Reports from the teacher indicated that scholastic performance suffered for all students during the phase in which a minimum of disruptive behavior occurred. It was therefore concluded that concurrent observation of academic achievement should be made an integrative part of future attempts to assess the effectiveness of such behavioral control procedures.

One of the greatest impediments to the dissemination of knowledge in the elementary school classroom is the relatively transient disruptive behavior that invariably emanates from one or more students. Although the distracting acts (e.g., talking, leaving the appointed seat, being inattentive, wiggling, attending to another's work, etc.) are not generally considered serious infractions, both the guilty party and those whom he distracts may suffer serious information loss. It seems, therefore, that one of the primary concerns of educational psychologists should be the development of techniques which tend to preclude such activity. Traditional approaches to these problems have employed corporal punishment and "penance" in the form of increased work loads or isolation. Many teachers agree that these methods are not completely effective or have unfortunate side effects, and that there is certainly room for more effective and more surreptitious methods of preventing disruptive behavior in the classroom.

A number of new techniques to control behavior have been developed in recent years, and for the most part have been extrapolated from the principles of behavioral control established from numerous operant conditioning experiments with lower animals. These new methods assume that behavior is governed by its consequences and that maladaptive behavior can be reliably preempted by adaptive behavior. Since it is not feasible to manipulate the primary needs of children in the classroom, more abstract or secondary reinforcements are typically used. Many studies (Clarizo and Yelon, 1967; Hall, Lund and Jackson, 1968; Woody, 1966; Ayllon and Azrin, 1965; and Azrin and Lindsley, 1956) have demonstrated that token reinforcement (e.g., stamps, chips, stars, etc.), which can later be used to obtain other rewards (e.g., candy, school supplies, novelties, toys, etc.), are quite adequate for shaping desirable behavior in young children.

Techniques of this sort typically involve monitoring the behavior of each child individually and meting out reinforcements on the basis of the frequency of occurrence of behavior defined as desirable. Even in nongraded classrooms with relatively little formal structure to the instructional schedule, the monitoring and decision-making activities inherent in the effective implementation of these methods necessitates a low student-teacher ratio. The size of most elementary school classes far exceeds this ratio and it becomes practically impossible to use a reinforcement system without modifying it somewhat. One way the teacher may make token reinforcement systems feasible in today's classroom involves enlisting the aid of the students to monitor each other's behavior. Patterson, Jones, Whittier and Wright (1965) reported that hyperactivity in the classroom could be reduced by manipulating peer influence, and Evans and Ozwalt (1968) have shown that peer approval was instrumental in accelerating academic progress in underachieving children. Surratt, Ulrich and Hawkins (1970) have demonstrated that elementary level students are quite capable of serving as behavioral engineers.

The aim of the present investigation was to assess the effectiveness of a behavioral control technique that was based on (1) reinforcing the absence of disruptive behavior, (2) the use of a token economy, and (3) peer rating procedures.

METHOD

Subjects

Thirty-two students in a remedial math section of an elementary school in Metairie, La., served as subjects. They were placed in this section on the basis of test scores on standardized math exams. The age range was from seven to 12 yrs. The teacher described them as a third-grade class working on a second-grade level, and as slow learners of low socioeconomic standing. The class was run on a nongraded system and met each weekday for 40 minutes.

Procedure

The study included three phases. Phase 1 was a baseline period which lasted five days. During this time the experimenter observed and recorded instances of disruptive behavior. In Phase 2, students were asked to rate others on the basis of their disruptive behavior and tokens were used as reinforcement. The experimenter recorded instances of disruptive behavior throughout the nine days that made up this period. The last phase (3) was identical to the first in that disruptive instances were recorded by the experimenter and no token reinforcements or peer ratings were carried out. This phase lasted for five days.

Disruptive Behavior

The same classroom was used every day and the desks were arranged in four rows. The two rows on the left side of the classroom faced the two rows on the right side with 10-15 ft separating these opposing seats. The experimenter used a sampling technique with a rapid recycling rate to record behavioral data. The rows were scanned at a rate of 1 per min and the frequency of disruptive behavior was recorded in a seating chart. The seating arrangements were the same each day. Disruptive behavior was defined as: talking, slouching or not sitting correctly at one's desk, not paying attention to the teacher, walking around the room or going to the teacher's desk without permission. During the token reinforcement and extinction phases, these rules were posted where all could read them in the form of "commandments" (e.g., 1. No talking. 2. Sit straight at own desk, etc.). This was called the "Good Behavior Chart." The relative frequency of each kind of disruptive behavior was not recorded. Total disruptive behavior scores are based on the conjunctive observations of all these forms of misbehavior.

Peer Ratings

After five days of baseline observation, the teacher informed the students that their classmates would rate them on the basis of their behavior and at the end of each day they would be classified as having been good or bad. To be rated "perfect," the students were told that they must follow the instructions on the Good Behavior Chart and that any reported instances of misbehavior would result in a rating of imperfect. At the end of the session the teacher gave the following instructions: "Now it is time to determine who was good and who was bad today. I want row 1 to rate row 3, and row 2 to rate row 4, row 4 to rate row 1, and row 3 to rate row 2. On these rating sheets are the names of the students on the row you are to rate. If you think John was good today and followed all of the rules for good behavior give him a check. If he did not follow these rules, give him an "X" for poor behavior. Do this for each student on your rating sheet. But if you rate a student as being good when the other students rate him as being bad, you will receive the "X" for rating the student unfairly. Also, if you give him an "X" when he was good, then you will get his "X" for rating unfairly." The last two sentences were intended to inhibit ratings based on other than behavioral criteria and at no time were any students' ratings actually corrected for "unfair" rating. The rating sheets were then collected by the teacher and scored by the experimenter.

Token Reinforcement

The students were informed, at the outset of the token reinforcement phase, that they would receive a blue star next to their name if they were rated as "perfect" (i.e., no reports of disruptive behavior) that day, that they would receive a red star if they were rated as "imperfect" (i.e., one report of disruptive behavior) and that if they received more than one report of disruptive behavior they would not receive any star. The chart was prominently displayed in the classroom, to which tokens were attached. The tokens were distributed on the basis of the peer ratings collected at the end of each class. Stars were displayed at the beginning of the following period. Students receiving blue stars were allowed to pick one item from a blue box and those receiving red stars chose from a red box at the end of each class. The blue box contained items (candy or story books) valued at 10¢ while the red box contained items (candy or ballons) valued at 1¢ or less.

RESULTS AND DISCUSSION

The frequency of disruptive responses recorded by the experimenter during each session has been plotted in Fig. 1. The mean number of disruptive responses per session for the baseline, token reinforcement, and extinction phases was 65.2, 25.9 and 74.2, respectively. Thus, the token reinforcement system resulted in greater than a 50% decrease in disruptive responses. Most of the day-to-day variability can probably be accounted for by differences in lesson plans and work assignments. On days when the teacher assigned seat work and quizzes, misbehavior was lowest and it was highest on days when general instruction and class participation occurred. The responses during the eleventh session are probably somewhat inflated due to the presence of a substitute teacher on that day. During this session "busy work" was assigned.

The finding that disruptive responding during the extinction phase was greater than during the baseline phase suggests that this relatively short period of token reinforcement resulted in only a transient reduction in disruptive behavior and was followed by a compensatory increase in disruptive responding. This pattern of response bears some resemblance to that found in situations where behaviors of high probability are punished (Holz, Azrin and Ulrich, 1963) or where the reinforcement density is manipulated in different components of a multiple schedule (Reynolds, 1961). Disruptive responses in this study were not directly punished and it is probably inappropriate to interpret the decrease and recovery of disruptive behavior as resulting from the suppression of misbehavior. A more feasible explanation might be that this system is essentially a situation in which differential reinforcement of other behavior (DRO) occurs. Thus, behavior which is incompatible with disruptive responding is reinforced during

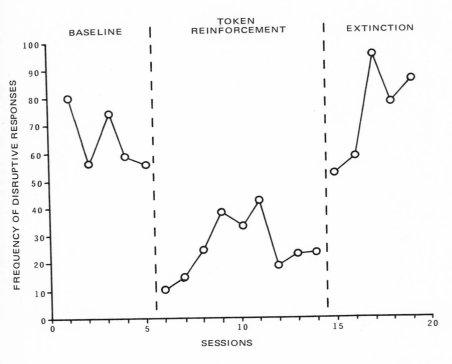

Fig. 1.

the token phase, and the extinction of responding in nondisruptive, incompatible ways allows the recovery of high rates of misbehavior.

Another point of interest concerns the way in which individual students may contribute to the effects noted. Fig. 2 presents the changes in mean number of disruptive responses over all three periods for 17 selected subjects. The lower panel represents the six students with the highest total disruptive behavior scores ("bad subjects"), the upper panel contains the records for six subjects with the lowest total disruptive behavior scores ("good subjects"), and the middle panel presents the behavior of five subjects chosen at random from the remaining group ("average subjects"). Two points are apparent. The decrement in disruptive behavior during the token reinforcement period is about the same in the "average" and "bad" groups, although the "bad subjects" begin at a higher baseline frequency and the decrease in disruptive behavior is proliferated in the extinction phase for "average subjects," while a pronounced rebound in disrupting responses is observed for the "bad subjects." The "good" subjects are

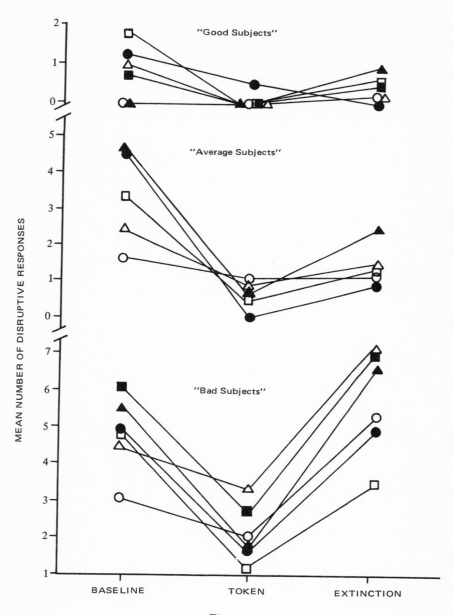

Fig. 2.

characterized by a lower overall level of disruptive behavior and the number of disruptive responses is not as markedly reduced during the token reinforcement phase. It must be emphasized at this point that disruptive behavior as defined in this study was often a social interaction. Informal observation of these children in class revealed that responses recorded as disruptive for "good" subjects were often the outgrowth of an interaction with "bad" or "average" subjects. Decreases in disruptive responses resulted from "good subjects" often refusing to interact with "bad" or "average" subjects. This points up the extremely important role of individual differences and seating arrangements in the occurrence of disruptive behavior.

These data offer unequivocal support for the notion that a system which utilizes token reinforcement contingencies distributed by the teacher on the basis of decisions by the students significantly reduces disruptive behavior in gradeschool children. Because the system is a relatively complex one, some questions remain about which components are most responsible for this effect. It is not clear, for example, whether the token reinforcements *per se* or the peer rating activity alone might have accounted for a large degree of decreased disruptive behavior. It is conceivable that the observing behavior necessitated by the peer rating system was incompatible with the disruptive responses that occurred in the absence of such a system.

Since the system was tested in only one grade at the elementary level, caution must be taken in predicting success at other ages and grades. Likewise, the effectiveness of the tokens used in this reinforcement system may well be limited to classes composed of students from socioeconomic levels commensurate with those employed in the present study (Terrell et al, 1959). These concerns do not detract seriously from the dramatic effect observed, and answers to these questions can be readily obtained through further research. Situations in which peer ratings are instituted throughout the experimental period (i.e., during the baseline, token reinforcement and extinction phases), or situations that involve peer ratings and no set contingencies during the token reinforcement phase would, when compared to results gathered by the present method, shed light on the relative importance of token reinforcement and peer ratings. Using these methods in other grades would establish the generality of this control procedure with respect to age, education level and socioeconomic status. Considering these points, most readers will probably agree that these methods offer some promise of improved control of classroom behavior. But it would be a mistake to conclude that these findings represent an *effective* use of behavioral control techniques.

While behavioral engineering offers an excellent means of supplementing existing instructional methods, there is also the temptation to consider the establishment of behavioral control as an end in itself. Our index of success in the present study was the degree to which disruptive behavior had been eliminated. That is not the primary aim of classroom instruction, however. It was indeed quite disheartening for us to learn, from spontaneous remarks from the teacher after the conclusion of the study, that she had observed a noticeable decrement in scholastic performance during the token reinforcement phase and an increment in such performance during extinction. An *effective* use of behavioral control techniques would certainly not result in decreasing disruptive behavior at the cost of decreasing scholastic performance. The most parsimonious explanation for that outcome in the present study is that the children shifted their attention from learning activities to "judging" activities and thus spent a predominant amount of time as Orwellian "big brothers."

This revelation should not be taken to indicate that the token reinforcement system implemented in this study is useless. Two very important points must be made here. First, the age of the group involved might be a critical factor. Perhaps older children could observe and judge their peers more subtly without becoming overly engrossed. If this is true, scholastic performance might not suffer markedly. Second, in situations where the main concern is custodial or disciplinary maintenance of nondisruptive behavior, determining token reinforcement contingencies by peer-rating procedures might be of great utility.

One pressing implication from this investigation centers around the practice of observing only one index of behavior while implementing behavioral control procedures. An adequate assessment of the utility of such methods in the classroom must take into account more than just the fluctuations in the behavior upon which reinforcement, or the lack of it, is based. Quantitative measures of other concurrent adaptive behavior should be made an integral part of the evaluation of these procedures.

REFERENCES

Ayllon, T. and Azrin, N. H. Measurement and reinforcement of the behavior of psychotics. *Journal of Experimental Analysis of Behavior,* 1965, 8, 357-383.

Azrin, N. H. and Lindsley, O. The reinforcement of cooperation between children. *Journal of Abnormal Social Psychology,* 1956, 52, 100-102.

Clarizo, H. F. and Yelon, S. L. Learning theory approaches to classroom management: rational and intervention techniques. *Journal of Special Education,* 1967, 1, 267-274.

Evans, G. and Ozwalt, G. Acceleration of academic progress through the manipulation of peer influence. *Behaviour Research and Therapy,* 1967, 5, 1-7.

Hall, R. V., Lund, Diane, and Jackson, Deloris. Effects of teacher attention on behavior. *Journal of Applied Behavior Analysis,* 1968, 1, 1-12.

Holz, W. C., Azrin, N. H., and Ulrich, R. E. Punishment of temporally spaced responding. *Journal of Experimental Analysis of Behavior,* 1963, 6, 115-122.

Patterson, G. R., Jones, J. W., Whittier, J., and Wright, M. A. A behavior modification technique for the hyperactive child. *Behavior Research and Therapy,* 1965, 2, 217-226.

Reynolds, G. S. Behavioral contrast. *Journal of Experimental Behavior,* 1961, 4, 57-71.

Surratt, P. R., Ulrich, R. E., and Hawkins, R. P. An elementary student as a behavioral engineer. *Journal of Applied Behavior Analysis,* 1969, 2, 85-92.

Terrell, G., Durkin, Kathryn, and Wiesly, M. Social class and the nature of the incentive in discrimination learning. *Journal of Abnormal and Social Psychology,* 1959, 59, 270-272.

Woody, R. H. Behavior therapy and school psychology. *Journal of Social Psychology,* 1966, 4, 1-14.

IV

Procedures for
Increasing Desirable Behavior

This section deals with procedures for increasing desirable behavior. Improved academic performance is obviously the goal of every teacher who uses behavior modification techniques, not just the people mentioned in the following articles. Lovitt, Guppy, and Blattner evaluate the use of a free-time contingency with fourth graders to increase spelling accuracy, with promising results. Lovitt and Curtiss studied academic response rates as functions of teacher- and self-imposed contingencies and found that self-imposed contingencies were usually more desirable. A study by Lovitt and Esveldt found that multiple-ratio schedules as opposed to single-ratio schedules generated superior performance on math problems. Further work on the use of self-determined reinforcement schedules by Glynn also suggests this is an excellent technique. McMichael and Corey used contingency management in an introductory psychology course; their results indicate the strength of contingency management as a learning technique.

Finally, all of the preceding theory and principles are brought together in the article by Ulrich, Louisell, and Wolfe. Observe carefully that not only are the students in the Learning Village of a heterogeneous background but also that the results of this program appear to be reliably superior to those obtained in the conventional public school. Does this suggest anything?!

18

The use of a free-time contingency with fourth graders to increase spelling accuracy

Thomas C. Lovitt, Tal E. Guppy, and James E. Blattner

This investigation was conducted in a fourth grade class of 32 pupils in a public school. The study assessed spelling performances of the group as a function of three conditions—(1) when traditional procedures were in effect, (2) when contingent free-time was individually arranged, and (3) when a group contingency, listening to the radio, was added to the individually obtained free-time. As a result of these procedures, the majority of the pupils' spelling performance increased, indicating that the use of contingent free-time and radio-listening were effective reinforcers.

The principles of contingency management have been widely demonstrated in clinical or therapeutic settings where one investigator manages the behavior of one child (Ullmann and Krasner, 1965; Ulrich, Stachnic and Mabry, 1966; Sloane and MacAulay, 1968; Bijou and Baer, 1967). The majority of these reports describe the efforts of one examiner managing the behavior of a single subject, and are generally concerned with the alteration of a social response such as hitting, throwing objects, crying, or having temper tantrums.

Other investigations have described the further extension of contingency management procedures. Recent reports have shown how the principles of systematic behavioral management may be applied by the classroom teacher not only to decrease inappropriate social behavior, but also to increase certain types of academic behavior. Clark, Lachowicz and Wolf (1968) demonstrated that when a token economy was instituted with a group of Neighborhood Youth Corps girls, their academic progress, as assessed by the California Achievement Test, surpassed a control group that functioned on a noncontingent basis. McKenzie, Clark, Wolf and Kothera (1968) further demonstrated that when parents granted contingent allowances for grades, the academic performance of children in special education classes increased. In both of these studies, where groups of children were involved and where the strategy was to increase some

From *Behavior Research and Therapy*, 1969, 7, 151-156. Copyright 1969 by the Society for the Experimental Analysis of Behavior, Inc. Reprinted by permission.

academic behavior, the managerial system was administered by a public school teacher.

The intent of the current report was to contribute further evidence that a single classroom teacher can initiate and administer a contingency system with groups of children for the purpose of increasing academic performance. Furthermore, this investigation attempted to illustrate how the acquisition of regular and continuous behavioral data could enable the classroom teacher to make objective programing decisions.

The current investigation assessed the spelling performances of a group of fourth graders as a function of three conditions: first, when traditional procedures were in effect; secondly, when contingent free time was individually arranged; and finally, when a group contingency was added to the individually obtained free time.

METHOD

Setting and Subjects

This investigation took place in a regular fourth grade class of 32 pupils in Seattle, Washington. The students in this class were from middle- or upper-middle-class homes and were of normal or above normal intelligence. The class was conducted entirely by the regular classroom teacher, who administered the spelling program, calculated and graphed the pupils' scores, and managed the contingency system. The teacher was advised by a member of a demonstration project aimed at initiating procedures for continuous measurement in the elementary schools.

Procedure

During the first phase of this study (11 weeks) spelling was scheduled in a rather traditional manner. On Monday of each week, Lesson A from the 4th grade *Spelling For Word Mastery* (1959) text was scheduled. This lesson required the children to read a story containing that week's spelling words, then to say and write the new words. For example, the pupil was required to use one word from a list of new words to fill in a missing blank. On Wednesday, a trial test was given. On Thursday Lesson D was programed, which involved completing an exercise containing about five answers, similar to Lesson B, and in addition, writing each of the spelling words. Each pupil's grade on the final Friday test was recorded in terms of percentage correct. Throughout this first phase the only contingencies in effect were report cards and unsystematic social approval from the teacher and peers.

During the second phase of the study, which extended for 10 weeks, the spelling procedures were the same—following the suggested plan in the text. Now, however, following the initial presentation of the words on Monday, the children were merely assigned spelling lessons B and D and were required to hand them in by Wednesday. No specific classroom time was allotted for the completion of the work during this phase.

Throughout Phase 2, final tests were given on Tuesday, Wednesday, Thursday, and Friday of each week. During this phase, when the pupil received a 100 percent score he was not required to continue taking spelling tests on the remaining testing days of that week. For example, if on the Tuesday test a pupil received a 100 per cent score he was allowed, during the Wednesday, Thursday, and Friday spelling test period, to either read a library book or engage in any other school relevant activity at his desk.

For those students who did not achieve a perfect score on the Tuesday test, their papers, with the corrections, were returned 15 min prior to the Wednesday test. This same procedure was practiced prior to the Thursday and Friday tests. The students were not required, however, to write or orally recite the misspelled words after the papers were returned. The returned papers may have simply functioned as a cue or discriminative stimulus that another spelling test was about to be given.

Throughout this phase the teacher recorded the pupil's score as 100 percent if he returned a perfect spelling paper on Tuesday, Wednesday, Thursday, or Friday; otherwise, if the pupil never achieved 100 percent, his Friday score was reported. Furthermore, the teacher recorded which day was represented by the score, 1=Tuesday, 2=Wednesday, 3=Thursday, and 4=Friday.

During Phase 3 of the study, which extended for three weeks, the procedures were the same as those in effect during Phase 2. On Monday the weekly words were presented; Lessons B and D were assigned to be submitted on Wednesday; and tests were given on Tuesday, Wednesday, Thursday, and Friday. The same contingency was in effect—when the pupil achieved a 100 percent score he was allowed to engage in a free time pursuit rather than required to continue being tested. An additional contingency was added, however. When on any given testing day all of the pupils received a 100 percent score, the total class was allowed to listen to the radio for 15 min.

RESULTS

Figure 1 illustrates the group data during the three experimental phases. Depicted in the figure are the total number of perfect papers recorded per week. As noted, during Phase 1, where the spelling was taught by traditional techniques, the range of 100 percent scores for the 11 week phase was 11—from four perfect papers on the second week to 15 during the ninth and tenth weeks. The median number of perfect papers during Phase 1 was 12.

A median number of 25.5 perfect papers was calculated in the 10-wk second phase, when obtaining free time depended upon obtaining a perfect score. The range of perfect papers throughout this phase was seven, from 22 to 29. When the median data from Phases 1 and 2 were subjected to the Fisher Test of Exact Probability, a probability score of 0.000002 was obtained.

During the brief third phase of the study, when a group contingency—listening to the radio—was added to the individually contingent free time, a median of 30 perfect papers was revealed. When this median was related to the median of Phase 2, a probability score of 0.01 was obtained.

Of the 32 members of the class, the median scores of 19 pupils improved in spelling accuracy from Phase 1 to Phase 2. The remaining 13 who did not improve were pupils whose median scores during Phase 1 were already 100 percent. Similarly, the median scores improved for only three pupils from Phase 2 to Phase 3, since the median scores for the 29 others were already at 100 percent during Phase 2.

Figure 2 depicts a pupil who improved greatly when the reward of free time was added during the second phase. As noted in the figure, S31's median percent correct throughout Phase 1 was 80 percent, but it increased to a median of 100 percent during Phase 2 and continued to be 100 percent in the final phase. When the data from Phases 1 and 2 were applied to the Fisher Test, a significance of 0.001 was revealed.

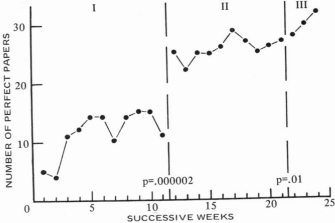

Fig. 1. Number of 100 percent papers recorded each successive week throughout the three experimental conditions. The p values reflect the degree of significance between adjacent conditions.

Figure 3, representing S15, reveals a pupil's record that also improved significantly from Phase 1 to Phase 2. During Phase 1 this pupil's range of scores was from 32-68 percent, whereas his range of scores in the second phase was from 72-100 percent. A median of 48 percent was calculated during Phase 1 and 80 percent in Phase 2. These median data, when subjected to the Fisher Test, revealed a probability value of 0.0001. During the three week third phase the S's three scores were 76, 100, and 100.

During Phase 1 of this study 125 perfect scores were recorded, an average of 11.4 100 percent papers per week. During Phase 2, however, 257 perfect papers were obtained, an average of 25.7 papers with 100 percent scores from the 32-member class per week. Of these 257 perfect papers, 150 or 59 percent were

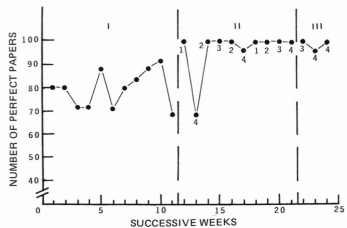

Fig. 2. S 31's percentage scores throughout the investigation. The numbers beneath the data points during conditions 2 and 3 correspond to the day of the week that S 31's score was recorded (1=Tuesday, 2=Wednesday, 3=Thursday, 4=Friday). The *p* value indicates the degree of significance between conditions 1 and 2.

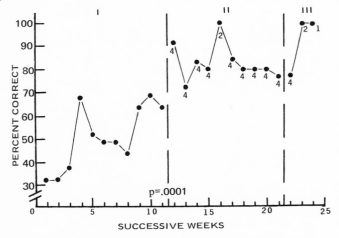

Fig. 3. S 15's percentage scores throughout the study.

recorded on Tuesdays, the first day for a spelling test. On Wednesdays, the second day of testing, 69 or 27 percent of the total 100 percent scores were recorded. Meanwhile, 24 papers (nine percent of the total) were recorded on Thursdays and 14 (five percent) on the final day.

During the final phase of the study, where, over a period of three weeks, 93 total tests were given, 85 perfect papers were submitted. Of these, 62 percent were recorded on Tuesdays, 28 percent on Wednesdays, 5 percent on Thursdays, and 5 percent on Fridays. Although a group contingency was in effect throughout Phase 3, the class never was allowed to listen to the radio, since the pupils did not all submit perfect papers on any one day. The nearest the class did come to being granted the radio contingency was on Tuesday of the final week, when 21 of the 29 who took the test received 100 percent scores.

CONCLUSION

When teachers are requested to maintain evaluative data and plot graphically the academic performances of pupils, spelling may be the best place to begin. Two reasons might support such a statement. One, spelling performance is probably tested more systematically and regularly than other academic skills. The procedures for testing spelling from week to week are essentially the same— present the words orally and request the pupils to write them. Furthermore, spelling performance is generally assessed at least once each week, whereas evaluations in other academic areas are usually obtained less often. The second reason for using spelling as the basis for graphically and continuously obtaining records of academic performance is that most teachers already record pupil performance in spelling. Many teachers indicate in their record books, in a tabular manner, the weekly percentage scores of the pupils. It becomes a simple matter for the teacher to convert these tabular record book notations to percentage points on a graph.

The contingencies employed in this study represented a natural extension of the classroom environment. Free time activities, allowing children to undertake an activity of their choosing, are often regularly scheduled classroom events. Many times, however, these activities are provided on a noncontingent basis—not dependent upon prior behavior of the pupils. When contingent leisure time reading was employed during Phase 2 and when the group reinforcement, listening to the radio, was added during the final phase, these were sufficient to alter the majority of the pupils' spelling accuracy. The classroom teacher did not have to resort to reinforcers that were more expensive or less natural to the classrooms to alter effectively the performance of the children.

Of equal importance throughout this study was that not only did pupil performance increase when contingencies were applied, but the classroom teacher began to consider individually the children in his class. By viewing the pupil's performance in graphic rather than tabular form, the teacher noted how some children changed dramatically when the consequences were imposed, while others were minimally affected by them. Some children were consistently superior in spelling, while others performed in a less remarkable manner, regardless of the rewards offered. As to the latter children, the teacher speculated that while the initiated contingencies were effective with most pupils, perhaps to increase the performance of some children other individualized rules should be attempted. Further, when viewing the graphic records of certain children the teacher noted that a program revision was called for. The data suggested to the teacher that perhaps the program was too difficult for some of the pupils and too easy for others.

As a function of this investigation, two rather basic behavioral principles were pointed out to the classroom teacher—one, that the use of systematic contingencies can affect behavior, and two, that data may be used to facilitate the making of classroom decisions. Hopefully, then, this classroom teacher's successful experience in obtaining and using group data regarding spelling will generalize to other academic areas.

REFERENCES

Bijou, S. W. and Baer, D. M. *Child development: readings in experimental analysis.* New York: Appleton-Century-Crofts, 1967.

Clark, M.; Lachowicz, J.; and Wolf, M. A pilot basic education program for school dropouts incorporating a token reinforcement system. *Behaviour Research and Therapy,* 1968, 6, 183-188.

McKenzie, H. S.; Clark, M.; Wolf, M. M.; Kothera, R.; and Benson, C. Behavior modification of children with learning disabilities using grades as tokens and allowances as back up reinforcers. *Exceptional Children,* 1968, 34, 745-752.

Patton, D. H. and Johnson, E. M. *Spelling for word mastery.* Columbus: Charles E. Merrill Books, 1959.

Sloane, H. N. and Macaulay, B. D. *Operant procedures in remedial speech and language training.* Boston: Houghton Mifflin, 1968.

Ullmann, L. P. and Krasner, L. *Case studies in behavior modification.* New York: Holt, Rinehart & Winston, 1965.

Ulrich, R.; Stachnic, T.; and Mabry, J. *Control of human behavior.* Glenview, Ill.: Scott, Foresman & Co., 1966.

19

Academic response rate as a function of teacher- and self-imposed contingencies

Thomas C. Lovitt and Karen A. Curtiss

The purpose of this study was to assess the effects of the contingency manager (teacher or pupil) on a pupil's academic response rate. The results of two such experiments disclosed that higher academic rates occurred when the pupil arranged the contingency requirements than when the teacher specified them. A third study manipulated only reinforcement magnitude to ascertain whether amount of reinforcement had interacted with pupil-specified contingencies to produce the increase in academic response rate. The latter findings revealed that the contingency manager, not reinforcement magnitude, accounted for this subject's gain in performance.

The management of one's own behavior has often been expressed as one of the prime objectives of our educational system. The problem in programming toward such an end has been one of definition—specifying those variables that constitute self-management. Until the skills or traits that lead to a self-managing individual are clearly detailed and explicitly defined, the objective of self-management may never be realized. If, however, certain subproperties of self-management can be determined, sequentially ordered, and systematically presented, the probability of realizing this objective is greatly increased.

An individual who can control or manage his own behavior may be a person who has the ability to assess his own competencies, set his own behavioral objectives, and specify a contingency system whereby he might obtain these objectives. Translated to a school situation, this would be an individual who knew his academic capabilities in terms of skill levels and rate of performance, could arrange a series of activities or steps to achieve a variety of self-imposed objectives, and could grant himself reinforcers on a prearranged schedule to accomplish certain behavioral sequences.

From *Journal of Applied Behavior Analysis,* 1969, 2, 49-53. Copyright 1969 by the Society for the Experimental Analysis of Behavior, Inc. Reprinted by permission.

Reprints may be obtained from Thomas C. Lovitt, Mental Retardation and Child Development Center, University of Washington, 4701 24th Ave. N.E., Seattle, Washington 98105.

This last behavior, self-specification of contingencies, has been a neglected area of investigation. Traditionally, it is the teacher who arranges the contingencies in the classroom, saying to the pupil: "If you do these arithmetic problems, you will receive a gold star", or, "If you correctly answer these questions you will be allowed to go out for recess." Infrequently is the student allowed to arrange his own educational environment.

The purpose of this study was to analyze functionally the effects of self-imposed *versus* teacher-imposed contingencies on the behavior of a particular pupil. In this study the specification of contingencies was the independent variable, while academic response rate was selected as the dependent variable.

METHOD

Student and Conditions

The student was a 12-yr-old member of a class for children with behavioral disorders at the Experimental Education Unit, University of Washington. The student had been a member of this class, whose management system was based on the Premack design of high- and low-probability behaviors (Haring and Kunzelmann, 1966; Haring and Lovitt, 1967), for two academic years. Contingent upon academic responses (low-probability behaviors), the students in this class were given points in each of the academic areas. These points were later converted to minutes of time in the high-interest (high-probability behavior) room. The ratios of points-per-answer were individually specified, not only among class members but also among subject matter areas for any one student.

Procedures

This investigation consisted of three separate experiments; two manipulated the contingency manager and one manipulated magnitude of reinforcement. During Exp. I, baseline data relevant to the student's academic response rate were obtained for nine days. Each day a response rate figure was calculated that represented the student's performance in all of his scheduled subject matter areas. Throughout this period no attempt was made to explain to the student the response-per-point ratio in each academic area.

After this baseline period, Stage 1 was instituted. It was the intent at this time to instruct the student as to the relationship between correct answers and contingent points. Each day in this 12-day stage the teacher verbally explained the contingencies and placed a written copy of them on the student's desk. Table 1 outlines the contingency system in effect throughout Exp. I. The contract was composed of nine agreements, each of which had a response-per-point ratio. For example, the student was granted two points for each page read (Sullivan Associates Program, 1963) and one point per 10 mathematics problems (Singer Mathematics Program, 1965). As the student completed each academic assignment, he was shown how many responses had been made and was asked to calculate the corresponding points he had earned.

Table 1. Contingency specifications during Experiment I.

Subject Area	Contingency Manager	
	Teacher-Specified	Child-Specified
MATH	10 problems: 1 min of free time	10 problems: 1 min of free time
SUPPLEMENTARY		
Math	10 problems: 1	10 problems: 1
READING		
(No errors)	1 page: 2	1 page: 2
(Errors)	1 page: 1	1 page: 1
SPELLING	18 words: 1	*10 words: 2
WRITING	20 letters: 1	*10 letters: 2
LIBRARY READING	1 story: 3	*1 story: 10
CYCLO-TEACHER		
Multiplication	1 side: 1	1 side: 1
Spelling	1 side: 2	1 side: 2

*Indicates where the child-imposed requirements differ from those imposed by the teacher.

In Stage 2, which extended for 22 days, the copy of the response-point requirements was removed from the student's desk. He was now asked to specify verbally his own payment in each of the nine areas and to record his decisions, which were then attached to his desk. As in Stage 1, when each assignment was completed the student was asked to calculate the points he had earned. Finally, in Stage 3, which lasted for seven days, the teacher-imposed contingencies were again in effect.

In Exp. I, as in all experiments of this study, the sequencing of academic areas was basically the same each day; reading was followed by math, then spelling, English, and writing. Furthermore, the time alloted to each subject was about the same each day: 2 hr for reading, 1 hr for math, and a total of 1.5 hr for spelling, English, writing, and library reading.

Regardless of any variability in the ordering of the subject areas or the time allotted to them, the teacher, not the student, always arranged the day's academic program. Thus, the subject could work only on each academic activity as it was scheduled, math during the math period and reading during the reading period. He could not switch freely from one academic area to another, regardless of the contingencies in effect from one activity to another, or who had imposed the contingencies.

After a period of four weeks, which separated the academic quarters at the University of Washington, Exp. II was begun. No baseline data were obtained during this second experiment, since the student was now fully acquainted with the response-per-point contingencies. Other procedures were carried out as detailed above, for the purpose of replicating Exp. I.

Teacher contingencies were explained, written out, and attached to the student's desk in Stages 1 and 3, while during Stage 2 the student's contingencies were in operation. The only difference between Exp. I and II was that in the first experiment, nine specific agreements were involved; in the latter investigation, eight were included. In both experiments, however, the student's complete program was included in the study. The response-per-point requirements of Exp. II are presented in Table 2.

Table 2. Contingency specifications during Experiment II.

Subject Area	Contingency Manager	
	Teacher-Specified	Child-Specified
MATH	10 problems: 1 min of free time	•10 problems: 2 min of free time
READING		
(No errors)	1 page: 2	•1 page: 3
(Errors)	1 page: 1	•1 page: 2
SPELLING	18 words: 1	•5 words: 1
WRITING	20 letters: 1	•10 letters: 2
LANGUAGE ARTS	10 answers: 1	•10 answers: 2
LIBRARY BOOK	1 story: 3	•1 story: 6
	3 questions: 1	•3 questions: 2

•Indicates where the child-imposed requirements differ from those imposed by the teacher.

Following this replication study, Exp. III was conducted. Since during Exp. II the student had altered all of the teacher-imposed requirements to grant himself more points per response, it was necessary to determine whether self-contingencies had affected the academic rate increase or whether this increase was due to increased payoff. Experiment III, therefore, consisted of three stages: (1) the teacher specified the response-per-point requirements she had placed in effect throughout Exp. I and II; (2) the teacher specified the requirements that the student had instituted during Exp. II; and (3) the teacher again specified her original requirements. These requirements were identical to those listed in Table 2. The only difference between Exp. II and III was that in Exp. III, the teacher imposed the contingency requirements throughout, whereas in Exp. II the student set his own contingencies during Stage 2.

RESULTS

Experiment I

During the baseline period (unspecified contingencies), the student's median rate of response was 1.8 while his median rate during Stage 1 was 1.65. The response range during the baseline observations, which lasted for nine days, extended from 1.1 to 2.7; during the 12 days of Stage 1 it extended from 1.1 to 2.4. Stage 2 consisted of 22 daily sessions; in this stage the student's median rate of response was 2.5, ranging from 1.4 to 3.6. A median of 1.9 was obtained in the final stage of the experiment, which consisted of seven daily sessions, while the student's performance extended from 1.0 to 2.2 responses per minute. The data from this experiment are displayed in Fig. 1.

Experiment II

Throughout the 13 days of the first stage, the student's rate of response ranged from 0.8 to 2.1, with a median response rate of 1.6. During the second stage of this experiment, which also lasted for 13 days, the student's median rate was 2.3 responses per minute. His range at this time was 2.0 to 2.6 responses per minute. In the nine days of the final stage, return to teacher contingencies, the

Experiment I. Teacher vs. self-contingencies.

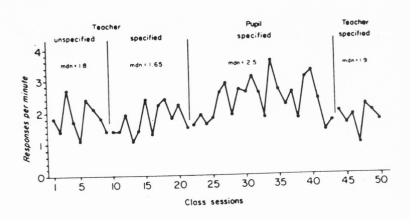

Fig. 1. Daily response rate throughout Exp. I.

student's median rate of response was 1.5; the range, 1.2 to 1.7. The results of Exp. II are shown in Fig. 2.

Experiment II. Teacher vs. self-contingencies.

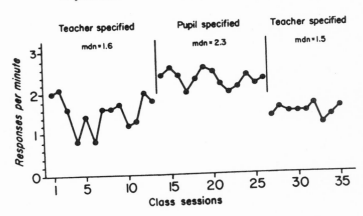

Fig. 2. Daily response rate throughout Exp. II.

Experiment III

The data from the final experiment are presented in Fig. 3. The student's median response rate was 1.5 for the 16 days of Stage 1. During Stage 2, which also lasted for 16 days, his median response rate was 1.2; and during the final stage, which consisted of 15 sessions, it was 1.4. The range during Stage 1 was from 1.1 to 2.1; from 0.6 to 1.7 during Stage 2; and from 0.6 to 1.6 during Stage 3.

Experiment III. Teacher vs. self-contingencies.

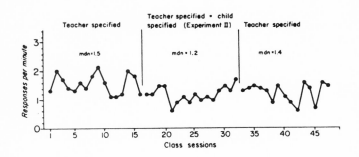

Fig. 3. Daily response rate throughout Exp. III.

DISCUSSION

The data from these experiments indicated that, for this student, self-imposed contingencies were associated with an increased academic response rate. This was evidenced in Exp. I and II; during Stage 2 of each experiment, the period of self-contingencies, the student's median performance was higher than during Stages 1 and 3, the periods of teacher-imposed contingencies.

That this response rate increase was attributed to the manipulation of the contingency manager, not to the contingency system being explained or not explained, was demonstrated in Exp. I. Although the latter manipulation might alter the response rate of some students, the data relevant to this variable indicated that, for this student, explaining or not explaining the contingencies produced nearly equal effects (see Fig. 1).

In addition, the data from Exp. III revealed that the response rate increase was due to manipulation of the contingency manager, and not to reinforcement magnitude. As mentioned earlier, although two experiments had demonstrated that during periods of self-specified contingencies the student responded at rates higher than during teacher-specified contingencies, this increased rate may have been due to mere magnitude of reinforcement. Indeed the contrary seemed to be the case; when the reinforcement ratios were increased by the teacher during Stage 2 of Exp. III, the student's response rate decreased, while it increased during Stage 3 when the original payment was in effect.

Throughout this study, response units from the various areas of reading, math, and spelling were grouped under a single category, "academic response." It may be, therefore, that the effects of the student specifying his own contingencies were more pronounced in certain academic areas than in others. It might also occur that a student, when allowed to specify his contingencies in one area but not in another, would, in fact, respond at an accelerated rate in both areas. Research is currently being conducted in which the effects of self-imposed contingencies are being analyzed within separate areas of academic responding in order to specify more precisely the effects of self-contingency management.

The evidence from the present experiment, that self-scheduling of events is associated with accelerated performance, is supported, in part, by a recent experiment (Lovitt and Curtiss, 1968). In order to investigate the effects of choice as an independent variable, students were given a number of daily sessions, each comprising three phases. One phase consisted of assigned mathematics, one of assigned reading, and one of a choice period in which the students could select either reading or mathematics. The results revealed that the students' rates of responding were greater during choice periods than during no-choice periods. It appeared that, for the students in this study, being allowed to choose (even between two academic tasks) was the critical variable.

If continued explorations with self-contingency management reveal similar findings, the educational implications appear rather obvious, for not only does the individual begin to develop self-managing skills by arranging certain aspects of his own environment, but in so doing his academic performance increases.

Research is now in progress to specify other components of self-management. Once these elements have been detailed, not only can they be scheduled sequentially, but each can be independently manipulated to evaluate its effect on academic responding. One study currently being conducted is comparing differences in student performance when a child has available a graph showing his daily performance rates *versus* when he is not provided a graph of these data. A second investigation is designed to evaluate the effects on academic performance when a student plots his own performance data *versus* when the teacher does the plotting. Another study is concerned with the function of specifying academic requirements. During certain phases of this study, the teacher sets the program limits, while during other portions, the student specifies the limits for daily performance.

Self-management no doubt involves behaviors other than those specified in this report. The fact remains, however, that if education is committed to educate students so that they can not only discriminate a number of teacher-arranged stimuli, but also arrange their own environment—hence control their own behavior—we must conceive of these self-controlling behaviors as capable of being taught and learned. The behaviors leading toward self-management, therefore, must be independently investigated and sequentially arranged to formulate a self-management curriculum.

REFERENCES

Haring, N. G. and Kunzelmann, H. P. The finer focus of therapeutic behavioral management. *Educational therapy,* Vol. 1. Seattle: Special Child Publications, 1966. Pp. 225-251.

Haring, N. G. and Lovitt, T. C. Operant methodology and educational technology in special education. In N. G. Haring & R. L. Schiefelbush (Eds.), *Methods in special education.* New York: McGraw-Hill, 1967. Pp. 12-48.

Lovitt, T. C. and Curtiss, K. A. Choice as an independent variable. Unpublished manuscript, University of Washington, 1968.

Sullivan Associates Program, *Programmed reading.* Cynthia Buchanan, Director. New York: Webster Division, McGraw-Hill, 1963.

Singer Mathematics Program. *Sets and Numbers.* Patrick Suppes, Director. New York: L. W. Singer Company, 1965.

20

The relative effects on math performance of single- versus multiple-ratio schedules: a case study

Thomas C. Lovitt and Karen A. Esveldt

This series of four experiments sought to assess the comparative effects of multiple- versus single-ratio schedules on a pupil's responding to mathematics materials. Experiment I, which alternated between single- and multiple-ratio contingencies, revealed that during the latter phase the subject responded at a higher rate. Similar findings were revealed by Exp. II. The third experiment, which manipulated frequency of reinforcement rather than multiple ratios, revealed that the alteration had a minimal effect on the subject's response rate. A final experiment, conducted to assess further the effects of multiple ratios, provided data similar to those of Exp. I and II.

In several recently reported studies, experimental analysis procedures were applied to classroom situations in an attempt to discover the effects of certain variables on different behaviors. They have: (a) described a behavior directly; (b) measured the occurrence of this behavior for an extended period of time; and (c) systematically manipulated a variable in order to analyze its effect.

The majority of these experimental analyses emanating from classrooms have been concerned with managerial behaviors such as inappropriate talking, disruptive, and out-of-seat behavior (Becker, Madsen, Arnold, and Thomas, 1967; Thomas, Nielson, Kuypers, and Becker, 1968). Other reports have described the manipulation of a variable when an academic behavior was the dependent variable (Lovitt and Curtiss, 1969). These studies are representative of current field investigations in that, generally, there is more concern given to the identification of the affecting variables than of the effects of the variables when they are intermittently scheduled.

Studies of contingencies or schedules of reinforcement involving children have been rare. Staats (1965), however, investigated the reading responses of

From *Journal of Applied Behavior Analysis,* 1970, 3, 261-270. Copyright 1970 by the Society for the Experimental Analysis of Behavior, Inc. Reprinted by permission.

Reprints may be obtained from Tom C. Lovitt, Child Development and Mental Retardation Center, Experimental Education Unit, University of Washington, Seattle, Washington 98105.

children under several reinforcement schedules and reported that, generally, higher response rates were produced under intermittent schedules. He added that: "Even the child under the variable-ratio and variable-interval schedule responded at a greater rate than the continuously reinforced children . . . [Staats, 1965, p. 45] ."

Staats' evidence would tend to corroborate the remarks of Morse (1966), who stated that contingencies of reinforcement are as influential in generating and maintaining behavioral patterns as the reinforcers themselves. Morse also noted that "powerful control of behavior by discriminative stimuli and by reinforcers such as food and water actually develops because they are favorably scheduled events [Morse, 1966, p. 59] ."

The present study, which was composed of a series of experiments, was prompted by a boy who responded academically at a very low rate. A previous attempt to accelerate the subject's response rate involved the manipulation of reinforcers by changing the consequences of his academic behavior from contingent time with games and crafts to social time with an adult male. This manipulation did not seem to affect significantly the dependent variable, academic rate.

The study sought to analyze the effects of contingencies of reinforcement on academic performance. To be precise, the purpose of this investigation was to compare performance rate when one reinforcement contingency was scheduled and when several reinforcement schedules were simultaneously available.

The dependent variables were correct and error performance rates on mathematics problems. The consequences or reinforcers for all studies were the same— points that were redeemable for minutes of free time. The independent variable was schedules of reinforcement.

During certain phases of these experiments, only one ratio was available—so many points contingent on correct math responses. In other phases, several ratios or contingency bands were available. During these latter phases, the subject was paid off from one or another ratio, contingent on his rate of responding. If his responses fell below a certain rate he received nothing. However, responses within a higher rate range were reinforced. Moreover, if he responded at a rate within the next higher band, he was paid off at a still higher rate. As the subject's response rate accelerated from one contingency range to the next, he was paid off with increasingly richer ratios.

EXPERIMENT I

Method

The subject was a 12-yr-old boy enrolled in a class for children with behavioral disorders at the Experimental Education Unit of the University of Washington. The material used was the subject's regular mathematics material *Sets and Numbers* (Suppes and Suppes, 1968).

During the 15-day baseline phase, data were obtained 1 hr daily on the subject's rate of responding to the math material. At this time the subject was on a 20:1 reinforcement schedule—1 min of free time in the "high-interest" room (Haring and Lovitt, 1967) contingent on 20 correct mathematics responses.

During the second phase (33 trials), four reinforcement bands were arranged. These new specifications were derived on the basis of the subject's performance during the first (20:1) phase. In order to receive any payoff during Phase 2 (multiple-ratio condition), the subject had to respond beyond his Phase 1 correct rate median of about one per minute.

Response rates higher than one per minute were reinforced at adjusted ratio schedules. The four ratio bands were:

(1) No points if fewer than 60 responses were emitted.
(2) Three points for 60 to 89 responses.
(3) Nine points for 90 to 119 responses.
(4) Fifteen points for more than 120 responses.

The sixtieth, ninetieth, and one-hundred-twentieth responses were marked on the subject's math sheet. These marks served as indicators to the subject only when all of his responses were correct. For example, if the subject passed the sixtieth problem, yet had answered four problems incorrectly, his point accumulation would be derived only from the 56 correct responses.

The ratio of points to responses was "richer" from one ratio band to the next. Within these bands, however, the ratios of reinforcement actually became leaner as the subject approached the next band. For example, as the subject passed into the second band, his 60 responses earned him three points, or a ratio of 20:1. Within the same band, his 89 responses still earned him three points, but now the ratio was 30:1.

The ratio conditions, either single or multiple, were explained to the subject each day. Table 1 describes the four ratio bands in terms of response requirements, rate equivalent, points earned, and the response-per-point or ratio equivalent that were in effect during the multiple-ratio phase.

Table 1. Multiple rate contingencies, Experiment I.

Responses	Rate/Minute	Points Earned	Ratio Equivalent
0-60	<1	0	0
60-89	1-1.48	3	20:1-30:1
90-119	1.5-1.98	9	10:1-13:1
120-240*	2-4.00**	15	8:1-16:1

*Subject's highest number of correct responses throughout Exp. I.
**Subject's highest rate throughout Exp. I.

In Phase 3, extending over seven trials, the initial contract was reinstated—1 point or 1 min per 20 correct mathematics responses. Throughout the experiment, the teacher calculated the subject's rate immediately after each session. Then, dependent on his rate of correct responses, he received a correspondent number of points that could be redeemed for minutes of free time.

Results

During the first phase, the subject's median response rate was 0.8 per min, in a range from 0.0 to 2.9. His median correct response rate during the multiple ratio stage was 1.7. His range of responding throughout this period was 3.8, extending from 0.2 to 4.0 responses per minute. A median response rate of 0.6 was calculated for the seven-day period when there was a return to initial, single-ratio conditions. The subject's range during this period was 1.3, extending from 0.2 to 1.5 problems per minute. Figure 1 presents the daily response rates throughout the experimental sessions.

Discussion

Although performance appeared to be sensitive to the experimental manipulation of the variable multiple ratios, two procedural matters could have spuriously influenced the findings. First, although the subject's overall response rate increased when multiple ratio bands were in effect and decreased after the variable was removed, the median difference from condition to condition was not great and the subject's response rate during all experimental phases fluctuated widely. The experimenters believed that this variability in response was partly because the math problems were not always sequentially arranged according to difficulty. The subject worked straight through his Suppes text where the types of problems varied from page to page. For example, on one page, problems such as $63 \div 7 = \square$ might appear, and on the next page narrative problems might appear. The subject's response rate was obviously affected by the type of problem.

Second, no error rate data were kept for this experiment. Since only correct rate of responding was recorded, it was impossible to determine whether the multiple ratios had any effect on the quality of the performance. Although the subject's correct rate was higher throughout the middle phase than in the first or last phases, the quality of responses (ratio of correct and error responses) was unknown. Because of these procedural concerns, the experimenters decided to conduct a second, more carefully controlled study.

EXPERIMENT II

Method

Since the major concern of this investigation was to assess the variable, multiple-ratio contingencies, and the subject's acquisition of mathematics responses was of secondary importance, the academic material was altered.

Experiment I. Single vs multiple ratios (Suppes Math Program).

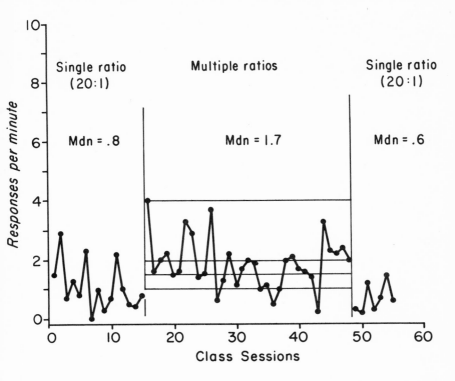

Fig. 1. Correct mathematics response rate throughout Exp. I where the Suppes Math Program was used and where single and multiple ratios were manipulated. The horizontal lines through the multiple-ratio phase indicate the four contingency bands.

Rather than require the subject to respond to mathematics material from the Suppes program, as in Exp. I, the subject was now given mathematics problems of the class 49 + 23 = _____, where the sum was ⩾198. Mathematics problems of this class were already in the subject's repertoire (Easy Math Program). It was hypothesized that material that was not only within his capabilities, but comparable from problem to problem, would be more sensitive to the experimental variable. It was also decided that error rate, as well as correct rate data, should be gathered.

During Phases 1 and 2, the subject's response-per-point requirement was 20:1 (the same ratio that prevailed during Phases 1 and 3 of Exp. I). In Phases 2 and 4, multiple-ratio bands were imposed. As in Exp. I, the four ratio bands were calculated on the basis of the subject's median performance in the first phase of the experiment. Since the subject's median rate was about three responses per minute during the initial phase of Exp. II, his responses had to exceed that rate to receive points during the multiple-ratio phases. Response rates of fewer than three per minute were not reinforced but rates over three were reinforced with successively richer ratios. For the four ratio bands the following adjusted rate requirements were specified:

(1) No points for 0 to 44 responses.
(2) Three points for 45 to 59 responses.
(3) Six points for 60 to 74 responses.
(4) Fifteen points for more than 75 responses.

Table 2 presents information concerning the multiple ratios, responses required, rate equivalent, points earned, and ratio equivalent.

Table 2. Multiple rate contingencies, Experiment II.

Responses	Rate/Minute	Points Earned	Ratio Equivalent
0-44	<3	0	0
45-59	3-3.93	3	15:1-20:1
60-74	4-4.93	6	10:1-13:1
75-126*	5-8.4**	15	5:1-8:1

*Subject's highest number of correct responses throughout Exp. II.
**Subject's highest rate throughout Exp. II.

If the subject responded at a rate of three problems per minute, his payoff would be at a ratio of 15:1, decreasing to 20:1 as his response rate approached four correct problems per minute. Then, if his rate of responding reached four per minute, the ratio would be 10:1.

Each session in Exp. II lasted for 15 min and, as in Exp. I, the single- and multiple-ratio conditions were explained daily to the subject. Throughout the multiple-ratio phases, the forty-fifth, sixtieth, and seventy-fifth mathematics problems were marked on the subject's worksheet.

Results

During the first phase, the subject's median rate of correct responses was 3.1, ranging from 2.0 to 4.5. A median rate of 5.35 correct responses per minute was obtained in the second phase, varying from 4.0 to 7.3 responses per minute. A median correct response rate of 3.9 was calculated for the third phase with responses ranging from 1.7 to 4.4. A median correct rate of 6.4 was obtained for the final multiple-ratio phase. The subject's response rate throughout this last phase varied from 5.5 to 8.4. The data from the four phases are presented in Fig. 2. The ranges of correct responses for the four experimental conditions were

2.5, 3.3, 2.7, and 2.9. This variability was virtually the same as that reported for Exp. I. The error-rate medians for the four phases were 0.2, 0.06, 0.1, and 0.15.

Experiment II. Single vs. multiple ratios (Easy Math Program).

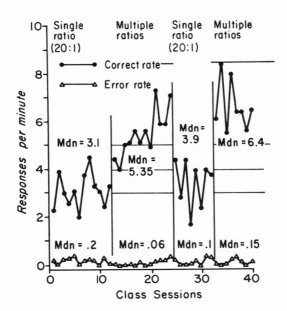

Fig. 2. Correct and error mathematics response rates throughout Exp. II where Easy Math problems were used and where single and multiple ratios were manipulated.

Discussion

It appears that the multiple ratios of reinforcement served to increase the rate of correct responses. It is also evident that no corresponding rise in error rate occurred. In fact, error rate variance was slight throughout the experiment.

The mathematics items throughout the second experiment were more uniform than those in Exp. I. The altered response rate from condition to condition could therefore be attributed more to the manipulated variable than to an irregular curriculum.

Although the variable—multiple-reinforcement ratios—apparently was effective in altering the subject's rate of mathematics responding, the possibility existed that sheer frequency of reinforcement was at least partially responsible for the performance increase. Figure 3 shows that the subject received much more reinforcement in terms of amount of points during the multiple-ratio phases of Exp. II than during the single ratio phases of the study. In fact, when a comparison is made between the subject's response rate and the rate at which points were dispensed during the second experiment, the patterns were very similar; i.e., when responses per minute were high, number of points received was also high (see Figs. 2 and 3).

Experiment II. Single vs. multiple ratio.

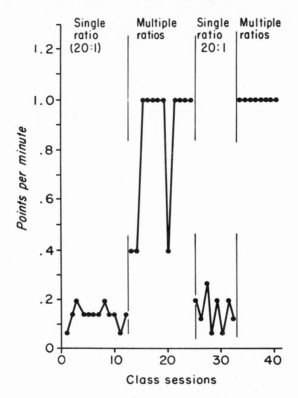

Fig. 3. Rate of points received per minute by the subject during the four phases of Exp. II.

To determine whether the multiple-ratio condition or frequency of reinforcement was the crucial variable in affecting response-rate differences, a third experiment was conducted in which frequency of reinforcement was the only variable manipulated.

EXPERIMENT III

Method

The first and third phases used the same base ratio as the first two experiments; for 20 correct responses the subject received 1 min of free time. A 5:1 ratio, the highest possible during previous multiple-ratio phases, was scheduled during the second phase of the study. The arithmetic materials were the same as those used in the second experiment (Easy Math Program).

Results

The results of Exp. III, illustrated in Fig. 4, reveal that frequency of reinforcement was apparently only a minimally affecting variable. His median correct rates were 5.65 during Phase 1, 5.9 during Phase 2, and 5.5 during Phase 3. The error-rate medians during the three phases were 0.06, 0.06, and 0.03. The subject's correct rate ranges were 3.2 (4.3 to 7.5), 2.7 (4.7 to 7.4), and 1.3 (5.2 to 6.5) during the first, second, and third phases respectively.

Discussion

As indicated by the data in Fig. 4, the subject's correct rate of responding was but slightly affected by the variable, frequency of reinforcement. Although "easy math problems" were used in both Exp. II and III and the 5:1 ratio was the richest ratio scheduled in both studies, the subject's performance in Exp. II was quite different from his effort in Exp. III. In Exp. II, his median correct rates were much higher in the manipulation phases (2 and 4) than during the control phases; this was not the case in Exp. III.

This difference in response rate between Exp. II and III could be attributed to the fact that during Exp. II, multiple-ratio bands were scheduled, whereas during Exp. III only one ratio was scheduled. It is also possible, however, that this performance difference was the result of "marking." During Exp. II, certain problems were marked, thus informing the subject that he had passed from one ratio band to another (if all his answers were correct). It is possible that marking served as a stimulus for accelerated performance. A further experiment was conducted to investigate this possibility.

EXPERIMENT IV

Method

The reason for conducting the fourth experiment was to determine whether marking certain problems to indicate multiple ratios was of itself accountable for the subject's rate increase.

During the multiple-ratio phases of Exp. II, the forty-fifth, sixtieth, and seventy-fifth responses were marked on the subject's math sheets to indicate

Experiment III. 20:1 vs. 5:1 (Easy Math Program).

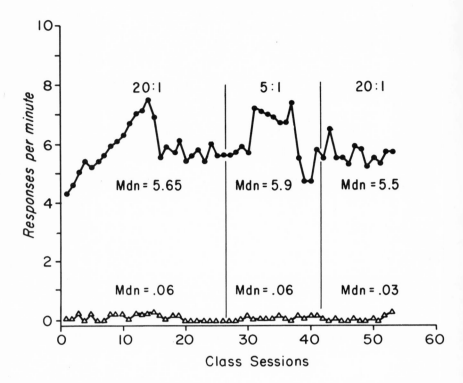

Fig. 4. Correct and error mathematics response rates during Exp. III where frequency of reinforcement was manipulated.

which schedule of reinforcement would prevail. These marks were included throughout all phases of Exp. IV.

The procedures were the same as those of Exp. II. Responses were reinforced on a 20:1 ratio during Phases 1 and 3, while multiple ratios were in effect in the second and fourth phases. The type of mathematics problems and the length of each experimental session were also the same as before: "easy" materials and 15-min sessions. The ratio conditions, either single or multiple, were explained daily to the subject.

The multiple ratios employed in Phases 2 and 4 were derived in the same way as in Exp. I and II. These rates were based on the subject's average response rate during the initial 20:1 phase, which during Exp. IV, was six responses per

minute.[1] In a 15-min session the subject was expected to emit 90 responses (15 x 6). Therefore, the four differential rate ratios were:
  (1) No points for 0 to 90 responses.
  (2) Six points for 90 to 99 responses.
  (3) Eight points for 100 to 119 responses.
  (4) Twelve points for more than 120 responses.
Table 3 presents information concerning the multiple ratios.

Table 3. Multiple rate contingencies, Experiment IV.

Responses	Rate/Minute	Points Earned	Ratio Equivalent
0-90	<6	0	0
90-99	6-6.6	6	15:1-16.5:1
100-119	6.7-7.9	8	12.5:1-14.9:1
120-144*	8-9.6**	12	10:1-12:1

*Subject's highest number of correct responses throughout Exp. IV.
**Subject's highest rate throughout Exp. IV.

Results

During the first phase (Fig. 5), the single-ratio phase, the subject's response rate ranged from 3.9 to 7.4; a median response rate of 6.1. Throughout the 15 sessions of Phase 2, his median rate of responding was 8.1, ranging from 7.5 to 9.6.

When conditions were reversed, the subject's response rate ranged from 5.5 to 7.8. His median rate throughout this phase was 6.8. The fourth phase of Exp. IV, the return to multiple-ratio bands, was characterized by a response range of 1.9 (from 7.6 to 9.5) and a median rate of responding of 8.4. The error-rate medians during the four phases of the study were 0.0, 0.0, 0.0, and 0.06.

Discussion

Apparently, the cue marks used in Exp. II did not influence response rate; for even though the forty-fifth, sixtieth, and seventy-fifth responses were marked throughout the single-ratio phases, his correct rates, during those phases, were

---

[1]In Exp. I, II, and IV the first ratio bands were similarly derived. The lowest rate of the first band was comparable to the subject's median rate in the first phase (single ratio) of the experiment. Subsequent ratio bands were rather arbitrarily established.

lower than during the multiple-ratio conditions. Furthermore, the forty-fifth, sixtieth, and seventy-fifth responses were marked throughout the multiple-ratio phases, when in fact the ratio bands corresponded to the ninetieth, one-hundredth, and one-hundred-twentieth responses.[2] Yet the subject's correct response rate was higher during these phases than when a single ratio was scheduled. It would appear then, that the marks on the pupil's paper, whether they corresponded to ratio changes or not, were totally nonfunctional.

Less variation was observed between the correct-rate medians of Phases 1 and 2, and 3 and 4 of Exp. IV than between the same phases of Exp. II. The differences between the correct medians of adjacent phases in Exp. II were 2.2 and 2.5. The differences in Exp. IV were 2.0 and 1.6. These data could indicate that the subject was perhaps reaching a performance ceiling. As noted earlier, the same materials were used in both experiments. Therefore, the more familiar the subject became with the materials, rate differences between experimental conditions would become increasingly more difficult to obtain.

The subject's gradual increase in response rate may be noted throughout Exp. II, III, and IV by analyzing the data in the single or 20:1 ratio phases. The correct-rate medians during these phases throughout the three experiments were 3.1, 3.9, 5.65, 5.5, 6.1, and 6.8. This acceleration across experiments may also be pointed out by presenting the data from the multiple-ratio phases of Exp. II and IV. The correct-rate medians during multiple-ratio phases through the two experiments were 5.3, 6.4, 8.1, and 8.4.

GENERAL DISCUSSION

The independent variable throughout this study, multiple-ratio contingencies, was a series of ratio bands. This arrangement of ratios was similar to a series of DRH schedules, where successively more rapid rates are reinforced by correspondingly richer payoffs. However, the similarity between the independent variable in this study and traditional efforts to reinforce high response rates differentially is appropriate for only the lowest portion of each reinforcement band. Since each contingency band represented a range of ratios, the higher the response rate within a band, the higher the reinforcement ratio. It can be argued that it would be most economical, in terms of work expended for points received for the subject to perform in the lower portion of each contingency band where the schedule is richer. In this series of experiments, the subject did not always behave in such a manner.

As may be noted in Phase 2 of Exp. I, of the 15 times the subject's rate was in the highest payoff band (over two responses per minute) his rates during 10

---

[2] In Exp. I and II, the multiple ratios were derived from the subject's median response rate in the first single-ratio phase. Since in Exp. IV marks were used in the first phase, before any knowledge of his performance, the same marks were used in the second phase. Therefore the marks in this experiment were not derived from the subject's median rate in the first phase and, correspondingly, did not describe the contingency bands that were in effect during multiple-ratio conditions.

Experiment IV. Single vs. multiple ratios (Easy Math Program).

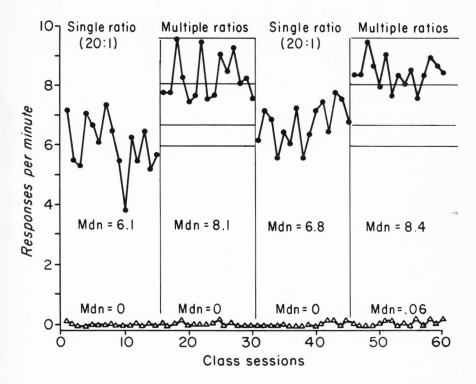

Fig. 5. Correct and error mathematics response rates during Exp. IV where Easy Math problems were scheduled and where single and multiple ratios were manipulated.

sessions were no higher than 2.5 responses per minute. It might be said, then, that in this experiment his behavior was very efficient. During Exp. II, Phase 2, the subject responded within 0.5 of the third payoff band twice and within 0.5 of the fourth band three times. Only once in Phase 4 was his response rate within 0.5 of the lower limit of any band. In Exp. IV, Phase 2, when the subject's rates fell within the third ratio band, they were invariably at the top of the band. When his rates fell in the highest band, he responded within 0.5 of the bottom of the band four of the eight times. During the final phase of the experiment the subject's rates, when in the highest payoff band, were within 0.5 of the lower limit six of the 12 times.

When the data from the first multiple-ratio phase of Exp. I, II, and IV were analyzed, it was noted that higher ratio bands generated more pronounced behavioral effects than lower bands. When the subject's responses were analyzed during the four bands of the multiple phases it was discovered that the subject was paid off more often from the highest rate band than from any of the others. During Phase 2 of Exp. I, the subject's response rate fell three times within the no-payoff band, seven times in the next higher, eight in the next to highest, and 15 in the highest. During Phase 2 of Exp. II, his rates fell three times in the next-to-highest and nine times in the highest band, while never falling in the no-payoff or next higher ratio bands. In Exp. IV, Phase 2, the subject was also paid off from only the top two bands—seven times from the next-to-highest and eight from the highest.

Numerous academic, social, and economic situations come to mind that are based on the rather complicated ratios investigated in this report. Circumstances where several reinforcement ratios are available and where the subject must exert more and more effort as he approaches the next ratio are common.

In social organizations like scouting, where several steps or ranks are sequentially arranged, this type of ratio is in operation. When the rank of Life Scout is reached, the scout does not have to increase his behavioral repertoire to retain the rank. But later, as he attempts to pass the skills required of an Eagle, he must first master the easiest tests, then the more difficult. As he approaches the next level of reinforcement, his rate of behavior must increase, although while it is increasing he is still recognized as a Life Scout and is paid off from that level.

A schedule of this type is noted in certain businesses. Civil service employees are also assigned ratings and are paid accordingly. If they wish to advance from one level to the next, they must become more competent, pass tests, or in some way increase their rates of behavior. While these rates are in the process of increasing, however, they are paid off from the initial reinforcement level. Thus, until the next reinforcement band is reached, the civil servant must do more work or more complicated work for the same reinforcement. Only when he is promoted does his reinforcement match his work efforts. And then the process begins all over again.

Rarely in the "real" social and economic worlds are reinforcement levels or promotions linearly related to behavior (too often promotions have no relationship to behavior). These promotions usually occur when a person has greatly accelerated his performance. Once elevated, however, the person's behavioral rate generally stabilizes (post-reinforcement pause).

On the basis of this series of studies it appears that multiple-ratio conditions should be considered an effective variable when the objective is to accelerate academic response rate. Teachers should, however, exercise some caution in scheduling multiple contingencies, as in this study, to accelerate performance. Such contingencies, if associated with reading or arithmetic, when the acquisition of new information is of prime concern, could indeed accelerate responding. However, although the response rate increases, the quality of performance is not necessarily improved; for as correct rate increases, so might error rate. Teachers, therefore, when measuring academic performance, must monitor error rate as well as correct rate and should, in some instances, to influence high-quality performance, associate some contingency with errors.

This study, besides exploring a condition that could serve to accelerate academic performance, also demonstrates a technique for the investigation of other independent variables. Educators, particularly educational researchers, have at least two responsibilities; (a) to arrange circumstances so that pupils acquire new behaviors, and (b) to discover what effects various environmental variables have on behavior.

In setting up experiments, the researcher must consider his objective; is he concerned with the pupil's acquisition of behaviors, or with the discovery of environmental relationships? These objectives are not necessarily the same. If his concern is for the former, measures of the pupil's performance before, during, and after training should be taken to determine the effects of teaching. If the training was successful (the pupil's correct rate increased and error rate decreased), the pupil's behavior is probably irreversible; a reversal condition would therefore serve no purpose.

In such instances, where learning occurs and where an independent variable such as points or tokens is also being manipulated, and if the rate of the measured behavior is altered, the reason for those effects would not be known. If the performance improved, it could be the function of the acquisition of additional skills, the manipulated variable, or some interaction.

However, if the researcher's objective is to ascertain the effects of some environmental condition—arrange situations where the variable is alternately available—he should arrange the setting so that possible effects of that variable can be detected. One way of arranging such conditions was the tactic employed throughout most of the present study—the use of easy or known materials. When the math or reading materials scheduled for a pupil are within his repertory and if a wide rate range of response is possible, the effects of an environmental manipulation on response rate can be isolated from the effects of learning. Such experiments may initially appear as too expensive for the classroom teacher who must be concerned with assisting pupils to acquire dozens of skills. However, unless educational researchers, either in classrooms, laboratories, or clinics, begin to explore the circumstances that may affect learning, the practice of teaching will continue to be nonempirically based.

REFERENCES

Becker, W. C., Madsen, C. H., Jr., Arnold, C. R., and Thomas, D. R. The contingent use of teacher attention and praise in reducing classroom behavior problems. *Journal of Special Education,* 1967, 1, 287-307.

Haring, N. G. and Lovitt, T. C. Operant methodology and educational technology in special education. In N. G. Haring and R. L. Schiefelbusch (Eds.), *Methods in Special Education.* New York: McGraw-Hill, 1967. Pp. 12-48.

Lovitt, T. C. and Curtiss, Karen A. Effects of manipulating an antecedent event on mathematics response rate. *Journal of Applied Behavior Analysis,* 1969, 1, 329-333.

Morse, W. H. Intermittent reinforcement. In W. K. Honig (Ed.), *Operant behavior: areas of research and application.* New York: Appleton-Century-Crofts, 1966. Pp. 52-108.

Suppes, P. and Suppes, J. *Sets and numbers.* New York: Singer/Random House, 1968.

Staats, A. W. A case in and a strategy for the extension of learning principles to problems of human behavior. In L. Krasner and L. D. Ullmann (Eds.), *Research in behavioral modification.* New York: Holt, Rinehart & Winston, 1965. Pp. 27-55.

Thomas, D. R., Nielsen, L. J., Kuypers, D. S., and Becker, W. C. Social reinforcement and remedial instruction in the elimination of a classroom behavior problem. *Journal of Special Education,* 1968, 2, 291-306.

21

Classroom applications of self-determined reinforcement

E. L. Glynn

Self-determined, experimenter-determined, and chance-determined token rein-forcement treatments were compared with a no-token treatment, in terms of effect on the learning of history and geography material in the classroom. Each treatment was assigned to one of four heterogeneous classes of grade nine girls. An initial baseline period preceded the differential reinforcement period, and a token withdrawal period followed. Subsequently, the self-determined treatment was employed in all three token reinforcement classes, before a final baseline period occurred. Findings included a similarity of initial baseline performance for all classes, an equal superiority of self-determined and experimenter-determined treatments to chance-determined and no-token treatments, and significant improvement from initial baseline to final baseline for self-determined and experimenter-determined treatments, but not chance-determined and no-token treatments. Differential token reinforcement experience was found to influence subsequent rate of self-determined token reinforcement.

There is confusion in the thinking of educators on the use of extrinsic reinforcers in the control of children's classroom learning.

Clearly, educators do not object to extrinsic reinforcers *per se,* since grades, promotions, degrees, diplomas, and medals appear to enjoy the same widespread usage that Skinner noted in 1953. Moreover, it is difficult to imagine a classroom where teacher praise and reprimand are not used in an attempt to control children's behavior. Despite this widespread use of extrinsic reinforcement, there is objection to the employment of certain forms (such as candy and tokens) on

From *Journal of Applied Behavior Analysis,* 1970, 3, 123-132. Copyright 1970 by the Society for the Experimental Analysis of Behavior, Inc. Reprinted by permission.

Reprints may be obtained from the author, Department of Education, University of Auckland, Box 2175, Auckland, New Zealand. Research reported in this paper was carried out in partial fulfillment of the Ph.D. degree at the Ontario Institute for Studies in Education (University of Toronto). The author is indebted to his chairman, Dr. S. B. K. Henderson, for his valued support and encouragement.

the grounds that the student will become dependent on them and will be unable to perform without them. (Anderson, 1967.) Yet, surely, the same objection should hold against all forms of extrinsic reinforcement, including teacher praise and reprimand.

Perhaps an explanation for this confusion is that the operation of a token reinforcement system, more than the generally inconsistent operation of teacher praise and reprimand, emphasizes the extent to which children's behavior is under the control of an external agent. External control of behavior is distasteful to many educators who would agree with R. M. Gagne, that "... the student must be progressively weaned from dependence on the teacher or other agent external to himself." (Gagne 1965, p. 213.)

It is suggested that some of the confusion has resulted from equating extrinsic reinforcement with external control of behavior. The two terms are not interchangeable. Skinner (1953), in discussing self-control, suggests the individual may be capable of controlling his own behavior by means of dispensing his own reinforcement contingent upon making certain classes of responses. Various studies of self-reinforcement (Kanfer, Bradley, and Marston, 1962; Bandura and Kupers, 1964; and Bandura and Perloff, 1967), have permitted human subjects to take over the reinforcing function of the experimenter, by signalling correct responses, or rewarding themselves from a supply of tokens. Such self-administered reinforcing systems do seem to possess behavior maintenance capabilities, at least for simple responses—cranking a wheel (Bandura and Perloff, 1967), and visual discrimination (Kanfer and Duerfeldt, 1967).

The present study attempted to apply self-administered reinforcement procedures to classroom learning. If these procedures were to prove effective, they may be more acceptable to educators because they suggest a way to wean children from dependence on an external agent, and at the same time, would permit the use of effective extrinsic reinforcers.

Three major purposes of the study were: (1) to compare the effectiveness of self-determined and experimenter-determined token reinforcement treatments in the classroom setting; (2) to examine the effects of token withdrawal following these treatments; and (3) to examine the effect of differential token reinforcement experience on the amount of subsequent self-determined token reinforcement. A distinction is made here between *determination* and *administration* of reinforcement. All token reinforcement in this study was self-administered, but the amount of reinforcement was experimenter-determined, chance-determined, or self-determined (within the limits imposed by the experimental procedure).

METHOD

Experimental Situation

The study was planned to require a minimum of accommodation on the part of teacher and children, since it was intended to test the practicality of token reinforcement within the regular classroom program. The study did not require the teacher to alter subject content or teaching methods. Four intact class groups were used, which meant that no changes in timetable were requested, and children were never removed from their usual class setting. The subject matter, history and geography, was taught to all four classes, in the same topical order, by the one teacher. The token reinforcement treatments were administered by one experimenter in all four classes.

Subjects

One hundred and twenty-eight ninth-grade girls, in four classes in a Toronto Separate School, served as subjects. Class size ranged from 30 to 34. Girls had been assigned to classes from an alphabetic list, which was divided into four sections. While not truly random, this procedure at least precluded deliberate stratification of classes according to ability.

None of the children presented any problem to the teacher with regard to disruptive behavior. The teacher considered all children "well-motivated" to learn, and interested in the subject matter. Having been present for a portion of the history and geography lessons of all four classes for the baseline period, the experimenter shared these opinions with the teacher.

Dependent Variables

1. Test Performance. Working from a list of history and geography topics supplied by the teacher, the experimenter prepared 40 reading sheets, each of approximately 500 words. The class history and geography texts provided source material. Accompanying each reading sheet was a sheet of 20 five-option multiple-choice questions, based on the factual content of the reading sheets. Hence, the major dependent variable for each of the five phases of the study was the average number of test items correctly answered by each girl.

An attempt was made to match the readings and tests closely with the teacher's program. This was not always achieved because of the occasional need for the teacher to revise a topic before going on to the next, and because the experimenter was requested to produce several readings on New Zealand, at a time when the teacher had almost completed her coverage of the topic. The four classes received all readings and tests, in the same order, with each phase of the study containing approximately five history and five geography readings.

2. Performance-token Ratios. The tokens were slips of paper, 2 by 1 in. (5 by 2.5 cm) bearing a star and the words "one credit." Tokens were exchanged for a variety of inexpensive prizes at the end of the first token phase, and at the end of the study. After each token reinforcement phase, a performance-token ratio was obtained for every girl. This ratio was formed by computing the total number of correct test items obtained in a particular phase, and dividing this number by the total number of tokens received in that phase.

Originally, it was planned to make the tokens exchangeable for the potentially reinforcing events available within the school program, and selected by children according to preference. Examples of such potentially reinforcing events are: time off a particular activity, library time, free time, homework exemptions, punishment exemptions, and the right to perform special duties. However, it was discovered that control of such events was out of the hands of the teacher concerned. Secondary school teachers do not have the same freedom in manipulating timetables and reinforcing events as do elementary school teachers, where one teacher handles one class for almost all the academic program.

In view of this difficulty, it was decided to provide a series of prizes, which could be obtained by turning in credits. An opportunity was taken to make the prizes relevant to some of the history and geography material, by using numerous inexpensive New Zealand souvenir items. When turning in their tokens, the girls were allowed to select a prize from the many items displayed, according to their mark order in number of tokens earned. There was a sufficient range of prizes for even the last-ranked child to have some choice.

3. Inter-class Communication. An attempt was made to measure the extent of inter-class communication that occurred during the study, since it was realized that performance of one class could also be influenced by the knowledge that other classes were receiving different treatments. A set of three open-ended questions was administered to all children at the end of the study, asking them whether the treatment given their own class differed from that given the other classes, and if so, to state how.

Procedure

1. First Baseline Phase (Baseline 1). This was a two-week period that served to establish basal measures of test performance in each of the four classes, and to accustom the children to the presence of the experimenter and the testing procedures. No tokens were issued.

Each day, the children were given a passage to read for 3 min, immediately after which the passage was collected, and a further 3 min were allowed for the multiple-choice test. (In considering these short time limits, it should be noted that the material encountered on the reading sheets would have been covered by current teacher lessons). When the 3-min test session was over, immediate feedback of results was given, by means of the experimenter reading out the letter code for correct answers. The children then counted the number of test items correct, and entered this on a slip of paper in individual envelopes supplied for the purpose. Finally, test sheets and envelopes were collected by the experimenter. Instructions stressed that information in the envelopes would not be made available to anyone other than the experimenter.

2. First Token Phase (Token 1). This was the only period in which token reinforcement procedures differed across classes. The procedures employed were:

(a) Experimenter-determined token reinforcement. Under this treatment, children received tokens according to an explicit rate of one token per four correct answers. During the token reinforcement periods, five tokens were placed in each envelope each day. The children were instructed to calculate the number of tokens earned by dividing their test score by four. An arbitrary rule permitted the taking of an additional token for a fractional number. (Thus a child would take four tokens if the number earned were 3¼, 3½, or 3¾.)

(b) Self-determined token reinforcement treatment. Under this treatment, children were invited to: "decide how many tokens you think you should award yourself. You can decide on any number from zero to five." No rules or suggestions were made concerning bases for decision making. The use of envelopes was intended to minimize the effect of social cues from peers, and of modeling peer standards, both of which are known to influence the rate of self-reinforcement (Marston, 1964; Bandura and Whalen, 1966; McMains and Liebert, 1968).

(c) Chance-determined token reinforcement. This was, in effect, an incentive-control treatment. Throughout the first token phase, the total number of tokens received by this class was kept identical with that of the self-reinforced class. Each day, chance-reinforced children were randomly assigned a "partner" from among the self-reinforced children. Regardless of performance of the chance-reinforced child, she found in her envelope the number of tokens that her self-reinforced "partner" for the day had taken. As well as providing an incentive control treatment, this procedure enabled the examination of the effect of such inconsistent experience of amount of reinforcement on extent of subsequent self-reinforcement.

(d) No-token reinforcement treatment. No token reinforcement was given under this treatment. The procedure was exactly the same as during Baseline I.

3. First Token Withdrawal Phase (Withdrawal 1). During this phase, token reinforcement was withdrawn from experimenter-reinforced, self-reinforced, and chance-reinforced classes.

4. Second Token Phase (Token II). Tokens were reintroduced for the experimenter-reinforced, self-reinforced, and chance-reinforced classes, but all three classes were now permitted to operate the self-reinforced procedure. The major question asked was whether the children previously reinforced according to an externally imposed standard (experimenter-reinforced) would subsequently display a rate of self-reinforcement close to this standard.

5. Second Baseline Phase (Baseline II). During this phase, the baseline readings and tests were readministered, in order to compare increase in performance on relearning among the four classes. Tokens were withdrawn for the first half (Withdrawal II), but included for the second half (Token III).

6. Review Test. A review test was constructed of items from each of the tests administered during the first token phase, the token withdrawal, and the second token phase, in order to determine whether treatment effects were of a long-term nature. Since the test was administered after the repeat of baseline, the test-retest interval was two to four weeks for items from the second token phase (Sections C), four to six weeks for items from the token withdrawal phase (Section B), and six to eight weeks for items from the first token phase (Section A). For the review test, seven tokens were provided in the envelopes of the experimenter-reinforced, self-reinforced, and chance-reinforced classes, and the self-reinforced procedure was applied in all three classes.

RESULTS

Daily test performance scores of all classes throughout the study are listed in Table 1. Also shown are the mean test performance scores for each phase of the study.

Table 1. Mean performance scores for all sessions and phases.

			Class		
Session		Non-Reinforced	Chance-Reinforced	Experimenter-Reinforced	Self-Reinforced
Baseline I:	1	10.60•	9.57	9.88	9.66
	2	11.60•	10.54	11.13	11.47
	3	9.69•	8.80	8.70	8.35
	4	9.82	8.63	8.91	9.91•
	5	10.71•	10.19	9.47	8.70
	6	12.21•	10.87	9.81	10.69
	7	9.72•	6.97	8.39	9.25
	8	10.55•	9.32	9.81	9.70
	9	9.46•	6.55	7.44	7.25
	10	9.63	9.42	8.78	9.97•
	Mean:	10.38•	9.02	9.13	9.47
Token I:	11	7.44	7.14	8.33•	8.33•
	12	10.08	9.37	11.29•	10.15
	13	9.38	9.53	11.08	12.66•
	14	10.30	9.37	11.32	11.45•
	15	8.07	6.28	9.14	10.14•
	16	10.53	10.41	11.62	12.54•
	17	9.57	8.07	10.32•	10.07
	18	11.50	11.33	13.97•	13.27
	19	11.17	11.13	12.41	12.56•
	20	10.07	10.09	12.06•	11.61
	Mean:	9.71	9.13	11.12•	11.09
Withdrawal I:	21	11.25	9.20	11.61•	10.67
	22	10.53	8.75	10.52	11.10•
	23	12.83•	12.52	12.75	12.39
	24	13.31	13.79	13.63	14.48•
	25	11.29	10.86	10.94	12.73•
	26	8.44•	7.39	8.44•	7.40
	27	10.62•	9.46	9.74	10.23
	28	10.31•	8.87	10.13	8.80
	29	10.69	10.03	9.70	11.23•
	30	8.59•	6.83	8.55	8.32
	Mean:	10.44	9.72	10.53	10.87•
Token II:	31	11.12•	9.42	9.48	10.16
	32	11.97	10.55	11.84	12.28•
	33	9.89•	8.58	9.48	9.33
	34	11.47	10.42	11.63•	11.10
	35	9.17	8.10	9.52	9.87•
	36	11.50	9.46	11.28	13.22•
	37	8.36	7.52	8.76	9.13•
	38	9.63	8.83	11.03•	9.38
	39	9.83	10.34	11.10	12.16•
	40	12.30	11.45	12.65•	11.80
	Mean:	10.47	9.33	10.64•	10.59
Baseline II:					
(a) Withdrawal II:	41	10.90	11.42	12.42	12.70•
	42	13.64	12.55	13.84	14.09•
	43	10.36•	8.13	10.06	10.00
	44	8.36	9.97	10.91•	10.90
	45	11.57	10.40	11.25	11.07
	Mean:	10.74	10.49	11.79	11.87•
(b) Token III:	46	11.38	11.04	12.78	13.19•
	47	10.29	9.50	10.42•	10.10
	48	10.72	10.72	10.83	11.57•
	49	10.59•	8.93	9.37	9.83
	50	11.14	10.41	11.23	12.35•
	Mean:	10.48	9.78	10.89	10.96•

*Indicates highest scoring class.

It was considered that the performance of the nonreinforced class provided the best available estimate of variations due to fluctuations in test difficulty. Accordingly, Fig. 1 was produced by depicting the daily performance of the three treatment classes, in terms of difference from the nonreinforced class, so that variation due to fluctuating test difficulty might be removed.

Baseline I

An analysis of variance performed on mean scores for Baseline I yielded a non-significant between-classes effect (F 3, 116 = 1.65, p> 0.05), and Hartley's test for homogeneity of variance yielded an F max. of 1.40 which is not significant. The four classes were thus regarded as being similar in performance during Baseline I.

Token I

An analysis of covariance was performed on Token I mean scores, using Baseline I mean scores as covariate. The between-classes effect was significant. (F 3, 115 = 16.69, p< 0.001). An analysis of variance for repeated-measures on test scores in every alternate session of the Token I phase yielded an insignificant classes-by-sessions interaction (F 12, 464 = 1.61, p> 0.05). Hence, analysis of mean Token I scores do not conceal any useful information about differential performance of classes across sessions.

The significant between-classes effect noted above is evident in Fig. 1. Token I mean scores were adjusted for the effect of the covariate (Baseline I performance), by the method suggested by Winer (1962, p. 592). Comparisons were made among the adjusted means by the Newman-Keuls procedure. The experimenter-reinforced and self-reinforced classes did not differ from one another, nor did the nonreinforced and chance-reinforced classes differ from one another. However, both the experimenter-reinforced and the self-reinforced classes differed significantly from the non-reinforced and chance-reinforced classes. The self-determined reinforcement procedure was equally as effective as the externally determined one, in producing an increase in performance.

Withdrawal I

The analysis of covariance performed on Withdrawal I mean scores (using Baseline I mean scores as covariate), yielded a significant between-classes effect (F 3, 115 = 3.24, p< 0.05), though the effect was weaker than that of Token I. This was expected, since in Token I, performance was directly influenced by differences in treatment procedures. Again, a repeated-measures analysis of variance yielded a nonsignificant classes-by-sessions interaction (F 12, 464 = 1.17, p> 0.05) so that analyses of mean scores for Withdrawal I did not conceal information about differential performance of classes across sessions. The significant effect reported above suggests that there remained some effects of Token I treatments during Withdrawal I. This can be seen in Fig. 1. After the

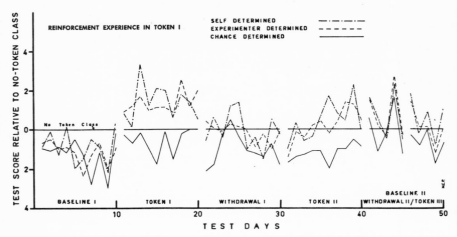

Fig. 1. Daily test performance of the three token classes relative to the no-token class.

mean scores from Withdrawal I had been adjusted for the effect of the covariate, Newman-Keuls comparisons were made among them. It was found that the experimenter-reinforced and self-reinforced classes performed better than the nonreinforced class, but not better than the chance-reinforced class.

Token II

The analysis of covariance performed on Token II mean scores (using Baseline I mean scores as covariate) yielded a significant, though weak, between-classes effect (F 3, 115 = 2.85, p< 0.05), but none of the possible comparisons among adjusted means yielded significant differences at the 0.05 level by Newman-Keuls tests. However, it can be seen from Fig. I that the experimenter-reinforced and self-reinforced classes were superior to the nonreinforced class for the greater part of Token II, while the chance-reinforced class always remained inferior to the nonreinforced class, suggesting some differences in performance between classes.

A repeated-measure analysis of variance of Token II data yielded a significant classes-by-sessions interaction (F 12, 464 = 2.47, p< 0.01). Hence, Token II mean scores obscure differential performance of classes across sessions. Figure 1 shows that the experimenter-reinforced and self-reinforced classes displayed a more obvious improvement in performance relative to the nonreinforced class than did the chance-reinforced class.

Baseline II

As the readings and tests administered during Baseline II were the same as those for Baseline I, comparisons of performance gains over the two administrations were made across classes.

Highly significant phase effects were found, for both the Withdrawal II and Token III halves of the repeated-baseline tests, but these may be readily attributed to general practice effects. However, significant classes-by-phases interactions were also found: F 3, 116 = 4.23, p< 0.01 (for Withdrawal II), and F 3, 116 = 2.80, p< 0.05 (for Token III). Newman-Keuls comparison were carried out to examine these effects further. Table 2 shows that the interaction effect is attributable to significant increases on Baseline II administration for the experimenter-reinforced and self-reinforced classes. This increase is not significant in the case of the nonreinforced and chance-reinforced classes.

Table 2. Newman-Keuls qr values for differences between Baseline I and Baseline II Mean Test performance scores.

Test Days	Class	Baseline I	Baseline II	qr
1-5	NR	10.49	10.74	0.84
and	YR	9.43	10.49	3.53
41-45	ER	9.55	11.79	7.42**
	SR	9.49	11.87	7.86**
6-10	NR	9.84	10.48	1.77
and	YR	8.58	9.78	3.32
46-50	ER	8.66	10.89	6.18**
	SR	8.81	10.96	5.96**

**$p < 0.01$;

Review Test

Analysis of variance performed on scores from each section of the Review Test yielded a significant between-classes effect (F 3, 108 = 4.47, p< 0.01) for Token I items (Section A). Newman-Keuls comparisons of class means revealed a pattern of significant results parallel to that of Token I performance. On Section A items, both the experimenter-reinforced and self-reinforced classes (x = 9.89 and 9.71) were slightly better than the nonreinforced and chance-reinforced classes (x = 8.21 and 8.00). There was no significant difference between the self-reinforced and experimenter-reinforced classes, nor between the nonreinforced and chance-reinforced classes. The performance increments resulting from differential reinforcement schedules evidently have some permanence.

Sections B and C of the Review Test (Withdrawal I and Token II items) yielded no between-classes effects that reflected earlier treatments.

Performance-Token Ratios

Table 3 presents data concerning number of tokens taken, and performance-token ratios of the three token classes throughout the study.

Table 3. Number of tokens taken and performance
token ratios in all token phases.

Phase	Chance Reinforced Class		Experimenter- Reinforced Class		Self- Reinforced Class	
	Number	Ratio	Number	Ratio	Number	Ratio
Token I	2.87	3.26	3.10	3.60	2.90	3.99
Token II	2.63	3.54	3.13	3.43	2.76	3.92
Token III	2.83	3.71	3.29	3.33	2.95	3.89
Review Test	3.82	7.77	5.82	5.77	3.57	9.50

Analysis of variance indicated no significant differences in number of tokens taken by the three classes during Token I (F 2, 90 = 0.453, p> 0.25). Hence, amount of token reinforcement can be regarded as similar across classes. Token I performance-token ratios were subjected to analysis by a median test for independent groups (Hays, 1962), since variances for the three groups departed widely from homogeniety (F max. 3, 30 = 9.05, p< 0.01). The observed Chi-squared value for the median test was 35.1 (p< 0.001). Hence, despite similarity of amount of token reinforcement during the Token I phase, the performance-token ratio for the self-reinforced class was higher than those of the experimenter-reinforced and chance-reinforced classes, indicating that the self-reinforced class had "worked hardest" per token.

Similar results emerged in Token II. Again, no significant difference in amount of token reinforcement was found (F 2, 90 = 2.37, p> 0.05), but significant differences were found in performance-token ratios (F 2, 90 = 3.18, p< 0.05), with that of the self-reinforced class being higher than those of the experimenter-reinforced or chance-reinforced classes.

In Token III, analysis of variance revealed that classes did differ in terms of amount of token reinforcement taken (F 2, 90 = 4.19, p< 0.05) with the self-reinforced class taking fewer tokens than the experimenter-reinforced class. Yet, as Table 3 shows, the self-reinforced class again displayed the highest performance-token ratio.

The above pattern of results was also found in the data from the Review Test. There were significant differences both in amount of token reinforcement taken by the three classes (F 2, 81 = 62.59, $p < 0.001$), and in the performance-token ratios (F 2, 81 = 9.20, $P < 0.001$). It can be seen from Table 3 that the self-reinforced class again took fewer tokens than the experimenter-reinforced and chance-reinforced classes, and displayed the highest performance-token ratio on the Review Test.

Table 4 supplies information on the variability in performance-token ratios for all token reinforcement phases. Clearly, the experimenter-reinforced class displayed the least variability throughout.

Table 4. Standard deviations of performance-token ratios.

Phase	Chance Reinforced Class	Experimenter- Reinforced Class	Self- Reinforced Class
Token I	0.98	0.43	1.31
Token II	1.01	0.59	0.63
Token III	1.12	0.62	0.76
Review Test	3.86	1.86	3.69

Communication Between Classes

On the openended questions concerning knowledge of the treatment of other classes, the maximum "information score" was 3.0. Mean scores for the four classes were: nonreinforced, 0.74; chance-reinforced, 0.73; experimenter-reinforced, 0.44; and self-reinforced, 0.27. Newman-Keuls comparisons showed the self-reinforced class mean to be significantly lower than those of the chance-reinforced and nonreinforced classes. This could indicate that reported performance differences might be confounded by other factors arising from amount of information about other classes. However, a detailed examination of responses to the openended questions suggested that the extent of any such confounding was not great. Children made surprisingly few statements about how procedures in any of the classes had differed from their own.

DISCUSSION

I. Effectiveness of Self-Determined Reinforcement

Restrictions must be placed on generalizing from the findings of this study, both in terms of the particular children involved, and in terms of the narrow range for self-determined reinforcement permitted by the procedure. It is an open question as to whether these results would be replicated with younger or underpriviledged children, without some modification of procedure—for example, providing a wider variety of more meaningful prizes. It is also an open question as to whether similar results would have been obtained with these children, had there been wider limits allowed on amount of reinforcement, and had there been no check by the experimenter on the amount of reinforcement taken. Furthermore, these results would appear more convincing, had there been a further nonreinforced control class at another school. This would have yielded direct information about the effect on the nonreinforced class, of knowledge of reinforcement contingencies in the other classes. More accurately than the self-report measures used in this study, it would determine whether the performance of the nonreinforced class during token phases was, in fact, only a reflection of test difficulty, or whether it was confounded with adverse motivational effects arising from knowledge of other treatments.

Nevertheless, the study does suggest that the concept of self-determined reinforcement is both applicable and appropriate for studies of academic performance in the classroom. Self-determined reinforcement, within the above-mentioned limits, proved to be at least as equally effective as experimenter-determined reinforcement, in terms of improving academic performance. Children were able to control successfully the token reinforcement for their classroom learning, when both social cues and specific instructions about extent of reinforcement were minimized. It would seem that the notion of systematic social reinforcement as a "critical component" of an effective token system (Kuypers, Becker, and O'Leary, 1968) may need to be qualified.

It is clear that token reinforcement procedures were less effective in Token II and Token III than in Token I, and since identical sets of prizes were available at the end of Token III, it is thought that the tokens dropped much of their value as reinforcers. There is a need for future studies to ensure a sufficiently varied set of reinforcing events to back up the tokens. The particular prizes used in this study were nevertheless effective during Token I, possibly because of their novelty.

2. Performance of the Chance-Reinforced Treatment Class

This class performed at a level generally below that of the nonreinforced class throughout the study. The inconsistent experience of this class in terms of amount of reinforcement during the Token I phase, seems to have not only precluded performance increments during this phase, but also to have prevented subsequent self-determined reinforcement procedures from having any incremental effect. This is certainly an indication that the ability to apply self-determined reinforcement is strongly influenced by the standards of externally determined reinforcement previously experienced. Hence, inconsistency of reinforcement can occur not only in terms of interpersing reinforcement with nonreinforcement as consequences of a given behavior, but also in terms of unpredictable amounts of reinforcement for a given behavior. These results suggest that parents and teachers, who function as major external reinforcing agents for children's behavior, should be aware that one consequence of maintaining such inconsistent standards of reinforcement may be impairment of the child's ability to apply self-determined reinforcement procedures effectively. If such an ability is considered as one component of self-control, as Marston and Kanfer (1963) suggest, then inconsistent experiences of amount of reinforcement would have a debilitating effect on the development of an individual's ability to control his own behavior.

3. Withdrawal of Tokens

Findings suggest that after token withdrawal, the four classes did not revert to the similarity of performance displayed during the baseline. Token reinforcement classes experimenter-reinforced and self-reinforced remained slightly superior to the non-reinforced class. There seems little evidence to justify the fear that children would become dependent upon token reinforcement so as to be unable to perform without it.

4. Performance-Token Ratios

Data on performance-token ratios provide further support that the operation of self-determined reinforcement is influenced by standards of externally determined reinforcement previously experienced. Table 3 shows that the experimenter-reinforced class adhered more closely to the performance-token ratio experienced during the Token 1 phase than did either the self-reinforced or chance-reinforced class. The experimenter-reinforced class had been supplied with an explicit ratio, whereas the self-reinforced and chance-reinforced classes had not. Yet, the self-reinforced and chance-reinforced classes moved towards a much higher performance-token ratio, especially on the Review Test. Table 4 indicates that the experimenter-reinforced class displayed the least variability in ratios throughout the study. This would be expected if members of this class were adhering to a common standard. The striking finding is that the children who had the greatest opportunity for leniency in taking tokens (self-reinforced class), actually imposed the strictest ratio on themselves.

The performance-token ratios observed in this study imply that an alternative to a teacher laying down explicit acceptable standards of performance for classroom learning, might be the provision of access to reinforcement on the basis of standards determined by individual children.

5. Applicability of Procedures

The token-reinforcement procedures employed proved to be well suited to classroom use. Tokens did not have to be paid out individually to each child (a saving of time and energy for the teacher). Handing out the envelopes took about 1 min each day, and children took about the same time to take their tokens and return the envelopes. Since envelopes contained a slip bearing daily performance scores, a continuous record was available showing performance and number of tokens taken. For experimental purposes, it can be noted that by including differential instructions in envelopes, several reinforcement procedures might be operated simultaneously.

REFERENCES

Anderson, R. C. Educational Psychology. *Annual Review of Psychology*, 1967, 18, 129-164.

Bandura, A. and Kupers, C. J. Transmission of self-reinforcement through modeling. *Journal of Abnormal and Social Psychology*, 1964, 69, 1-9.

Bandura, A. and Whalen, C. K. The influence of antecedent reinforcement and divergent modeling cues on patterns of self reward. *Journal of Personality and Social Psychology*, 1966, 3, 373-382.

Bandura, A. and Perloff, B. Relative efficiency of self-monitored and externally imposed reinforcement systems. *Journal of Personality and Social Psychology*, 1967, 7, 111-116.

Gagne, R. M. The conditions of learning. New York: Holt, Rinehart & Winston, 1965.

Kanfer, F. H., Bradley, M. M., and Marston, A. R. Self-reinforcement as a function of degree of learning. *Psychological Reports*, 1962. 10, 885-886.

Kaufer, F. H. and Duerfeldt, P. H. Motivational properties of self-reinforcement. *Perceptual and Motor Skills*, 1967, 25, 237-246.

Kuypers, D. S., Becker, W. C., and O'Leary, K. D. How to make a token system fail. *Exceptional Children*, October 1968, 101-117.

Marston, A. R. Variables affecting incidence of self-reinforcement. *Psychological Reports*, 1964, 14, 879-884.

Marston, A. R. and Kanfer, F. H. Human reinforcement: experimenter and subject controlled. *Journal of Experimental Psychology*, 1963, 66, 91-94.

McMains, M. J. and Liebert, R. M. Influence of discrepancies between successively modeled self-reward criteria on the adoption of a self-imposed standard. *Journal of Personality and Social Psychology*, 1968, 8, 166-171.

Skinner, B. F. *Science and human behavior*. New York: Macmillan, 1953.

Winer, B. J. *Statistical principles in experimental design*. New York: McGraw-Hill, 1962.

22

Contingency management in an introductory psychology course produces better learning

James S. McMichael and Jeffrey R. Corey

For the contingency mangement techniques first devised by Keller (1966, 1968) to become a widely accepted teaching method, it is necessary that they be shown (1) to be applicable to general subject matter and (2) to be superior to traditional lecture methods. The present study demonstrated (1) by successfully teaching the material from a standard psychology text. The superiority of contingency management was established by direct comparison of final examination scores from comparable groups taught the same subject matter by either Keller's method or traditional methods. Students taught by Keller's method also rated the course more favorably.

Since Keller (1968) first introduced the systematic application of principles of learning derived from laboratory studies to the teaching of a college subject, his techniques have seen increasing use. Several studies have been done or are in progress to determine the factors most critically responsible for the effectiveness of the method (see Farmer, Lachter, and Blaustein, 1968). But certain basic questions remain to be answered, questions which would be among the first to be asked by a professor who is considering adopting these techniques.

The first concern would be: can the techniques be applied to any organized body of knowledge? Many of those who now employ the techniques either use textbooks that focus upon the area of the experimental analysis of behavior (e.g., Farmer et al., 1968) or have prepared materials that they deem particularly

From *Journal of Applied Behavior Analysis,* 1969, 2, 79-83. Copyright 1969 by the Society for the Experimental Analysis of Behavior, Inc. Reprinted by permission.

Authorship is considered equal. Reprints may be obtained from either author at the Department of Psychology, C. W. Post College, Greenvale, New York 11548. The authors wish to thank Andrew P. Spiegel, Dean of the College, for his encouragement and for providing financial assistance where it was needed to carry out the project. We also wish to thank the graduate students, Mr. George Dos Santos, Mr. William D. Siegfried, and Mr. George Whitehead, who helped supervise the undergraduate proctors and who aided in the collection and analysis of the data. Professor Richard M. Malott of Western Michigan University provided us with valuable advice in the initial stages of this project.

appropriate to the use of contingency management techniques (e.g., Malott, personal communication). Since most introductory courses, including those in psychology, rely upon a general textbook, one purpose of the present study was to test whether contingency management techniques could be used to teach the subject matter of a standard textbook, Kendler's *Basic Psychology* (1968).

Secondly, and of fundamental importance, the question naturally arises as to whether students will learn more when these techniques are used. Ancillary to this is the question as to whether students would, by their own criteria for a good course, rate a course using these techniques higher than they would a course taught by traditional methods. Thus, the second major purpose was to assess the effectiveness of contingency management techniques in these respects.

Before the experiment itself, a feasibility study was conducted. During the summer of 1968, a general introductory course based on Kendler's *Basic Psychology* (1968) was administered to 165 students in five separate classes. It was found that: (1) general material, i.e., statistics, physiological psychology, verbal learning, forgetting, etc., could be presented using Keller's method; (2) Students tended to achieve relatively high grades on objective final examinations; (3) The students rated the course very highly. We were favorably impressed with these results but felt that more data were needed to justify the expansion of this program to our regular introductory course. Consequently, the purpose of the present study was to compare directly the results of a course section using contingency management techniques to results obtained by comparable students in conventional lecture sections covering the same material.

METHOD

Subjects

Students. At C. W. Post College 880 students registered in four introductory psychology sections without prior knowledge of what method would be used to teach the course. The initial registration figures were as follows: Experimental class, 221; Control class A, 229; Control B, 213; and Control C, 217. Twenty-seven students withdrew from the experimental class, 36 from Control A, 29 from Control B, and 20 from Control C before the final exam.

Staff. In the experimental class, one of the authors supervised two graduate assistants and 19 undergraduate proctors. The proctors received academic credit for their duties; each proctor was responsible for about 12 students (range 7 to 18).

In each of the control sections, the instructor was assigned one graduate assistant. Nine additional graduate assistants were available, when needed, from a grading pool.

Procedure

Specific details of procedure used in the experimental class may be found in Keller (1968). The course was the first of a two-semester introductory sequence.

To make the course compatible with the second semester, which was to be taught by conventional techniques, the second edition of Kendler's *Basic Psychology* (1968) was divided into twelve 20-page units, with the assignments covering chapters 1, 3, 4, and 7 through 11. The control classes used the same textbook and covered the same material.

The control classes met three times a week for 50-min lectures and were tested three or four times; the experimental students were assigned two 50-min proctoring sessions a week in which to take unit tests and to receive a proctor's help.

Students were required to pass, with a perfect score, each unit test, consisting of 10 fill-in questions, before receiving a study guide for the next unit. Each study guide was designed by the authors to call the students' attention to concepts we considered central to the topic of the unit. On the average of once a week the instructor presented a lecture, demonstration, or film. It was stated that only those students who had passed the appropriate number of units were to attend these presentations, but no attempt was made to enforce this ruling.

At the end of the semester, the instructors from all the sections selected 50 multiple-choice questions from the instructor's manual for use as a common final exam. All items were agreed to be appropriate and representative of the material covered in each course. While some of these items had previously appeared on 1-hr examinations in all the control sections, none had been seen by the experimental class. All final examinations were given at the same time and were closely proctored. To guard against contamination of the results by cheating, alternate forms of the exam were appropriately distributed. The exams were graded by graduate students using a punched answer key and were spot-checked by the instructors. Before the exam date, students were told how the final exam would weigh in the determination of course grades as follows: Experimental group, 40%; Control A, 40%; Control B, 50%; Control C, 50%.

Included with the exam was an anonymous rating sheet, handed in separately from the exam. The students were asked to rate the overall quality of the course on a 0 to 10 scale, with 0 labelled as "extremely poor" and 10 as "extremely good." Other scales were included to provide more detailed information for the individual instructor.

RESULTS

The distribution of final exam scores in the experimental and control groups appears in Fig. 1. The mean score out of 50 possible points for each of the groups was: Control A, 35; Control B, 34; Control C, 34; Experimental, 40.

An analysis of variance showed the overall effect to be highly significant ($F = 35.5$, $df = 3$, 764; $p < 0.005$). *Post hoc* t-tests revealed that the most substantial differences among groups existed between the experimental group and each of the control groups ($p < 0.0001$ for each comparison). By contrast, the differences among the control groups were slight, with none reaching the 0.01 level of significance in spite of the large number of subjects.

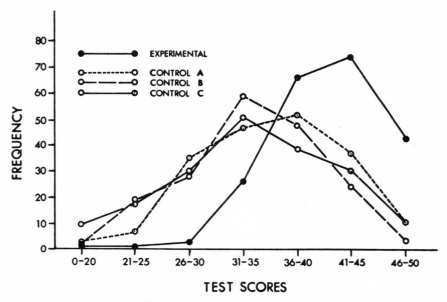

TEST SCORES

Fig. 1. Distribution of test scores for the three control classes and the experimental class. The mean score for the experimental class was 40; for Control A, 35; Control B, 34; and Control C, 34.

Likewise, the student ratings showed that the experimental group rated the course higher than did the control groups. These data are seen in Fig. 2, and an analysis of variance showed the overall effect to be highly significant ($F = 78.9$; df = 3, 706; $p< 0.005$). The mean ratings were: Control A, 6; Control B, 7; Control C, 5; Experimental, 9. *Post hoc* t-tests again showed that the experimental-group ratings were higher than each of the control-group ratings ($p< 0.0001$). At the same level of significance Control B was higher than either of the other control groups, which did not differ significantly from each other ($p = 0.31$).

DISCUSSION

The data indicate that students in the experimental group learned more and rated the course higher than did comparable students taught by conventional methods. The data from the final examination are especially convincing in light of several aspects of the procedure which, if anything, would have favored students in the control groups. First, the questions on the final examination were multiple-choice items selected by the instructors from the commercial test-item file. Students in the control groups had been given multiple-choice tests throughout the semester and, therefore, would have been more practiced in

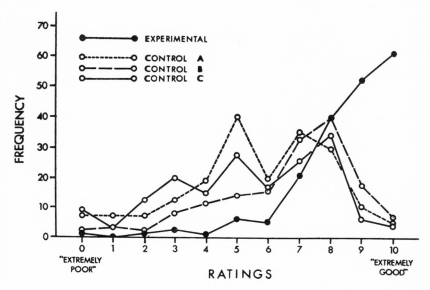

Fig. 2. Distribution of ratings for the three control classes and the experimental class. The mean rating for the experimental class was 9; for Control A, 6; Control B, 7; and Control C, 5.

studying for this kind of final exam. Second, some of the items on the final examination had previously been given to the control groups on 1-hr examinations. Third, while bias could not be introduced by students selectively registering for sections of their choice, students could drop the course from their schedules. If there were greater numbers of dropouts in the experimental group than in the control groups, a bias favoring the experimental group could have been introduced by leaving students who were better able to handle the material or more favorably disposed toward the course. To the contrary, the experimental course was dropped by fewer students than on average dropped the control sections.

One aspect of the experimental design produced a confounding which cannot entirely be dismissed. There were different instructors for the various groups, and it is possible that the instructor for the experimental group was a substantially "better teacher." However, we do not think this to be a likely explanation of the data, since his students in the previous year had achieved scores on objective examinations which were no higher than those of the present control groups. The instructors varied considerably in factors which could relate to teaching effectiveness (e.g., orientation toward the field of psychology, amount of teaching experience, and sex). Since no substantial differences were seen among the control groups on final examination scores, we conclude that the method, rather than such confounded factors, produced the present results.

From the data which showed that the students in the experimental section rated the course highly, we merely conclude that students will readily accept the use of contingency management techniques. Clearly, there are many possible sources of variability in students' ratings of courses, and these were not systematically studied in this experiment.

Since this study was designed to compare two teaching methods, our data do not bear directly on the question of which factors are responsible for the efficacy of contingency management techniques. However, in the course of this study, certain potential improvements in technique were suggested. For example, to reduce procrastination, attendance at all proctoring sessions is strongly encouraged for students who are behind in unit tests. A further contingency now allows accelerated students to perform a laboratory experiment or to write a paper on an area of special interest. After the initial investment of time and institutional resources, this course now functions smoothly and with no additional costa as part of our general introductory psychology program.

REFERENCES

Farmer, J., Lachter, G. D., and Blaustein, J. J. *The effect of proctoring in a structured teaching situation.* Paper presented at the meetings of the Eastern Psychological Association, Washington, D.C. 1968.

Keller, F. S. A personal course in psychology. In R. Ulrich, T. Stachnik, and J. Mabry (Eds.), *Control of human behavior.* Glenview, Ill.: Scott, Foresman, Inc., 1966. Pp. 91-93.

Keller, F. S. "Goodbye, teacher. . . . . ." *Journal of Applied Behavior Analysis,* 1968, 1, 79-89.

Kendler, H. H. *Basic psychology.* 2nd ed.; New York: Appleton-Century-Crofts, 1968.

23

The learning village:
a behavioral approach to
early education

Roger E. Ulrich, Stephen E. Louisell,
and Marshall Wolfe

During this century, scientific understanding of the nature of the learning process has tremendously increased. Following the early work of Pavlov, Thorndike, Watson and Skinner, laboratory studies of the interaction between environmental stimuli and observable responses have proliferated. The corpus of data and principles of behavior resulting from this research provide a rich source of methodology for the person interested in changing any type of behavior. When applied in nonlaboratory settings, the methodology is known by various names: operant conditioning, behavior modification and contingency management perhaps being most popular.

From the point of view of the public, the main virtue of the methodology has been its striking effectiveness. It has been used to reverse psychotic symptoms (Ayllon and Michael, 1959), to teach autistic children to talk (Risley and Wolf, 1966), to increase time college students spend studying (Fox, 1962; Goldiamond, 1966), to help people lose weight (Goldiamond, 1966), to decrease aggressive behavior (Brown and Elliott, 1965), and to accomplish many other good works (see Ulrich, Stachnik, and Mabry, 1966, 1970; Ullmann and Krasner, 1965). In preschool and grade school settings, the techniques have been applied, most commonly, to remediate behavior problems and deficits (Homme, deBaca, Devine, Steinhorst, and Rickert, 1963; Zimmerman and Zimmerman, 1962; Packard, 1970; Hall, Lund and Jackson, 1968; Thomas, Becker, and Armstrong, 1968; Hart and Risley, 1968; Madsen, Becker, and Thomas, 1968; Buell, Stoddard, Harris, and Baer, 1968; Schwarz and Hawkins, 1970; Ulrich, Wolfe, and Bluhm, 1968; Surratt, Ulrich, and Hawkins, 1969; Schmidt and Ulrich, 1969).

From *Educational Technology*, 1971, 11, 32-45. Copyright 1971 by the Society for the Experimental Analysis of Behavior, Inc. Reprinted by permission.

Any program such as that described here requires the support of many people and many institutions. In this regard, the authors would like to acknowledge the support of Western Michigan University, the Kalamazoo Community Mental Health Services Board, the Kalamazoo Valley Intermediate School District, the Michigan Department of Social Services, the Michigan Department of Mental Health, the Michigan Department of Education, the National Institute of Mental

Since one of the principal concerns of behavior modification is with the acquisition of new behaviors, the method is especially appropriate to educational settings. A comprehensive application of the principles of learning to the education of children is currently being made in a private, experimental school system known as the Learning Village. The purpose of the Learning Village is to accelerate and enhance the development of children by applying scientifically sound educational procedures as soon after birth as possible and by continuing their application for as long as the person remains involved in the educational system.

The Learning Village is designed to deliberately create in children the behaviors that most parents hope their children will eventually acquire through ordinary experiences at home and in school. An important group of these

Health and the Office of Naval Research. In the initial stages, the Learning Village programs were helped especially by Dr. Thomas Stachnik, Dr. Philip Smith, Dr. Vernon Stehman and many other people connected with the Michigan Department of Mental Health. Additional advice came from the Governor's executive staff, namely from Charles Orlebeke, William Whitbeck, Ted Blizzard, David Duncan and Charles Greenleaf. The initial proposal for the Learning Village programs was submitted to the Michigan Department of Mental Health by the senior author, Mr. Paul Surratt and Mr. Marshall Wolfe. Major responsibility for the day-to-day direction and implementation of the Learning Village program is presently assumed by Marilyn Arnett, Helen Brewer, Arlyne Gutmann, Carmen Hren, Madelon Lewis, Alex Luvall, Dorothy Marine, Robert Pierce, James Scherrer, Richard Spates, Carole Ulrich and Robert Wiggins. Teachers and other staff include Marcia Beard, John Bird, Melanie Blanks, Bette Boulding, Debra Briley, Bernice Brown, Janice Brown, Sondra Curry, Lola Dangerfield, Robert Dyche, Anne Farmer, Richard Fearon, Janine Fockler, Margaret Gilligan, Gerald Harper, Ruth Harper, Marie Harris, Red Hartmen, Russell Jones, Tom Louisell, Lois Martin, Delores McGinnis, Mona Mitchell, Fran Pietras, Ruth Shafer, Marilyn Shaw, Brenda Sherburn, Carol Siep, Sharon Sowers, Lois Speck, Joan Spindler, Sue Steiner, Darwin Stier, Paula Van Valkenburg, Opal West, Kathleen Williams, Mary Williams, Cheri Yeager and Mary Ann Zender. Former staff members who rendered indispensable service in establishing the Learning Village program include Sue Anger (our first graduate), Jim Anthony, Al Birdsall, Michael Boyle, Donald Clark, Tony Colasacco, Richard Cole, Jim Cossingham, Sibyl Daniels, Mary Fullmer, Alan Gonick, Tom Kucera, Jan Lindenberg, Helaine Nelson, Chris Nuttall, Paul Surratt and W. Scott Wood. To Judy Favell, Wade Hitzing, John Martin, Max Maultsby, Paul Mountjoy, Roger Pulliam, Donald Roberts, Paul Surratt, Lewis Walker, Velma Watts and Jim Yore on the Behavior Development Corporation Advisory Board and to Ron Hutchinson, Behavioral Development Corporation vice president, we extend a special thanks.

Any attempt to name the people who have been helpful in such a program will probably leave someone unmentioned. To these persons, the authors extend their apologies and appreciation. Special thanks goes to Kay Mueller, who helped prepare and edit the manuscript. Sylvia Dulaney made many useful and essential suggestions. Galen Alessi, Joe Auffrey, Carmen Hren and Lynne Peters were especially helpful in collecting and preparing data.

behaviors comprises the academic behaviors so necessary to the individual's survival in modern Western society. These include effective use of language and abstract concepts, the ability to extract information from the environment, and the acquisition of information—all of which might be combined under the label of "intelligence." Another group of behaviors is the personal behaviors, such as the ability to keep oneself healthy and productive, and to understand the causes of one's own behavior. Perhaps the most important group of behaviors is that which includes the social and emotional responses important to the individual's, and indeed to society's, survival. Among these are the ability to work cooperatively with others, the ability to demonstrate affection toward others, a concern with the welfare of others, and the skills required to identify and make necessary changes in social systems. When a comprehensive program designed to create desired behaviors is applied very early in children's lives, the children hopefully will develop without many of the behavioral problems and deficits all too familiar to educators. More positively stated, the program of the Learning Village is designed to insure the development of children who read and write well, who think well, who can make the most of their environment, and who love themselves and their fellow men.

THE BEGINNING

The Learning Village grew out of efforts by the Department of Psychology at Western Michigan University to make university training and experience more relevant to cultural concerns (Ulrich and Kent, 1970). Since the education of children is one such concern, an effort was made to institute programs which would permit the involvement of university faculty and students in extra-university educational settings. One program was developed by the Behavior Research and Development Center at Western Michigan University in the Indian Lake Public School, Vicksburg, Michigan, under the jurisdiction of the Kalamazoo Valley Intermediate School District. Initially the program dealt with behavior problems of individual children (Ulrich, Wolfe and Bluhm, 1968). The effort was later expanded to include training programs in behavior modification for teachers in the Kalamazoo public schools (Wood, 1968) and for parents. In addition, work in the public schools gave university students an opportunity to participate in behavior modification in classroom settings. Concurrent with the efforts made in local public schools, a nursery school program was begun, first in a private home and later at Western Michigan University (Wood, Ulrich, and Fullmer, 1969). These forays into behaviorally-oriented education were subsequently expanded and consolidated into the private system known as the Learning Village. The private status of the Learning Village allows, within the limits of present knowledge and human frailty, for a rigorous application of behavioral methodology to all aspects of education (Ulrich, Wolfe, and Surratt, 1969; Ulrich, Wolfe, and Cole, 1970). In addition, private status allows the application of behavioral methodology to the education of people from a wide range of ages. The Learning Village enrolls children as young as two months of age and hopes eventually to develop strategies of comprehensive education which might be applied to the continuing education of adults within an experimental community setting.

Soon after entering the field of nursery school and elementary education, the organizers of the Learning Village encountered the formidable array of traditional ideas, rigid regulations and extensive licensing procedures enforced by local, state, and federal agencies which license programs that involve children (Wolfe, Ulrich and Ulrich, 1970; Mabry, Stachnik and Ulrich 1970). Although the regulations and procedures are intended to better conditions in society, they undoubtedly discourage many persons in their efforts toward the same goal. Complete familiarity with the regulations in the community might prevent some problems. However, unexpected delays and expenses seem, at present, to be inherent in interactions between established institutions and any group that hopes to use new methods to solve old problems.

THE MATTER OF PRIORITIES

No new programs can begin or exist, however, without some support from established institutions, both public and private, and from individuals. The Learning Village receives financial assistance from federal, state, and local agencies, as well as from individuals. Some parents pay tuition. The tuition of many infants and nursery school children is paid by the Michigan Department of Social Services. Initial capital was provided by bank loans to founders of the Behavioral Development Corporation and by private funds. Although the support received to date has been greatly appreciated, and the support appears to be increasing, the Learning Village has experienced the shortage of funds inevitably encountered by any daycare center or private school facility that attempts to go beyond minimal care. Programs that are innovative, both in terms of the methods used and the population reached, are especially difficult to finance. The difficulties have been compounded by the stress the Learning Village places on the prevention, rather than the remediation, of educational mental health and other social problems. Adults soon forget the inadequacies of their early experiences. The problems presented to society by the uneducated teenager or adult generate more concern than the establishement of a system designed to prevent such problems. For example, funds seem easier to obtain when one can alarm the public with exhibits of school failures, extreme mental illness or retardation, drug abuse or crime. Efforts to develop a strategy of education which would make remedial expenditures unnecessary are somehow less inspiring. As anyone involved in education knows, funds are scarce. The education of our children should be one of our top national priorities. At present it is not.

ALL DAY AND YEAR 'ROUND

Children attend the Learning Village all day and on a year 'round basis. A substantial portion of the children's time in school is spent learning academic material. Thus the amount of time spent by the children in school and in structural learning situations is unusual in comparison with traditional educational practices. However, this type of program is gaining support. For example, the Westinghouse Learning Corporation (1969), in its report entitled, *The Impact of Head Start,* makes several pertinent recommendations. It recommends that preschool programs be structured with heavy emphasis on teaching necessary skills; that preschool programs be operated on an all day and year 'round basis; and that special preschool programs be extended downward into infancy and upward into the primary grades. Hopefully an increase in comprehensive, structured early education will follow such "official" endorsement.

Enrollment in the Learning Village does not require that a child be gifted either academically or economically. The Learning Village is also committed to the belief that experience with people of various cultural backgrounds is essential to the true education of any child. The children and staff of the Learning Village, therefore, come from a wide range of economic and cultural backgrounds. In addition, many students, when they enroll in the Learning Village, might be described as academically disadvantaged. They lack the language and conceptual skills usually considered essential to success in school. Although many of the academically disadvantaged come from the less affluent families, academic deficits occur in children from all socioeconomic backgrounds.

THE EDUCATIONAL PROGRAM

The educational program at the Learning Village begins in the infant nursery, which enrolls children aged from two to 30 months. The infant program is designed to teach motor skills, such as sitting, walking, and use of the hands; perceptual skills, such as appropriate responses to stimuli differing in quality or intensity; conceptual skills, such as identification of objects and understanding simple concepts; and language skills, such as speech, vocabulary, and sentence structure. An effort is made to lengthen the child's attention span, develop imitative behavior, and develop memory. Emphasis is also placed on personal and social skills, such as eating, use of the toilet, cooperative play, and affectionate responses to other children and to adults. Creative responses to the environment are also identified and encouraged. Some of these skills and concepts are taught semiformally in the infant nursery. During such "study" periods each teacher supervises approximately four children. Within this context, the teacher instructs each child individually for periods of approximately 10 minutes. The overall staff-to-student ratio in the infant nursery is 1:3. Since the staff's time is devoted almost entirely to caring for and teaching children, the children in the infant nursery probably receive far more attention from adults than they would in their own homes. In addition, the children are encouraged to interact constructively with the other children in the infant nursery as well as with older children (Ulrich, Wallace and Dulaney, unpublished manuscript). The result is a social environment far richer than that encountered by the infant confined to the typical home environment.

A special effort was necessary to become licensed by the State of Michigan to include infants in the program of the Learning Village. Many psychologists and social workers believe that group daycare for children of these ages is damaging, no matter how rich and intensive the care. This unfortunate belief is often based on studies of the development of children in institutional environments that would be considered inadequate by any standards (e.g., Bowlby, 1953; Spitz & Cobliner, 1965). The fact that the environments included group care was secondary to the fact that the children were neglected in countless ways. In the absence of further information, the results of such studies should not be extrapolated to condemn situations which might provide truly constructive experience for infants. Other objectives to scientifically based programs for the early education of children may have impeded licensing. These objections relate to philosophical issues such as man's nature and freedom. The issues are beyond the scope of this paper. However, they are frequently encountered by people engaged in modifying human behavior and have been treated elsewhere (Skinner, 1953; Ulrich, 1967; Ulrich, Stachnik and Mabry, 1966, 1970).

Probably because of the difficulty in obtaining a license, infant daycare programs, and hence, data on their effectiveness, are rare. However, one infant program which has been in operation for four years at Syracuse University recently reported a study of the attachment behavior of the children enrolled in the program and of their mothers (Caldwell, Wright, Honig, and Tannenbaum, 1970). No significant differences were found between the attachment between mothers and the children enrolled in the program and the attachment between mothers and children in typical home environments. However, a relationship was found between the developmental level of children and their attachment behavior. Children at more advanced developmental levels seemed to exhibit a stronger attachment toward their mothers. The stronger attachment was evident both in children enrolled in group daycare and in children who spent their days at home. Since the developmental level of the infants at the Learning Village is greatly enhanced by the program, one might expect an accompanying enhancement of the infants' responsiveness both to their mothers, and to other individuals in their environment.

A rich, well-designed, well-staffed group daycare program for infants is certainly preferable to a deficient home environment. It is also preferable to daycare by a single, "babysitting" agent who may not be qualified to give the infant the experiences he needs. Hopefully, as the pressure from mothers for these services increases and as the effects of properly designed and implemented daycare for infants become known, the number of centers will increase until the educational and social experiences of children during these crucial months of their development need no longer be left to chance.

At the age of approximately two and one-half years, Learning Village children enter the nursery program (2½ to 5 yrs). The personal and social goals of the nursery program are continuations of those of the infant nursery. The nursery program includes four 20-min study periods each morning. Study periods are devoted to language skills, reading, arithmetic, science, social studies, and the scientific exploration, manipulation and analysis of the environment. "Distar" programs (Englemann and Bruner, 1969; Englemann, Osborne and Englemann, 1969; Englemann and Carnine, 1969) are used in the nursery reading, language and arithmetic instruction. During the study periods, the children are divided, according to their *current* progress, into classes of approximately five children each. The small, individualized groups allow the teacher to give attention to each child, and allow the child to progress at his own rate while remaining in the social context of his own age group.

At the age of approximately five years, the children progress to grade school, where study periods become longer, more time is spent in study groups, and the material, of course, becomes more advanced. Studies (Westinghouse Learning Corporation, 1969) have shown that the continuation of successful educational techniques into grade school is essential to the consolidation of gains made in preschool programs. The staff of the Learning Village anticipates that, as its educational techniques are both implemented earlier in the child's life and continued later in the child's education, results as yet unparalleled in education may be achieved.

The program of the Learning Village is deliberately designed to teach the children certain skills. The emphasis on these skills and the clear structuring of the study periods would be regarded with alarm by some educators (e.g., Neill, 1960). The conviction exists in "humanistic" educational circles that it is some-how damaging to children to *deliberately* teach them the skills which can currently be of use and which certainly will be needed in the future. Such instruction is often thought to stifle children's creativity. When children learn academic skills happily and effectively, they are characterized as being "tricked" or "bribed" into learning these things. Somehow such learning is thought to interfere with the development of a creative personality.

At the Learning Village, quite the opposite seems to be true. Far from stifling the child's personality, the development of skills, even at very early ages, seems to promote active interaction with the environment, to help the child feel good about himself and his abilities, and in general to make the child a happier, more effective, more creative individual. It is difficult to prove scientifically that such effects occur and why. However, it is equally impossible to prove that certain academic deficits promote creativity and freedom. Many adults in our society cannot functionally read or write or work with numbers. These extreme deficits can hardly make these people more free or contribute to their experience as human beings.

Study periods at the Learning Village are designed to be fun and rewarding, just as play periods are designed to be fun and rewarding. During play periods the children are physically more active than during study periods, when they more or less sit in one place and say specific things at specific times. However, the children do not love to play and hate to study. The aversion which some educators have to traditional academic instruction probably relates more to the unpleasant way in which their own educational instruction was enforced rather than to any intrinsically damaging quality in the process of acquiring skills and knowledge. The program at the Learning Village is arranged so that the process of acquiring skills, in itself, enhances the child's development as a human being.

THE BEHAVIORAL METHODOLOGY

The program of the Learning Village, especially of the infant nursery and nursery, allots an unusually large amount of time to the structured learning of academic skills. However, the acceleration of learning which occurs in the Village exceeds that which would occur if the children were simply "exposed" to academic stimuli for the amount of time stipulated in the program. Nor would attempts to promote the social and personal development of the children be as successful if traditional methods were used. As mentioned earlier, the success of the Learning Village depends on the application to the school setting of the principles of learning discovered in the laboratory. The resulting methodology involves arranging the environment, including the behavior of the staff, in such a way that the occurrence of desired behaviors will increase and the occurrence of undesired behaviors will decrease.

The first step in a program of behavior modification is to specify the behaviors ultimately desired. In the Learning Village these "terminal" behaviors include proficiency in reading; correct and creative use of language; acquisition of knowledge about the environment; the ability to use basic concepts of arithmetic and mathematics; a scientific approach to the environment; cooperative, affectionate social behavior; an understanding of the factors which control behavior; an understanding of the factors which make social systems viable and reinforcing to their members; and a good opinion of oneself and one's abilities.

These ultimate goals are translated into specific behaviors which receive daily attention in the Village. The specific behaviors constitute the small steps, or approximations, from which the terminal behaviors are built. The specification of behaviors is clearly apparent in the academic program, which is systematically broken down into many small steps. In order for a child to learn to speak, read and write, he must make a long sequence of specific responses. Infants imitate sounds, older children make statements about their environment, still older children learn to recognize written symbols, and finally to read and understand words, sentences and stories. The specific behaviors expected of a child are determined by his current behavioral repertoire. If a child is not mastering the material in his study group, he can be moved to a group where more simple responses are required. A special effort is made to match the required responses with the child's progress to insure that the child's experience will include many opportunities for successful responding.

Specific, desired social behaviors include playing with other children, smiling or laughing, absence of crying or aggressive behavior, sharing toys, and being quiet and following instructions when appropriate. Desired personal behaviors include picking up toys at the end of play periods, cleaning up one's own spills, appropriate use of the bathroom, eating a nutritiously balanced diet, and having adequate table manners. The behaviors involved in self-esteem are more difficult to specify, but must certainly involve a willingness to do and learn new things. When a child has a good opinion of himself, he expects to succeed at untried behaviors. He therefore greets new experiences as opportunities for success and good feeling.

Staff members constantly attempt to think about the children in terms of the behavior they exhibit. A child who is sullen or shy is, after all, a child who frowns a lot and plays by himself. If the teacher can arrange conditions so that the child smiles a lot and plays a reasonable amount with other children, the child would no longer be called sullen or shy. When a child does not make the appropriate academic responses, one does not blame the child, or say he is not "motivated," or say he doesn't "need" to learn. One asks, "Does the child have in his repertoire the behaviors prerequisite to the desired behavior?" or, "Is the teacher providing the stimuli which will cause the child to make the desired responses?"

The most important tool used in the Learning Village to promote desired behaviors is positive reinforcement. Nontechnically, a positive reinforcer may be equated with a reward. Technically, a positive reinforcer is any environmental event that increases the probability of reoccurrence of the behavior it follows. In other words, the frequency at which a behavior occurs is determined by the events that have followed the occurrence of the behavior in the past. Positive reinforcers must be identified by observing the behavior of children. Events which might not be considered pleasant, such as scolding from an adult, may actually reinforce some children's behavior (Madsen, Becker, Thomas, Koser, and Plager, 1968). Conversely, events assumed to be pleasant, such as praise, are not always effective reinforcers (Becker, Thomas, and Carnine, 1969). When a child is not responding as expected, one of the questions to be asked is: are the stimuli used as reinforcers indeed reinforcing?

At the Learning Village, the procedure known as contingency contracting (Homme, 1969) is often used to arrange for the reinforcement of students' behavior. "If you do 'X,' I will give you or let you do 'Y,' " is the basic form of any contingency contract. In this paradigm, "X" is the response that is to be made in order to receive the reinforcer "Y." A good example of contingency contracting is found in the interaction between teachers and school boards. At the beginning of each school year, local school boards or their agents contract with the teachers in their district for a certain salary (Y). If the teachers accept, they must, in turn, make certain responses (X's) during the next nine or 10 months. This process is no different from the contingency contracting that goes on every day between teachers and students at the Learning Village. At the beginning of a lesson, the teacher might say, "Class, if you study hard today for 20 minutes, you may, immediately after the lesson, play with a toy for 10 minutes." In this case, studying hard has previously been defined as paying attention to the teacher, responding with a high percentage of accuracy, answering and asking questions, and not disrupting the class. Such explicit reinforcement contingencies are readily accepted by the children and, indeed, have become part of the "culture" of the Learning Village.

Of course, not every desired response made by the children is reinforced. Such a procedure would not only exhaust the teachers, but would soon render almost any reinforcer ineffective. Continuous reinforcement is sometimes used to establish behaviors that have a very low probability of occurrence. For most behaviors, however, intermittent reinforcement makes far more effective use of reinforcers. The rate of responding maintained on most schedules of intermittent reinforcement is higher than the rate of responding maintained on continuous reinforcement. In addition, responses maintained on intermittent reinforcement are less likely to fall out of the child's repertoire should a temporary lapse in reinforcement occur.

At the Learning Village, various types of events are used to reinforce behavior. Social reinforcement, such as praise and attention for appropriate behavior, is used lavishly. Attention is given, for example, to the children who are attending during lessons, who are picking up toys after play periods, or who are eating their lunch. The teachers become very adept at delivering enthusiastic social reinforcers. As mentioned above, social reinforcement is not uniformly effective for all children (Baer, 1962; Harris, Wolf and Baer, 1964). However, it is effective for most children. Heavy use of social reinforcers does much to make school a happy, supportive place to be. Since the behavior desired of the child is broken down into small steps which the child can master, the environment is arranged so that the child emits desired responses at a high rate. Many of these small "successes" are greeted with statements acclaiming the child's intelligence, his capabilities, and his willingness to work hard. The result is an atmosphere in which the child feels he is indeed a capable, intelligent human being.

The opportunity to engage in a "fun" behavior is also used as a reinforcer. Such behavioral reinforcers are derived from the Premack principle, which states that a behavior which has a high probability of occurrence can be used to reinforce a behavior which has a lower probability of occurrence (Premack, 1959). Most children find the opportunity to play with certain toys or to go on field trips reinforcing. Other behavioral reinforcers used in educational settings have included the opportunity to push the teacher around the room in a swivel chair, the opportunity to help the janitor sweep the halls, and the opportunity to read a novel. In another nursery school setting, a period in which the children could run and scream was used to reinforce periods of quiet (Homme, deBaca, Devine, Steinhorst and Rickert, 1963).

In order for a reinforcer to be effective it must follow closely the behavior it is designed to reinforce. Physical and temporal limitations often prevent the immediate delivery of reinforcers such as field trips or access to certain toys. To allow immediate delivery of reinforcement, and to provide flexibility in the reinforcement system, a token economy (Ayllon and Azrin, 1968) has been instituted in the Learning Village. When a teacher wishes to reinforce a behavior, he may give the child a token. A token is any small item, such as a poker chip or a piece of play money, that is easily dispensed. The child later exchanges his tokens for a reinforcer of his choice. A designated amount of tokens may buy a field trip, a novel, a puzzle, or the use of a certain toy. Because the tokens can be used to buy so many different reinforcers, they become in themselves powerful reinforcers. The token system not only allows convenient and immediate delivery of reinforcers, but allows the children, within limits, to select their own reinforcers. Different children prefer different toys and activities, and the preferences of children are often surprising. The token economy relieves the educator of the necessity of predicting and standardizing the reinforcers he uses.

The event which occurs most frequently at the Learning Village is the positive reinforcement of a child's behavior. The children come to school expecting many pleasant experiences, and they do, in fact, have these experiences. The traditional academic system is simply not reinforcing enough to make school attractive to many children. For positive reinforcers, schools have traditionally relied on social reinforcers which the teacher may or may not use effectively, on grades, and on the ability of the learning process to reinforce itself. Many educators feel that these are the only reinforcers which can be decently or wisely used. They feel that if the children are rewarded with toys, tokens, or exuberant praise for their good work, they may become dependent on these reinforcers and insensitive to the reinforcers inherent in the learning process. Indeed many teachers refer incorrectly to such reinforcers as bribes. Those with a better understanding of the term "bribe" know that it refers to a reward given to perform an illegal act. Perhaps underlying this general attitude is a sort of Puritanism which dictates that things should be done because one is told to do them, or because they are "good"—not because they may also be really fun.

Nearly everyone has from time to time been reinforced by solving a difficult puzzle or by acquiring new information. However not all the academic behavior required of children is similarly reinforcing. In learning to read, children must learn many things that are of little immediate use to them and which are, after all, not very interesting. There is no harm in "dressing up" this material to make it as interesting as possible. However, the most effective way to make the material truly interesting and important to the child is to make its acquisition necessary to obtain something which the child wants. Deliberate, frequent reinforcement is especially important when very young children are required to learn very simple things. The fact that a reinforcer follows the acquisition of some information does not necessarily reduce whatever "intrinsic" interest that information may have for the child. Rather, the reinforcer makes the child's learning of the material more pleasant and effective and thereby should enhance whatever "intrinsic" interest there is in the material. As the child grows older, some reinforcers should be faded out. Many fade naturally. Children in the Learning Village who initially would not sit in a chair for five min without some kind of extrinsic reinforcer, now will sit and read for 45 min or longer simply because they now find reading, itself, to be a reinforcing activity. However, one should never assume that everything that even adults are required to learn or do will be so intrinsically reinforcing that no special efforts should ever be made to enhance a person's experience by adding other reinforcers when necessary and possible.

When one neglects positive reinforcers as a means of controlling behavior, one must rely on punishment or other methods which involve aversive stimuli. Neglect of reinforcers has indeed forced on the schools excessive use of aversive control. Problems arise when children are forced to learn because they are shamed or given bad grades and parental censure when they fail. Under such circumstances, even learning material that would otherwise be interesting and exciting, becomes associated with unpleasant experiences and may in itself become unpleasant. The results of this type of aversive control exhibit themselves in many ways, from more dramatic behaviors such as school vandalism, and aggression (Ulrich and Favell, 1970; Ulrich and Wolfe, 1969), to less dramatic but equally deleterious behaviors such as tardiness, nonattentiveness in class, clockwatching, and failure to complete assignments. School should be a place where children find they can use their skills and intellects to acquire many things which they desire and enjoy. The best way to make learning pleasant and exciting is to reinforce it with a wide variety of satisfying and exciting experiences.

TREATMENT OF UNDESIRED BEHAVIORS

The positive reinforcement of specific, desired behaviors forms the core of the educational program at the Learning Village. The reinforcement procedures build in the children a repertoire of skills; appropriate academic responses; appropriate verbal behavior; cooperative, nonaggressive play; and good eating, toilet and other personal behaviors. In short, the reinforcement procedures help the children develop as happy, active, effective individuals. The emphasis placed on the development of desirable behaviors in itself precludes development of many of the undesirable responses encountered in educational settings. A child who is reinforced for appropriate academic responses, for smiling and saying, "I like *so and so*," for playing cooperatively with other children, and for eating his lunch will not lag academically, cry and complain, hoard toys, or throw his food. The preventive approach to problem behavior is by far the most efficient and the most pleasant and constructive from the child's point of view (Ulrich, Wolfe and Cole, 1970; Ulrich, Wolfe, and Bluhm, 1968; Ulrich, Stachnik, and Mabry, 1970). Time and effort need not be spent on the difficult and unpleasant business of eliminating undesired behaviors. The child seldom needs to be reprimanded, or punished in any way. The development of happy, competent children precludes the development of unhappy, problem children.

However, problems do arise in the Learning Village. When a problem behavior occurs, an attempt sometimes is made to restructure a specific feature of the environment to prevent its reoccurrence. For example, some children would only eat their desserts and drink their milk, without eating the other food in their lunches. The lunch procedure was therefore changed so that the opportunity to eat the food *always* eaten followed the consumption of the food *sometimes* eaten.

The general procedure used most frequently to eliminate undesired behaviors is a combination of extinction (ignoring) of the undesired behavior and reinforcement of behavior incompatible with the undesired behavior. If a child cries and it is known that he is in no physical danger or discomfort that could readily be corrected, he is ignored. Crying of the learned variety thus occurs less frequently. Crying now, when it does occur, contains more information for parents and teachers. When he smiles and plays, he is reinforced. A child who stays by himself and interacts almost entirely with adults is given adult attention only when he plays with another child (Hart, Reynolds, Baer, Brawley, and Harris, 1968). A child who is disruptive in a classroom is ignored, and the children who attend to the teacher are praised and otherwise reinforced. Failures to make correct academic responses are ignored and correct responses are reinforced. This procedure gradually eliminates the undesired behaviors and substitutes desired behaviors.

In the case of some behaviors, such as aggression, gradual elimination of the behaviors is not always acceptable, and an attempt must sometimes be made to immediately eliminate the behavior. When absolutely necessary, nonphysical punishment is used to attempt to control these behaviors. The punishment may involve loss of tokens in a token economy, or "time out" from the school envrionment in the form of sitting in an isolated or semi-isolated area. Such aversive control is at the bottom of the list of procedures used at the Learning Village. It is used only when no other method is appropriate. Physical punishment such as hitting the children is never used. Indeed, the use of positive reinforcement, in combination with extinction of undesired behaviors, makes the use of aversive control seldom necessary. As mentioned previously, aversive control can create its own problems in the form of emotional behavior and other undesired behavioral effects. By far the best method of approaching problem behavior is to prevent its occurrence by the deliberate development of incompatible, desired behaviors.

THE TEACHING STAFF

Classes at the Learning Village are very small, and the overall staff-to-student ratio is maintained at 1:5. This desirable state of affairs is achieved, in part, not by hiring numerous people who have been through traditional certification procedures, but by utilizing to the fullest extent possible the teaching capabilities of everyone involved with the Learning Village. Certified teachers, professional psychologists, college students, high school students, parents (41 percent of the Learning Village students have parents on the staff), grade school students, cooks, nurses, in short everyone who crosses the threshold, can become involved in the educational program of the Village.

Most educational systems are isolated from the environment children encounter outside school. The behaviors expected of the children and the methods used to develop the behaviors while in school have little resemblance to the behaviors and environmental controls which the child will encounter during the greater part of his life. The restriction of teaching to individuals who have been through a rigid certification procedure furthers the isolation of the usual educational setting. The traditional methodology of education has been vague and difficult to communicate. Because the behavior somehow expected of teachers has not been adequately specified in traditional education, the system has fallen back on extensive and rigid requirements in the hope that spending years in college or passing an examination will produce skilled teachers. In contrast, the procedures of behavior modification not only specify the behavior expected of the children, but also specify the behavior desired from teachers.

Teachers can be taught quite readily to attend to specific, clearly defined behaviors, and to reinforce, extinguish, or perhaps punish those behaviors as necessary. When nearly everyone can be trained to be an effective teacher, the educational setting need no longer be restricted to certain individuals who have been university trained. Newspaper editors, politicians, garage mechanics, law enforcement agents or anyone can teach their skills to children if they are aware of and can apply the principles which control behavior. As more people become teachers, the barrier between community and school, and indeed between student and teacher, can disappear. The entire community can become truly involved in the education of its children.

The formal staff of the Learning Village at present includes a professional psychologist on the Ph.D. level, psychologists and educators on the master's level, psychologists and educators on the bachelor's level, certified teachers, parents, undergraduate college students, high school students, a cook, a nurse, a custodian, and bus driver.

The core of the teaching staff is made up of college students who major in psychology and education. Before beginning work at the Learning Village, these people usually have acquired a background in behavioral psychology. An inservice training program helps them identify and develop the specific teaching behaviors they will need in their work. For many of the students, the Learning Village serves as a laboratory in which they may apply the information they acquire in the college setting (Stachnik and Ulrich, 1969).

High school students are another source of teaching staff. A program has been instituted which identifies and trains high school students interested in education (Arnett, Clark, Spates, and Ulrich, 1969; Ulrich, Arnett and DeLoach, in press). These students come both from backgrounds which virtually assure them of a college education and from those which have not typically produced college graduates. Even among the latter group, half the trainees have gone on to enroll in college, planning to specialize in either education or psychology.

To simply describe the students as adequate teachers is to vastly underrate them. The teaching techniques used in the Learning Village are relatively easy to communicate, and the students have successfully mastered them. Most students approach their work with a thoughtful, critical, creative attitude. In fact, the teaching behavior of a trained high school student is in some cases indistinguishable from that of a certified teacher. In other instances it is distinguishable in that the high school student is much better. The success of these students provides strong evidence that the ability of people in this age group to produce work truly satisfying to themselves and valuable to society is presently being squandered by an extended and isolated educational system. Efforts must be made to liberate our younger colleagues, both by accelerating their formal education and by integrating their formal education with experiences that will allow them to make full use of their knowledge and capabilities.

Yet another source of teaching staff is parents of children attending the Learning Village. Training programs in behavior modification are available both to parents who do and do not intend to teach in the Learning Village. The Michigan Department of Social Services has recently contracted with the

Learning Village to train parents and interested lay persons in child care techniques. Parents, even with little formal education behind them, can be trained to be effective teachers and modifiers of their own children's behavior. The training of parents makes an important contribution to the education of children. Continuity is provided between the conditions in force in the home and the school environments. Tantrum behavior may be successfully extinguished at school only to be unwittingly reinforced at home. The training program makes parents aware of the effects of reinforcement and how they can be applied in both the school and the home settings. The training program also serves as a source of enrichment of the parents' lives. Many times it provides a gateway for reentering the educational system at the high school, or more often at the college level. Finally, the training of parents can make an important contribution to the relationship between the parents and their own children. As parents learn to diminish the undesired behaviors of their children, many sources of friction may be eliminated. As parents become able to identify and respond to the behaviors they desire from their children, a new, more positive type of interaction enters many homes.

PYRAMIDAL INSTRUCTION

The use of high school and college students as teachers in the Learning Village is one facet of a program which could eventually have a profound impact on the process of education. Throughout American education, the involvement of students in the educational process is inadequate. A fundamental, rigid distinction is made between teacher and learner. Traditional educational methodology requires that students be, for the most part, passive recipients of the wisdom of their teachers or professors. Students are expected to postpone active, constructive participation in the world around them until they have relinquished any identification as learners.

The success with which behavioral teaching methodology can be communicated and effective teaching behavior developed makes rigid segregation of teacher and learner unnecessary. High school and college students have, in the Learning Village, demonstrated that they can be effective teachers. In the Psychology Department of Western Michigan University, a program has also been developed that utilizes college students to teach other college students (Ulrich and Kent, 1970). For example, after completing the first semester of the introductory psychology course, students become eligible to serve, during the second semester, as teaching assistants for the same course (Malott and Svinicki, 1968). This system extends throughout the undergraduate and graduate curriculum. Advanced graduate students teach less advanced graduate students. Graduate students teach upper level undergraduate courses. Advanced undergraduates teach introductory courses, and so forth. Each time a group of students completes a course, a pool of potential teachers of that course is created. At Western Michigan University, an attempt is made to utilize this source of teaching staff to its fullest extent.

A natural extension of the system downward into the high schools and grade schools can easily be envisioned. College students could teach high school students. Upper class high school students could teach first and second year students. Ultimately grade school children could teach kindergarten and nursery children. In fact, grade school children have proved capable of effective teaching behavior. In one study conducted in a public school setting, older grade school children monitored and reinforced the study behavior of younger children (Surratt, Ulrich, and Hawkins, 1969). In the Learning Village, grade school children have successfully taught infants to identify pictures (Ulrich, Wallace, and Dulaney, unpublished manuscript). In this second study, a programmed booklet was developed to introduce the grade school children to the principles of learning. Several frames from the booklet are shown in Fig. 1. The children had had considerable experience with programmed materials and successfully completed the booklet. Each participating child then took an infant aside, determined the number of pictures the infant was able to identify before the teaching procedure was instituted, reinforced subsequent identifications, and recorded the subsequent increase in correct identification. Further development of training materials, and further experience with use of grade school children as teachers, should allow much broader use of the teaching ability of these children.

The use of students as teachers not only teaches new material to the learner, but allows the teaching student to make use of the material he has previously learned. Many educators, among them Dewey and Montessori, have stressed the importance of the "need to know" in learning. Furthermore, use of sound behavioral principles in a teaching situation demonstrates most dramatically to the teaching student the effect that his behavior has on the behavior of others. Such a behavioral "laboratory" experience (Stachnik and Ulrich, 1969) is a valuable contribution to education at all levels. At the Learning Village it is used especially to help children attain the understanding of behavior which is a primary objective of the program.

The possibility of training people of all ages to teach younger people could allow a restructuring of education so that it is carried on to a great extent by the students themselves. The adult or postgraduate teacher could serve as a source of design, consultation, and training. His experience could pyramid downward to create increasing numbers of potential teachers at each descending level. Conceivably, a teacher-to-student ratio comparable to that presently in force in the Learning Village would be possible. When the behavior of children is so developed that they become an active part of the educational environment, they do not cause the discipline problems which now take up much of the teachers' time. Thus teachers could teach more students and teach them well. The restructuring of education to allow complete participation of students would not only relieve educational systems of some personnel and financial problems, but would provide a rich and constructive educational experience for the students themselves.

Teachers have learned to use rewards when they teach. A reward is anything that the student likes; such as praise, a piece of candy, or a five minute play period. So, something that a student likes can be used as a r - - - - - by the teacher. [REWARD]

You are now going to learn another name for a reward. The other name is positive reinforcer. Please print these two words here: - - - - - - - - - - - - - - - - - - - [POSITIVE REINFORCER]

In this little book we will use the words posi- - - - reinf - - - - - in the place of the word reward. Remember, a positive reinforcer is about the same as a r - - - - d. [POSITIVE REINFORCER AND REWARD]

A piece of candy, or praise, or a chance to play a game are all examples of types of p - - - - - - - r - - - - - - - - -s. [POSITIVE REINFORCERS]

Positive reinforcers should come after a behavior; it is the job of the teacher to give the student a positive - - - - - - - - - - - after the student has behaved in a way that the teacher wants him to. [REINFORCER]

Positive reinforcers cause the behavior which they follow to happen more often in the future.

Therefore, positive reinforcers are given by the teacher to cause the behavior of the student to happen - - - - often in the future. [MORE]

Let's say that you want your student to increase the number of times he spells his name correctly. If you give a - - - - - - - - - - - - - - - - - to the child after his behavior, it will happen - - - - often in the future. [POSITIVE REINFORCER and MORE]

It is easy to see why a behavior which is followed by a - - - - - - - - - - - - - - - - - - - would happen more in the future. Let's say that you were given a nickel after every time you printed your name neatly. Don't you think that your behavior of printing neatly would happen more often in the future? [POSITIVE REINFORCER]

Let us say that you gave a piece of candy to a child after he clapped. Wow! He would be clapping his hands all the time. The behavior of hand clapping would happen - - - - often in the future. [MORE]

Fig. 1. Sample frames from a programmed booklet designed to train grade school children to teach children in the infant program.

ASSESSMENT OF THE PROGRAM

Assessment of the effects of the program at the Learning Village has just begun. Indeed, it will not be adequate until the school has been in operation for some time and the longterm development of the children has been observed. As of this date, the nursery school program has been in operation for only two years, and the infant and elementary programs for a little more than one year. Anecdotal information obtained from teachers, parents, and visitors as well as test data suggest that the academic behaviors of the students at the Learning Village have indeed been accelerated. At the same time, the children appear to be happy and well adjusted. The undesired emotional behaviors and impeded development predicted as the result of infant daycare and the instruction of young children have not been observed. Parents and teachers have reported no incidents of excessive tantrum behavior or regression to behaviors such as bed-wetting or thumbsucking. Instead, they are amazed by the gaiety and sophistication of the students at the Learning Village. One mother, who is also a fourth-grade teacher at a local public school, was delighted when she discovered that her three-year-old was learning the same science material that she was teaching her fourth graders. Another mother, whose two children were essentially "expelled" from a local daycaré center because of their excessive tantruming, now reports that the Learning Village experience has completely eliminated her children's maladaptive behavior.

Although the staff of the Learning Village is not convinced that a standardized testing program is the best way to evaluate a student's progress, a testing schedule has been implemented. Because nursery programs that teach academic skills are rare, tests scored on the basis of large-group norms are not available for children who are currently in the nursery program. However, results of the Wide Range Achievement Test (WRAT) (Jastak, Bijou and Jastak, 1965) are available for children who are presently enrolled in the kindergarten program. Some of these children have had two years of behaviorally oriented instruction, whereas others have had only one year. The results for the kindergarten children are shown in Table 1. Of the 18 kindergarten children, two are reading at the fourth-grade level, and five children are reading at the third-grade level. The children who scored lowest in reading placed well into the first grade. With one exception, all of these children's reading scores ranked at least in the 90th percentile of their age group's scores. In arithmetic, the results are a little less spectacular, but are consistently good. More than half the children placed in the 90th percentile or better. Spelling has never been explicitly taught in the nursery or kindergarten program, yet the spelling scores, with two exceptions, range from good to adequate. With due respect to the abilities of the children, however, some additional comments are necessary to explain their spelling scores. The children are taught to read *and* spell, but they are initially taught reading and spelling phonetically. As the child progresses, phonetic symbols are faded out and replaced with standard letters of the alphabet. Based on the fact that the children have not altogether reached that stage as yet, they will frequently spell phonetically. Phonetically spelled words, although correct to the children, were not correct by WRAT standards.

For the convenience of readers concerned especially with teaching economically less advantaged children, the children who are supported through some financial assistance plan are indicated in Table 1. All of these children placed in the 90th percentile or better in reading. The arithmetic scores have a wider range, the highest being in the 99th and the lowest in the 34th percentile. In spelling the range of scores is extremely wide.

Some data comparing the program of the Learning Village with a more traditional educational experience is provided by tests given in conjunction with the nursery program which was a forerunner of the Learning Village (Wood, Ulrich, and Fullmer, 1969). Prior to and during the 1968-69 school year, Western Michigan University operated a traditionally-oriented Campus Nursery School. Concurrent with the operation of the Campus Nursery School, some of the founders of the Learning Village operated an experimental nursery in the same building. Most of the children enrolled in the Experimental Nursery were taken from the waiting list of the Campus Nursery School. Thus neither the Campus Nursery School nor the Experimental Nursery School populations were typical of most educational settings. Most of the children were well-off economically and many came from homes which stressed academic achievement. In the

Table 1. Performance of Learning Village kindergarten students on the
Wide Range Achievement Test.

Child	Number of Years in the Program	Age: Years Months	Reading Grade Level: Grade.Month	Reading Percentile in Age Group	Arithmetic Grade Level: Grade.Month	Arithmetic Percentile in Age Group	Spelling Grade Level Grade.Month	Spelling Percentile in Age Group
K1	1	4-11	2.5	99	1.8	98	Kg.9	66
K2	1	5-0	1.4	90	1.4	90	Pk.7	04
K3*	1	5-1	1.4	90	1.2	82	Kg.9	66
K4	1	5-3	2.5	99	2.1	99	1.2	82
K5	1	5-5	1.7	97	1.8	98	1.0	70
K6*	1	5-5	1.4	90	1.0	70	Pk.2	01
K7*	1	5-10	2.5	99	2.2	99	1.5	87
K8*	1	7-1	3.8	95	1.9	39	2.3	53
K9	2	5-7	2.6	99	2.4	99	1.8	95
K10	2	5-10	4.2	99	1.9	96	1.8	95
K11*	2	5-11	1.6	90	1.4	82	1.3	79
K12*	2	6-1	3.0	99	Kg.9	34	1.4	63
K13*	2	6-1	2.3	96	1.0	39	1.0	39
K14	2	6-2	3.1	99	2.1	92	2.3	96
K15	2	6-2	3.9	99	2.4	97	1.8	82
K16	2	6-4	4.2	99	2.8	99	2.3	96
K17	2	6-6	1.7	53	1.0	21	1.1	25
K18*	2	6-7	3.6	99	1.9	63	2.0	68
MEAN		5-9	2.6	89	1.7	77	1.3	64
MEDIAN		5-10	2.5	99	1.8	69	1.3	86

*Received financial assistance

Experimental Nursery, however, five children were added who required financial assistance. At the Campus Nursery School, little attempt was made to teach academic skills. At the Experimental Nursery School, the program was similar to that of the Learning Village. The teacher-to-student ratio was also higher at the Experimental Nursery School.

After approximately one year of half-day attendance, children from both schools were given the Metropolitan Reading Readiness Test and the Weschsler Pre-School and Primary Scale of Intelligence Test Battery. At this point, nearly all of the children from the Campus Nursery School began to attend public school kindergarten. Some of the children from the Experimental Nursery School also enrolled in public school, and some of them enrolled in the newly founded Learning Village. After the kindergarten year, the reading readiness and IQ tests were again administered to those children who could be located and whose parents gave permission for testing. Subsequently, the Wide Range Achievement Test was administered to both groups.

The scores of the children who were able to take the post-nursery school and post-kindergarten IQ tests are shown in Table 2. The IQ scores show no glaring differences, yet some trends are apparent. After a year of nursery school education, the mean IQ score of the children from the Experimental Nursery School was 7.49 points higher than that of the children from the Campus Nursery School. Such a difference in itself is not remarkable. However, the scores of the children who subsequently attended the Learning Village kindergarten show a mean increase of 9.4 points from the post-nursery to the post-kindergarten tests. These means were based only on the scores of children who took both tests. The direction of all changes was positive. In contrast, the scores of the children from

Table 2. Post-nursery school and post-kindergarten scores on the Weschsler Pre-School and Primary Scale of Intelligence of children who attended (a) the Experimental Nursery School and Learning Village Kindergarten, (b) the Experimental Nursery School and Public School Kindergarten, and (c) the Campus Nursery School and Public School Kindergarten.

	Experimental→Learning Village				Experimental→Public School				Campus→Public School		
Child**	Post-Nursery School	Post-Kinder-garten	Change	Child	Post-Nursery School	Post-Kinder-garten	Change	Child	Post-Nursery School	Post-Kinder-garten	Change
K9	118	139	+21	EP1	122	120	- 2	CP1	102	122	+20
K10	124	131	+ 7	EP2	124	121	- 3	CP2	110	108	- 2
K11*	105	122	+17	EP3	116	118	+2	CP3	115	U	-
K12*	102	104	+ 2	EP4	114	116	+2	CP4	105	119	+14
K13*	96	101	+ 5	EP5	114	116	+2	CP5	114	115	+ 1
K14	132	135	+ 3	EP6	121	122	+1	CP6	109	119	+10
K15	124	133	+ 9	EP7	114	115	+1	CP7	102	116	+14
K16	127	147	+20	EP8*	78	73	- 5	CP8	133	134	+ 1
K17	99	99	0	EP9	124	U		CP9	110	112	+ 2
K18*	120	130	+10					CP11	116	R	-
								CP12	83	U	-
								CP13	108	116	+ 8
								CP14	86	91	+ 5
								CP15	106	107	+ 1
								CP16	104	109	+ 5
								CP17	108	R	

*Received financial assistance.
**These children's scores on the Wide Range Achievement Test appear in Table 1.
U-Unavailable
R-Testing refused by parent

the Experimental Nursery School who attended public kindergarten uniformly show no real change. In fact, the mean change of those children taking both tests was -2. However, one child, EP8, did not attend school that whole year. The scores of most of the children who went from Campus to public school show a fairly consistent but smaller increase than did the Experimental to Learning Village children. Of those taking both tests, average improvement was 6.58. Finally, the mean IQ score for those children tested who were involved in behavioral education for two years was 10.1 points higher than that of the children involved in traditional education for two years.

The effects of a first encounter with structured education may be reflected in the slight edge which the Experimental Nursery School children had over the Campus Nursery School children after the initial year, and in the slight increase in the scores of the Campus School children after a year in kindergarten. The failure of the experimental school children who transferred to public school to match the increase in IQ scores of the Learning Village children may reflect the importance of continuing special programs of early education for more than one year. Finally, the difference between the mean post-kindergarten scores of the Learning Village and the public school children does suggest that gains in IQ scores are possible through extended programs of effective early education.

The distribution of percentile ranks of the children given the reading readiness test is shown in Figs. 2 and 3. The reading readiness test is designed for administration between kindergarten and first grade. The percentile ranks are therefore not corrected for age. The reading readiness test is not a test of reading ability. Rather it tests knowledge of word meaning, knowledge of numbers and the alphabet, and listening, matching and copying skills. On the post-nursery test

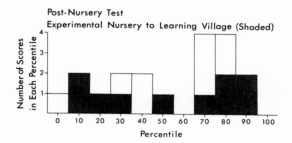

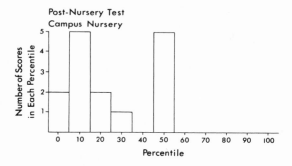

Fig. 2. The top graph depicts the distribution of the post-nursery Metropolitan Reading Readiness Test (MRT) scores by percentile for the children who attended the Experimental Nursery. The shaded area represents the scores of the children who attended the Learning Village kindergarten the following year. The bottom graph depicts the distribution of the post-nursery MRT scores by percentile for the children who attended the Campus Nursery. The scores of the children who attended the Experimental Nursery are widely distributed, while those of the Campus Nursery cluster around the lower end of the scale. Ten Experimental Nursery children scored above the 50th percentile while none of the Campus Nursery children scored above the 50th percentile. The MRT is typically administered to children at the end of their kindergarten year. The children in this study were given the MRT a full year before it is normally given.

(see Fig. 2), the scores of the children who attended the Experimental Nursery are widely distributed, whereas those of the Campus School children tend to cluster near the low end of the distribution. After a year of kindergarten, a change occurred in nearly all the scores (see Fig. 3). The mean percentile rank of the children who attended the Experimental Nursery and public kindergarten was 80.1 (top graph); of the children who attended the Experimental Nursery and the Learning Village, 82.2 (middle graph); and of the children who attended the Campus Nursery and public kindergarten, 75.9 (bottom graph). The distributions of the three groups given the post-kindergarten test are also very much alike. Apparently, both the public school kindergarten and the

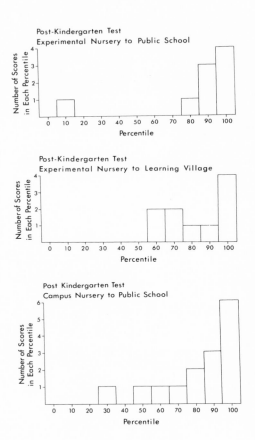

Fig. 3. The top graph depicts the distribution of the scores by percentile on the Metropolitan Reading Readiness Test for the children who attended the Experimental Nursery and a public school kindergarten. The mean percentile score was 80.1. The middle graph depicts the distribution of the scores by percentile on the Metropolitan Reading Readiness Test for the children who attended the Experimental Nursery and the Learning Village kindergarten. The mean percentile score was 82.2. The bottom graph depicts the distribution of the scores by percentile on the Metropolitan Reading Readiness Test for the children who attended the Campus Nursery and a public school kindergarten. The mean percentile score is 75.9.

Table 3. Mean grade level and percentile scores on Wide Range Achievement Test of children who attended (a) the Experimental Nursery School and Learning Village Kindergarten, (b) the Experimental Nursery School and Public Kindergarten, and (c) the Campus Nursery School and Public Kindergarten.

School Experience	Reading		Arithmetic		Spelling	
	$\bar{X}$ Grade Level: Grade.Month	$\bar{X}$ Percentile in Age Group	$\bar{X}$ Grade Level: Grade.Month	$\bar{X}$ Percentile in Age Group	$\bar{X}$ Grade Level: Grade.Month	$\bar{X}$ Percentile in Age Group
Experimental Nursery School → Learning Village	3.02	93.64	1.78	72.20	1.68	73.80
Experimental Nursery School → Public School	1.22	44.20	1.25	45.00	.98	30.71
Campus Nursery → Public School	1.25	45.70	1.37	54.40	1.07	42.10

Learning Village gave the children the skills they needed to score well on the reading readiness test. Indeed, the skills emphasized by the reading readiness test are often part of the public school kindergarten curriculum.

The scores obtained on the Wide Range Achievement Test present quite a different picture. The mean percentile rank and grade level scores on this are compared in Table III.

The children who attended the Learning Village kindergarten had a mean reading rank above the 90th percentile and placed, on the average, at the beginning of the third grade. The mean reading scores of the children who attended the public school kindergarten fell at approximately the 45th percentile and in the second month of the first grade. Although the public school curriculum did teach the children the skills needed to perform on the average as well as the Learning Village children on the reading readiness test, it did not teach them to read at nearly the same level. In contrast, the program of the Learning Village taught not only the skills measured by the reading readiness test, but actual reading, arithmetic and spelling skills as well. In arithmetic and spelling the mean percentile ranks of the children who attended the Learning Village are above the 70th percentile. The mean percentile ranks for the children who attended public kindergarten are around or below the 50th percentile. In terms of grade level, the mean scores in arithmetic and spelling of the children who attended the Learning Village fall near the end of the first grade. The grade level scores of the children who attended public school fall closer to the beginning of the first grade.

Although the Experimental Nursery children had, in the reading readiness skills, a "head start" on the Campus Nursery children, the Campus Nursery children were ultimately able to "catch up." A similar "catching up" in actual reading skills might be proposed for the children attending the public school. The apparently low ceiling of the reading readiness test, plus the superior home and, to some extent, school situations of nearly all the children tested may account for the final similarity of the reading readiness scores. However, some

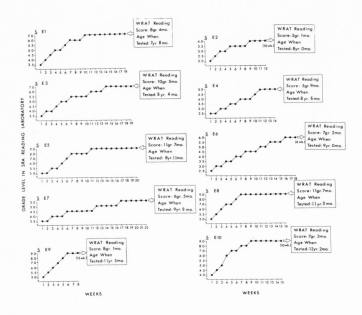

Fig. 4. The above graphs indicate the grade level progression by weeks on the Science Research Associates (SRA) Power Builders and the Wide Range Achievement Test (WRAT) scores for the Learning Village Elementary School students. All subjects except E9 and E10 scored higher on the WRAT than their progression level on the SRA Power Builders. This can probably be explained by the fact that the SRA Power Builders place greater emphasis on comprehension skills. The arrows that point toward the last data point indicate that the WRAT was given during that week. For example, the WRAT was administered to Subject E1 during the 19th week of the SRA program. Arrows that point away from the last data point indicate that there was a time lapse between the last week that a student worked on the SRA Power Builders and the date that he took the WRAT. The amount of time between the completion of the last SRA Power Builder and the administration of the WRAT is indicated in parentheses. Temporary "regressions" to previous grade levels are built into the SRA program, which requires some repetition of grade levels. These repetitions appear as level segments (e.g., SEI weeks 10-18) on the graphs. They do not necessarily represent any lack of progress.

picture of the future reading performance of the Learning Village children might be obtained by examining the current reading performance of the children who have spent one year in the elementary school of the Learning Village.

Perhaps the best picture of reading progress in the elementary school can be obtained by examining the progress of the children of the Science Research Associates (SRA) Reading Laboratory Power Builders. The Power Builders involve reading a story and answering questions designed to develop comprehension and verbal skills. The Power Builders are not tests, but are reading experiences designed to improve the students' skills. In the Language Laboratory, students progress from one grade level to another according to their performance on individual Power Builders. The grade level at which the child begins is determined by administering the Starter Level Guide, an SRA test coordinated to the Reading Laboratory. Fifteen or 20 Power Builders are included in each grade level, depending on the level. However, if a student meets criteria, he may progress to the next level without completing all of the Power Builders. Criteria are set by the teacher and, in part, by the student. Mrs. Carmen Hren, the elementary school reading teacher, usually requires that the children complete at least six Power Builders at 80 percent accuracy, or three or four Power Builders at 90 or 100 percent accuracy. Incidentally, completion of a Power Builder at 80 percent or better accuracy is reinforced by tokens.

Figure 4 shows the grade level progress of the Learning Village elementary school children on the SRA Power Builders. Temporary "regressions" to previous grade levels are built into the SRA program, which requires some repetition of grade levels. These repetitions appear as level segments in Figure 4, and they do not represent any real set-back in the student's progress. The elementary school children also took the Wide Range Achievement Test near the time of the last entry in the progress charts. The WRAT grade level scores for these children are also shown in Figure 4. For completeness, Table IV gives the full set of WRAT scores of the elementary school children.

Table 4. Performance of Learning Village elementary school children on the Wide Range Achievement Test.

		Reading		Arithmetic		Spelling	
Child	Months	Grade Level: Grade.Month	Percentile in Age Group	Grade Level: Grade.Month	Percentile in Age Group	Grade Level: Grade.Month	Percentile in Age Group
E1	7-8	8.4	99	3.6	77	5.0	98
E2	8-0	5.1	92	3.9	68	3.5	58
E3	8-4	10.5	99	4.2	75	6.3	99
E4	8-6	5.9	96	4.2	68	4.7	81
E5	8-11	11.7	99	7.2	99	11.5	99
E6	9-0	7.2	98	4.2	53	5.3	79
E7	9-9	6.5	86	4.7	50	3.7	27
E8	11-0	11.7	99	6.1	53	10.9	99
E9	11-5	8.1	86	6.3	55	7.2	73
E10	12-1	7.3	53	7.4	53	5.5	22
MEAN	9-6	8.2	91	5.2	65*	6.4	73
MEDIAN	8-8	7.7	97	4.4	61	5.4	80

As Fig. 4 shows, the progress of the children in the SRA Reading Laboratory has been substantial. Within weeks, children progress several grade levels. That this progression is not an artifact peculiar to the SRA program is indicated by the Wide Range Achievement Test grade level scores. In most cases, the children

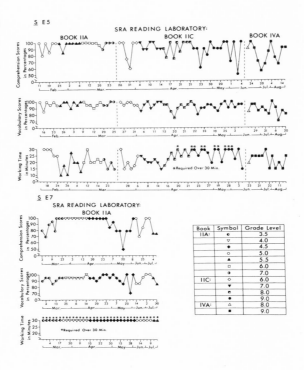

Fig. 5. The lesson-to-lesson progressions of two Learning Village Elementary School students are depicted in the above graphs. On each Power Builder, the student graphs his own comprehension and vocabulary scores as well as his working time. Subject E5's graphs closely resemble those of a superior learner (Parker, 1969, p. 58). The graphs of Subject E7 resemble those of a typical slower learner. While Subject E7 always had a working time of over 30 minutes, his accuracy in both the comprehension and vocabulary portions of the Power Builders was quite high. Both subjects are reading above grade level. For each Power Builder, the child records his own score on two types of questions; comprehension (top graphs) and vocabulary (middle graph) as well as on working time (bottom graphs). The chart at the lower right hand side of the figure shows the SRA book from which the child was working and the symbol used in the figures for depicting the grade level.

scored at a higher grade level than the grade level of the Power Builders with which they were currently working. Those children who scored below were the oldest, had less experience with the Power Builders and terminated well before the reading test was administered.

Some idea of the lesson-to-lesson performance of the children may be obtained from Fig. 5, which shows the scores of two representative children on the individual Power Builders. For each Power Builder, the child records his score on two types of questions (Comprehension and Vocabulary) and records his working time. Child E5's record is typical of the children who progressed rapidly. Accuracy was very high (usually above 80 percent) on both comprehension and vocabulary, even by the SRA standards for the superior learner (Parker, 1969, p. 58). Earlier lessons were completed with apparent speed and ease, several lessons often being completed in a single day. More time was sepnt on later lessons, but accuracy did not deteriorate. In these later lessons, this eight-year-11-month-old child was doing work designed for use in the ninth grade. His WRAT reading score placed him almost at the senior high school level.

The lesson-to-lesson progress typical of another child is also shown in Fig. 5. Child E7 spent more time on each lesson and did fewer lessons per day. However, his accuracy is excellent. Although this nine-year-old child initially placed below the grade level appropriate to his age, he has now "caught up." In addition, the quality of his work is superior, and the child's reading scores on the Wide Range Achievement Test suggest that his actual reading skills may be above his SRA grade level. A slower worker does not have to be a poor reader.

The reading performance of virtually every one of the children now in the Learning Village elementary school by far exceeds normal achievement in public elementary school. The children who attended the experimental nursery school and the Learning Village have already finished kindergarten with superior reading ability. If they make progress typical of the children now in the Learning Village elementary school, the future contrast with the reading ability of the children who entered public school should be even greater.

One might prefer comparative data showing the effects of the Learning Village program and of traditional education on a more typical population of school children. However, the comparative data do indicate that a Learning Village type program can make a significant difference even in the education of children destined for an above-average academic experience. As mentioned earlier, the general population of the Learning Village is not preselected for academic achievement or "intelligence." However, even children who enter the Learning Village with academic deficits are soon indistinguishable in performance from children who enter with good academic backgrounds.

The results of the academic program at the Learning Village are most dramatic in the area of reading. If it is true, as many educators claim, that reading is the key that unlocks the door to knowledge, the students are well on their way to success in education. The experience at the Learning Village has caused the children to learn far more than they would have from the usual elementary school kindergarten to nursery school-plus-kindergarten program. The staff of the Learning Village believes that the results achieved are due primarily to the behavioral methodology used. In the past, attempts to improve the education of children have suffered from a fundamental ignorance of the nature of learning. Technologies of education, to be consistently effective, must be based on a scientific understanding of their subject. Once the results of scientifically based educational methodology become known, a tremendous growth in and refinement of the technology of behavioral education should follow. The ultimate results of long term, comprehensive behavioral education must be consigned to the void of future happenings. The results could surpass the most fanciful goals of current educators. Indeed, behavioral education may create the very kind of people needed to cope with the extremes of technical advancement and social crisis characteristic of the twentieth century. Whether or not today's children will be given the chance to eventually prove or disprove the above conjecture, of course, as always, depends upon the decisions of those adults who control our present educational systems.

REFERENCES

Arnett, M.; Clark, D.; Spates, R.; and Ulrich, R. An in-service training program for high school students. Paper delivered at American Psychological Association, Washington, D.C., September 1969.

Ayllon, T. and Azrin, N. H. *The token economy: a motivational system for therapy and rehabilitation.* New York: Appleton-Century-Crofts, 1968.

Ayllon, T. and Michael, J. The psychiatric nurse as a behavioral engineer. *Journal of the Experimental Analysis of Behavior,* 1959, 2, 323-334.

Baer, D. M. A technique of social reinforcement for the study of child behavior: behavior avoiding reinforcement withdrawal. *Child Development,* 1962, 33, 847-858.

Becker, W. C.; Thomas, D. R.; and Carnine, D. *Reducing behavior problems: an operant conditioning guide for teachers.* Urbana, Ill.: ERIC Clearinghouse on Early Childhood Education, 1969.

Bowlby, J. *Child care and the growth of love.* Baltimore: Penguin Books, 1953.

Brown, P. and Elliot, R. Control of aggression in a nursery school class. *Journal of Experimental Child Psychology,* 1965, 2, 103-107.

Buell, J.; Stoddard, P.; Harris, F. R.; and Baer, D. M. Collateral social development accompanying reinforcement of outdoor play in a preschool child. *Journal of Applied Behavior Analysis,* 1968, 1, 167-174.

Bushell, D., Jr.; Wrobel, P. A.; and Michaelis, M. L. Applying "group" contingencies to the classroom study behavior of preschool children. *Journal of Applied Behavior Analysis,* 1968, 1, 55-62.

Caldwell, B. M.; Wright, C. M.; Honig, A. S.; and Tannenbaum, J. Infant day care and attachment. *American Journal of Orthopsychiatry,* 1970, 40, 397-412.

Englemann, S. and Bruner, E. C. *Distar reading.* Chicago: Science Research Associates, 1969.

Englemann, S. and Carnine, D. *Distar arithmetic.* Chicago: Science Research Associates, 1969.

Englemann, S.; Osborne, J.; and Englemann, T. *Distar language.* Chicago: Science Research Associates, 1969.

Fox, L. Effecting the use of efficient study habits. Journal of Mathematics, 1962, 1, 75-86, and in R. E. Ulrich; T. Stachnik; and J. Mabry (Eds.) *Control of Human Behavior: I. Expanding the Behavioral Laboratory.* Glenview, Ill.: Scott, Foresman, 1966. Pp. 85-93.

Goldiamond, I. Self-control procedures in personal behavior problems. In R. E. Ulrich; T. Stachnik; and J. Mabry (Eds.) *Control of Human Behavior: I.*

Expanding the Behavioral Laboratory. Glenview, Ill.: Scott, Foresman, 1966. Pp. 115-127.

Hall, R. V.; Lund, D.; and Jackson, D. Effects of teacher attention on study behavior. *Journal of Applied Behavior Analysis,* 1968, 1, 1-14.

Harris, F. R.; Wolf, M. M.; and Baer, D. M. Effects of adult social reinforcement on child behavior. *Young Children,* 1964, 20, 8-17, and in R. E. Ulrich, T. Stachnik and J. Mabry (Eds.) *Control of Human Behavior: I. Expanding the Behavioral Laboratory.* Glenview, Ill.: Scott, Foresman, 1966, Pp. 130-137.

Hart, Betty M.; Reynolds, Nancy J.; Baer, D. M.; Brawley, Eleanor R.; and Harris, Florence R. Effects of contingent and noncontingent social reinforcement on the cooperative play of a preschool child. *Journal of Applied Behavior Analysis,* 1968, 1, 73-76.

Hart, B. M. and Risley, T. R. Establishing use of descriptive adjectives in the spontaneous speech of disadvantaged preschool children. *Journal of Applied Behavior Analysis,* 1968, 1, 109-120.

Homme, L. E. *How to use contingency contracting in the classroom.* Champaign, Ill.: Research Press, 1969.

Homme, L. E.; deBaca, P. C.; Devine, J. V.; Steinhorst, R.; and Rickert, E. J. Use of the Premack Principle in controlling the behavior of nursery school children. *Journal of the Experimental Analysis of Behavior,* 1963, 6, 544; and in R. E. Ulrich, T. Stachnik and J. Mabry (Eds.), *Control of Human Behavior: I. Expanding the Behavioral Laboratory.* Glenview, Ill.: Scott, Foresman, 1966. Pp. 93-94.

Jastak, J. F.; Bijou, S. W.; and Jastak, S. R. Wide Range Achievement Test. Wilmington, Del.: Guidance Associates, 1965.

Mabry, J. H.; Stachnik, T. J.; and Ulrich, R. E. Cultural impediments to the implementation of a behavioral technology. In R. E. Ulrich, T. J. Stachnik, and J. A. Mabry (Eds.) *Control of Human Behavior: II. From Cure to Prevention.* Glenview, Ill.: Scott, Foresman, 1970.

Madsen, C. H., Jr.; Becker, W. C.; and Thomas, D. R. Rules, praise and ignoring: elements of elementary classroom control. *Journal of Applied Behavior Analysis,* 1968, 1, 139-150.

Madsen, C. H., Jr.; Becker, W. C.; Thomas, D. R.; Koser, L.; and Plager, E. An analysis of the reinforcing function of "sit down" commands. In Parker, R. K. (Ed.) *Readings in Educational Psychology.* Boston: Allyn & Bacon, 1968.

Malott, R. and Svinicki, J. Contingency management in an introductory psychology course for 1000 students. Paper presented at the American Psychological Association, San Francisco, 1968.

Neill, A. S. *Summerhill: a radical approach to child rearing.* New York: Hart, 1960.

Packard, R. G. The control of "classroom attention": a group contingency for complex behavior. *Journal of Applied Behavior Analysis,* 1970, 3, 13-28.

Parker, D. H. Teachers Handbook. SRA Reading Laboratory. IIa. Science Research Associates, 1969.

Premack, D. Toward empirical behavior laws: I. Positive reinforcement. *Psychological Review,* 1959, 66, 219-233.

Risley, T. and Wolf, M. M. Experimental manipulation of autistic behaviors and generalization into the home. Paper read at American Psychological Association, September, 1964, and in R. E. Ulrich, T. Stachnik and J. Mabry (Eds.)

Control of Human Behavior: I. Expanding the Behavioral Laboratory. Glenview, Ill.: Scott, Foresman, 1966, Pp. 193-198.

Schmidt, G. W. and Ulrich, R. E. Effects of group contingent events upon classroom noise. *Journal of Applied Behavior Analysis,* 1969, 2, 171-179.

Schwarz, M. L. and Hawkins, R. P. Application of delayed conditioning procedures to the behavior problems of an elementary school child. In R. E. Ulrich, T. Stachnik and J. Mabry (Eds.) *Control of Human Behavior: II. From Cure to Prevention.* Glenview, Ill: Scott, Foresman, 1970. Pp. 271-283.

Skinner, B. F. *Science and human behavior.* New York: Macmillan, 1953.

Spitz, R. A. and Cobliner, W. G. *The first year of life.* New York: International Universities Press, 1965.

Stachnik, T. J. and Ulrich, R. E. A laboratory section for educational psychology. *The Psychological Record,* 1969, 19, 129-132.

Surratt, P.; Ulrich, R. E.; and Hawkins, R. P. An elementary student as a behavioral engineer. *Journal of Applied Behavior Analysis,* 1969, 2, 85-92.

Thomas, D. R.; Becker, W. C.; and Armstrong, M. Production and elimination of disruptive classroom behavior by systematically varying teacher's behavior. *Journal of Applied Behavior Analysis,* 1968, 1, 35-46.

Ullmann, L. P. and Krasner, L. (Eds.) *Case studies in behavior modification.* New York: Holt, 1965.

Ulrich, R. E. Behavior control and public concern. *The Psychological Record,* 1967, 17, 229-234.

Ulrich, R. E.; Arnett, M.; and DeLoach, T. G. Teaching the disadvantaged. In J. Bergeson and G. Miller (Eds.) as yet untitled. New York: Macmillan, in press.

Ulrich, R. E. and Favell, J. E. Human aggression. In C. Neuringer and J. L. Michael (Eds.) *Behavior Modification in Clinical Psychology.* New York: Appleton, 1970, Pp. 105-132.

Ulrich, R. E. and Kent, N. D. Suggested tactics for the education of psychologists. In R. E. Ulrich, T. Stachnik, and J. Mabry (Eds.) *Control of Human Behavior: II. From Cure to Prevention.* Glenview, Ill.: Scott, Foresman, 1970.

Ulrich, R. E.; Stachnik, T.; and Mabry, J. (Eds.) *Control of human behavior: I. expanding the behavioral laboratory.* Glenview. Ill.: Scott, Foresman, 1966.

Ulrich, R. E.; Stachnik, T.; and Mabry, J. (Eds.) *Control of Human Behavior: II. From Cure to Prevention.* Glenview, Ill.: Soctt, Foresman, 1970.

Ulrich, R. E.; Wallace, F.; and Dulaney, S. Pyramidal instruction: a proposed solution to an educational problem. Unpublished manuscript.

Ulrich, R. E. and Wolfe, M. Research and theory on aggression and violence. *The Science Teacher,* 1969, 36, 24-28.

Ulrich, R. E.; Wolfe, M.; and Bluhm, M. Operant conditioning in the public schools. *Educational Technology Monographs,* 1968, 1 (1).

Ulrich, R. E.; Wolfe, M.; and Cole, R. Early education: a preventive mental health program. *Michigan Mental Health Research Bulletin,* 1970, 4, (1).

Ulrich, R. E.; Wolfe, M.; and Surratt, P. New methods for treatment delivery. *Michigan Mental Health Research Bulletin,* 1969, 3, 41-44.

Westinghouse Learning Corporation. *The impact of head start, an evaluation of the effect of head start on children's cognitive and affective development.* Office of Economic Opportunity Publ. No. B894536. Springfield, Va.: U.S. Govt. Clearinghouse, June 1969.

Wolfe, M.; Ulrich, R.; and Ulrich, C. Administrative hurdles blocking preventive mental health programs for children. *Michigan Mental Health Research Bulletin,* 1970, 4, 44-48.

Wood, W. S. The Lincoln Elementary School Project: some results of an in-service training course in behavioral psychology. *Educational Technology Monographs,* 1968, 1, (2).

Wood, W. S.; Ulrich, C.; and Fullmer, M. Early education: an experimental nursery school. Paper read at Michigan Academy of Arts, Letters and Sciences, Ann Arbor, 1969.

Zimmerman, E. H. and Zimmerman, J. The alteration of behavior in a special classroom situation. *Journal of the Experimental Analysis of Behavior,* 1962, 5, 59-60, and in R. E. Ulrich, T. Stachnik, and J. Mabry (Eds.) *Control of Human Behavior: I. Expanding the Behavioral Laboratory,* Glenview, Ill.: Scott, Foresman, 1966, Pp. 94-96.